# THE POISONED CHALICE OF US DEMOCRACY

# THE POISONED CHALICE OF US DEMOCRACY

## Studies from the Horn of Africa

John Young

BLOOMSBURY ACADEMIC
LONDON • NEW YORK • OXFORD • NEW DELHI • SYDNEY

BLOOMSBURY ACADEMIC
Bloomsbury Publishing Plc
50 Bedford Square, London, WC1B 3DP, UK
1385 Broadway, New York, NY 10018, USA
29 Earlsfort Terrace, Dublin 2, Ireland

BLOOMSBURY, BLOOMSBURY ACADEMIC are trademarks of
Bloomsbury Publishing Plc

First published in Great Britain 2024

Copyright © John Young, 2024

John Young has asserted his right under the Copyright,
Designs and Patents Act, 1988, to be identified as Author of this work.

For legal purposes the Acknowledgements on p. vii constitute an
extension of this copyright page.

Cover design by Grace Ridge
Cover image © Adobe Stock

All rights reserved. No part of this publication may be reproduced or transmitted
in any form or by any means, electronic or mechanical, including photocopying,
recording, or any information storage or retrieval system, without prior
permission in writing from the publishers.

Bloomsbury Publishing Plc does not have any control over, or responsibility for,
any third-party websites referred to or in this book. All internet addresses given
in this book were correct at the time of going to press. The author and publisher regret
any inconvenience caused if addresses have changed or sites have ceased
to exist, but can accept no responsibility for any such changes.

A catalogue record for this book is available from the British Library.

Library of Congress Cataloging-in-Publication Data
Names: Young, John, 1951- author.
Title: The poisoned chalice of US democracy: studies from the Horn of Africa/John Young.
Description: New York: Zed Books, an imprint of Bloomsbury Publishing, 2024. |
Includes bibliographical references and index.
Identifiers: LCCN 2023020311 (print) | LCCN 2023020312 (ebook) |
ISBN 9781350374584 (paperback) | ISBN 9781350374591 (hardback) |
ISBN 9781350374607 (epub) | ISBN 9781350374621 (pdf) | ISBN 9781350374614
Subjects: LCSH: Democracy–Horn of Africa–Case studies. | Democracy–Economic
aspects–Horn of Africa. | Economic policy–Political aspects–Horn of Africa. |
Horn of Africa–Politics and government–20th century. | Horn of Africa–Politics and
government–21st century.
Classification: LCC DT367.8.Y68 2024 (print) | LCC DT367.8 (ebook) |
DDC 962.4042–dc23/eng/20230426
LC record available at https://lccn.loc.gov/2023020311
LC ebook record available at https://lccn.loc.gov/2023020312

| ISBN: | HB: | 978-1-3503-7459-1 |
|---|---|---|
| | PB: | 978-1-3503-7458-4 |
| | ePDF: | 978-1-3503-7462-1 |
| | eBook: | 978-1-3503-7460-7 |

Typeset by Integra Software Services Pvt. Ltd.
Printed and bound in Great Britain

To find out more about our authors and books visit www.bloomsbury.com
and sign up for our newsletters.

CONTENTS

| | |
|---|---|
| Acknowledgements | vii |
| Acronyms | viii |
| INTRODUCTION | 1 |
|    Organization of the book | 5 |
| Chapter 1 | |
| RISE AND DECLINE OF US DEMOCRACY | 11 |
|    US liberal international order | 12 |
|    Rise and decline of US elections | 20 |
|    Propagation of Western democracy | 26 |
|    Decline of US democracy | 30 |
|    Conclusion | 34 |
| Chapter 2 | |
| SCRAMBLE FOR THE GREATER MIDDLE EAST IN THE WAKE OF US DECLINE | 37 |
|    An ascendent China | 38 |
|    Middle Eastern States in the Horn of Africa | 46 |
|    Conclusion | 52 |
| Chapter 3 | |
| ETHIOPIA AND THE CHALLENGE OF DEMOCRACY | 55 |
|    Origins and development of the TPLF | 56 |
|    Capitalism (reluctantly) embraced | 61 |
|    Revolutionary democracy versus liberal democracy | 63 |
|    National federalism | 69 |
|    State-led development | 73 |
|    Meles: The making of an autocrat | 77 |
|    Countdown to the Abiy counter-revolution | 82 |
|    Conclusion | 92 |
| Chapter 4 | |
| SUDAN, THE UNITED STATES AND THE PROPAGATION OF DEMOCRACY | 97 |
|    US relations with Sudan in historical context | 98 |
|    US relations with the Sudanese Islamists | 100 |
|    US pursuit of democracy and peace in Sudan | 105 |
|    Decline of Islamist radicalism | 108 |

United States and Islamists find common ground
in commitment to capitalism 114
The post-al-Bashir era 121
Conclusion 131

Chapter 5
SOUTH SUDAN: ANOTHER FAILED US DEMOCRACY PROJECT 133
Historical context 134
US enters the fray 135
Mythologizing South Sudan's conflicts 137
US-sponsored South Sudan peace process 139
Civil war in South Sudan 145
South Sudan's future 148
Conclusion 150

CONCLUSION 153
Ethiopia and compromises with the West 154
Sudan: Change without fundamental change 160
South Sudan and national self-determination 166
Final words 168

Bibliography 171
Interviews 191
Index 192

## ACKNOWLEDGEMENTS

This book draws on the support, advice and engagement of countless people over the period of thirty-seven years that I have been involved in the Horn of Africa and thus I can only acknowledge a fraction of those I am indebted to. I must begin, however, with Mahgoub Mohamed Salih and Bona Malwal, respectively, the publisher and editor of *The Sudan Times* of Khartoum, where I worked as a journalist between 1986 and 1989 and were my teachers on Sudan and southern Sudan and provided the window through which I was introduced to Tigray and Ethiopia. They also, however inadvertently, provided the introduction to the two organizations that would most influence my understanding of the Horn – the Sudan Communist Party and the Tigray People's Liberation Front and this study can in some respects be considered an extended debate with these two organizations.

In addition, I must thank Riak 'Franco' Pouk Nyab and Bol Gatkouth Chuol for their help in understanding southern and South Sudan's tumultuous politics and complex national cultures. As well, I learned a lot about South Sudan from the best president the country never had, Dr Lam Akol.

In Ethiopia I must foremost thank General Gebretensae Tsadkan for helping me appreciate military realities and the TPLF and Professor Assefa Fishea for his insights into Ethiopian federalism. Also, very helpful has been Patrick Gilkes.

Professor Siddig Tawer, Siddig Yousif and Samia Ahmed were crucial to my understanding of Sudan.

I also want to thank Professor Steve McBride of McMaster University for his assistance.

Lastly, I want to thank my wife, Thea Geddert, for reading drafts of this book and being an audience as I endeavoured to make sense of a range of regional and global issues.

# ACRONYMS

| | |
|---|---|
| Afar National Democratic Front | ANDF |
| Africa Command | AFRICOM |
| African Union | AU |
| Agreement for the Resolution of Conflict in South Sudan | ARCSS |
| Amhara Democratic Movement | ANDM |
| Australia, UK and the US | AUKUS |
| Benishangul-Gumuz People's Democratic Unity Front | BGPDUF |
| Boycott, Disinvestment, and Sanctions | BDS |
| Chinese Communist Party | CCP |
| Comprehensive Peace Agreement | CPA |
| Eritrean Liberation Front | ELF |
| Eritrean People's Liberation Front | EPLF |
| Ethiopian People's Revolutionary Democratic Front | EPRDF |
| Ethiopian Peoples' Democratic Movement | EPDM |
| Ethiopian People's Revolutionary Party | EPRP |
| Ethiopian Somali People's Democratic Party | ESPDP |
| Ethiopian Student Movement | ESM |
| Forces of Freedom and Change | FFC |
| Gambella People's Democratic Movement | GPDM |
| General Agreement on Tariffs and Trade | GATT |
| Global War on Terror | GWOT |
| Gulf Cooperation Council | GCC |
| Harari National League | HNL |
| Heavily Indebted Poor Country | HIPC |
| Horn of Africa | HOA |
| International Commission on Intervention and State Sovereignty | ICISS |
| International Criminal Court | ICC |
| International Financial Institutions | IFIs |
| Inter-governmental Authority Development | IGAD |
| Internally Displaced Persons | IDP |
| International Monetary Fund | IMF |
| Marxist-Leninist League of Tigray | MLLT |
| National Congress Party | NCP |
| National Democratic Alliance | NDA |
| National Intelligence and Security Services | NISS |
| National Islamic Front | NIF |
| New Partnership for African Development | NEPAD |
| North Atlantic Treaty Organization | NATO |
| Ogaden National Liberation Front | ONLF |

| | |
|---|---|
| Organisation for Economic Co-operation and Development | OECD |
| Oromo Liberation Army | OLA |
| Oromo Liberation Front | OLF |
| Oromo People's Democratic Organization | OPDO |
| Popular Congress Party | PCP |
| Rapid Support Forces | RSF |
| Relief Society of Tigray | REST |
| Responsibility to Protect | R2P |
| Southern Ethiopia Peoples' Democratic Front | SEPDF |
| SPLM-In Opposition | SPLM-IO |
| SPLM-North | SPLM-N |
| Stockholm International Peace Research Institute | SIPRI |
| Strategic Initiative for Women in the HOA | SIHA |
| Structural Adjustment Programs | SAPs |
| Sudan Communist Party | SCP |
| Sudan People's Liberation Army | SPLA |
| Sudan People's Liberation Movement | SPLM |
| Supreme Allied Commander Europe | SACEUR |
| Tigray People's Liberation Front | TPLF |
| Transitional Military Council | TMC |
| United States Institute of Peace | USIP |
| US Agency for International Development | USAID |
| Universal Declaration of Human Rights | UDHR |
| United Nations Development Programme | UNDP |
| United Nations Mission in South Sudan | UNMISS |
| World Trade Organization | WTO |

INTRODUCTION

The United States and its Western allies first invaded Iraq in 2003 to remove their former ally, Saddam Hussein, and eliminate the Weapons of Mass Destruction (WMD) which did not exist. The objectives of the invasion then expanded to bringing democracy to Iraq and for the country to become a showcase for the spread of democracy in the greater Middle East. But this project failed dismally, and Louise Fawcett concluded that the Iraq War 'ended an era of Western hubris about the theory and practice of democracy promotion' (Daniel Williams, 20 March 2023).

In 2001 a US-led NATO coalition launched a war against the Taliban who the Americans had previously supported to undermine a progressive Soviet-backed government. Here too the rationale became couched in terms of democracy and state building. And like Iraq, the project proved to be a fiasco. As a result, President Biden was compelled to endorse the decision of his predecessor, Donald Trump, to evacuate the country and turn state power over to the Taliban in late 2021.

The botched efforts of US democracy promotion in Afghanistan and Iraq have important implications for the Global South and this is explored in three case studies drawn from the Horn of Africa (HOA). Like Iraq and Afghanistan these case studies demonstrate the failure of Western democracy to take roots in societies very different from those in which democracy originated and developed. The failure is also a reflection of the decay of Western democracy in its American heartland and the waning US international liberal order which was constructed to defend US hegemony and propagate Washington's version of democracy.

The crisis within American democracy is increasingly recognized in the recent academic literature.[1] The expressions of this crisis are manifold: the election of the right-wing populist Donald Trump to the presidency in 2016, the refusal of large

---

1. See for example, Yascha Mounk, *The People vs. Democracy*, 2019; Steven Levitsky and Daniel Ziblatt, *How Democracies Die*, 2018; *Adam Przeworsk, Crises of Democracy*, 2020; Richard Posner, 2011; William G Howell and Terry M Moe, *Presidents, Populism, and the Crisis of Democracy*, 2020; Suzanne Mettler and Robert C. Lieberman, *Four Threats: The Recurring Crises of American Democracy*, 2020; Margaret Sullivan, *Ghosting the News: Local Journalism and the Crisis of American Democracy*, 2020; and Christian Lammert, *The Emergence of Illiberalism*, 2020.

numbers of Americans to accept the outcomes of the 2016 and 2020 elections, the exponential growth of inequality, the 2020 summer of riots, the never-ending wars of successive US governments, the failure to effectively deal with the environmental crisis, and the growing danger of a nuclear conflict as a result of the US and NATO proxy war in Ukraine. But the crisis is perhaps most evident in the declining faith of ordinary Americans in US democracy. A majority of American voters across nearly all demographics and ideologies believe their system of government does not work, with 58 per cent of those interviewed for a New York Times/Siena College poll saying that the world's oldest independent constitutional democracy needs major reforms or a complete overhaul (New York Times, 13 July 2022).

The crisis of democracy is in turn a reflection of a crisis of capitalism with which democracy, as it is understood in the West, is intimately linked. This is in part due to the decline of US economic power from the end of the Second World War when the United States accounted for almost one-half of the global GDP to 15.83 per cent in 2020 (Aaron O'Neil, 23 November 2021). US supremacy and the legitimacy of the democracy it promotes have been based on its unchallenged military and economic power, domination of the world's energy reserves and maintaining the dollar as the world's reserve currency.

Political processes in the Global South have long been shaped by developments in the metropoles and Western-dominated globalization. The present state structures of most countries in the Global South were established by the Western colonial powers, their national economies are largely a product of global capitalism and they have a subordinate position in a Western-dominated hierarchy of states. That has been the case for more than a generation, but what is striking in the present era is how developments in the Global South are being influenced by the crisis in Western democracy, the decline of US power, the rising power of China and Russia, the proxy war in Ukraine, and – in the case of the HOA – economically powerful and politically ambitious Middle Eastern states no longer controlled by the United States.

Although capitalism and imperialism have universalized Western democracy, it has only rarely proved viable or sustainable in the Global South. This can be attributed to the malevolence of individual dictators or the failure of the people, but the argument developed here is that Western democracy is an inappropriate model of governance for these societies. The struggle for democracy should not be dispensed with, but Western democracy has not proved workable in much of the Global South and trying to introduce it as the experience of Ethiopia, Sudan and South Sudan amply demonstrates will be costly and detract from efforts to break free from Western hegemony and construct forms of democracy rooted in indigenous cultures. It will be contended here that the structural changes necessary to achieving political equality, dramatically improving living standards, overcoming national repression, ending unequal development and confronting systemic economic injustice are unlikely to be achieved through Western democratic government institutions and instead should be tackled by institutions developed of, by and for the people of the Global South.

Respect for individual human rights is essential to democratic governance, but there also needs to be an appreciation of group rights, particularly of nations to self-determination, which are typically given short shrift in Western human rights discourse or models of governance. Human rights organizations have usually followed powerful groups in the West and adopted a neoliberal framework that views politics as violent and oppressive and considers civil society and the market as the realm of individual freedom. This perspective either ignores or does not give due attention to economic, social, cultural and national oppression that is endemic in the HOA and common in the Global South.

Struggles to realize internal national self-determination and secession have been a major cause of conflict in the HOA. While the rest of Africa has managed to maintain its colonial dictated boundaries, the HOA has witnessed the secession of two states – Eritrea and South Sudan and the de facto independence of Somaliland – and in light of Ethiopia's November 2020 war, the possible eventual secession of Tigray. The struggle for national self-determination must be understood as fundamentally democratic struggles for collective human and civil rights, and that is not usually the case in the Western discourse on democracy.

With capitalism and neoliberalism now integral to Western democracy, raising abysmal living standards in the Global South is to be left to the market, the role of the state is relegated to that of a 'night-watchman', and this typically produces impoverishment, economic polarization within and between societies, and uneven development, all of which generate conflict. Moreover, through the spread of liberal peacemaking, notions like the Responsibility to Protect and failed states, and neoliberalism in the West have undermined national sovereignty and provided an ideological basis for its interventions. Contrary to Western conceptions, strong states and governments are essential to control powerful and largely economic elements in society and ensure the public good.

Lastly, democracy is meaningless if national governments do not have the authority or capacity to respond to the interests of their citizens, and that is the case under regimes of neocolonialism which fosters weak states beholden to the West and its international institutions and not their own citizenry. As a result, the propagation of Western democracy has become a trap in which the United States and its allies pursue the latest phase of neocolonialism and increasingly democracy is reduced to a form of neoliberalism.

Indeed, with the advent of neoliberalism and the decline of Keynesian economics in the 1980s, alternatives to development models based on hyper-capitalism and subject to US hegemony have withered. This in turn precipitated the collapse of Western social democracy which has endorsed neoliberalism, the US international order and the US-led proxy war in Ukraine. It also led to increased Western aggression in the form of trade wars, sanctions, destabilization, organizing coups, inciting civil wars, confiscation of assets, proxy wars and full-scale invasions against states in the Global South that refused to accept Western rules and Western-dominated international institutions like the World Bank and the International Monetary Fund.

Apart from China it is only on the fringes of the international community that alternative forms of governance and economic organization can be found, and most of them have not proved viable nor attractive. The 1979 Iranian Revolution presents itself as a Shia-Islamist theocratic alternative to the West, but it has never broken from global capitalism or produced a radically different society. The regime, however, survived sustained attacks by Israel and the United States because of support from regional allies and the belated assistance of Russia and China fearful that such a strategically important country could become a US client state. Meanwhile, the rise to power of the National Islamic Front in Sudan in 1989 claimed to represent a Sunni alternative, but as we will see the civilizational project of the NIF failed and in the face of US opposition the regime never seriously attempted to develop an alternative economic system. Crucially neither the Iranian nor Sudanese models were taken up elsewhere in the Islamic world. Ethiopia's Ethiopian Peoples Revolutionary Democratic Front (EPRDF) was on track to introducing an alternative socialist model, but coming to power in 1991 at the end of the Cold War it could not expect support from Russia or China and thus it compromised its transformative plans.

Indeed, in the post-Cold War era the United States and its Western allies have largely had the capacity to either foreclose non-Western approaches or make those pursuing such approaches pay a high price. As a result, only a handful of states – North Korea, Cuba, Syria, Nicaragua, Venezuela and Eritrea – have managed to break free of Western hegemony and most have only survived because of support from Russia and China. North Korea and Cuba can be considered to constitute genuinely alternative social systems. Afghanistan's Taliban may be on the path to an alternative, albeit a dystopia, but its military defeat of the United States may produce the same kind of destabilization that Vietnam endured for decades after it defeated the United States. In any case the very clear message that the West conveys to the Global South is that any attempt to assert national autonomy and construct alternative modes of governance and economy will be violently opposed. Operating under the constant threat of elimination by the United States, these states have become pre-occupied with security and rarely serve as examples for other countries.

However, the power of the West and the United States to direct the affairs of the Global South in pursuit of its own interests is in decline, a new era of multipolarity is emerging and is likely to take form even quicker than could have been imagined before the outbreak of the Ukraine War in February 2022. The failure of the collective West to gain the support of the Global South in its conflict with Russia over Ukraine, the dramatic moves to peace in the Middle East in early 2023 despite Western opposition and the failure of the same collective West to crash the Russian economy with the most severe sanctions ever imposed on any country are indicative of the declining power of the US-led West. What follows, however, is not an attempt to imagine that future or the alternatives that might emerge, but to analyse conditions during what is likely to be a messy transitional period, or as

Gramsci put it, 'The crisis consists precisely in the fact that the old is dying and the new cannot be born; in this interregnum a great variety of morbid symptoms appear' (Antonio Gramsci, 1989).

## Organization of the book

The book begins with a chapter on the 'Rise and Decline of US Democracy'. Democracy as it is pressed on the Global South is Western democracy, and given the extent of its promotion, it is largely US democracy. A comprehensive critique of US democracy is not possible, but it is important to understand the model and means by which it is pressed on the HOA and other countries of the Global South. That involves an examination of the US liberal international order, the primacy given to elections, the propagation of Western democracy and its decline in the present era.

Democracy developed in conjunction with capitalism and imperialism, and for many Western political theorists, democracy is the political form of capitalism. However, capitalist democracy is an oxymoron since they have different and even conflicting value systems. The tensions between capitalism and democracy produced multiple crises in the nineteenth and early twentieth centuries but they were muted by the steady expansion of the vote and periodic application of state violence. However, the 1917 Bolshevik revolution made clear that unless carefully managed capitalism could produce its own grave diggers. From 1917 through the Great Depression until the Second World War an anti-capitalist revolution in the West looked like a distinct possibility.

But the Second World War ended unemployment, fostered trade unionism, increased workers' power, and, in an environment of war-induced hyper-nationalism, the prospects of revolution in the leading capitalist countries declined. This intensified in the post-war period by a widespread attack on left wing parties and left-led trade unions. Anxious that the end of the war should not produce an economic and political crisis as had occurred after the First World War and fearful of Soviet socialism, Western governments adopted Keynesian economic policies. These policies muted the class struggle and oversaw thirty years of what has been called the 'golden age of capitalism' when the economy grew, services expanded and the standard of living of workers improved. This was also the period in which the European empires were dissolved, the independent states of the Global South were largely brought under the control of the United States and its mega corporations which dominated the international economy, and the United States under the guise of NATO led the European states into a confrontation with the socialist bloc.

During this period the United States constructed and propagated a liberal world order to protect capitalism and ensure US hegemony. This involved a set of global, rule-based, structured relationships based on political liberalism, economic liberalism and liberal internationalism. By the late 1970s the bloom was coming off capitalist expansion: corporate profits were declining, workers' militancy was increasing, a growing number of countries in the Global South were embracing socialism and aligning with the Soviet Union. Meanwhile at home feminist, Black, campus and a host of protest movements demanded fundamental changes while a major peace movement developed in response to the Vietnam War. Against this background neoliberalism was introduced to reassert the power of capital, contain dissent and undermine state sovereignty in favour of the market.[2] This led to increasing economic polarization, the decline of the 'welfare state' and for most lowered living standards.

As a result of the West's victory in the Cold War it was assumed that the vast sums devoted to the military by the United States and its NATO allies would end and there would be a peace dividend. But that did not happen, and the first Gulf War made clear that there was to be no draw down in the commitment to US military hegemony. The Soviet rump state of Russia, a resurgent China, along with a host of other countries, were viewed as enemies of the United States which necessitated a continuing devotion to security. 9/11 led to NATO coming to the aid of the United States by invoking Article 5 which states that any attack on a member state will be considered an attack against the entire group. This in turn set the stage for the Global War on Terror (GWOT) and provided the rationale for the suspension of civil liberties, while the promise of democracy and freedom supplied the justification for the US-led invasion of Iraq and Afghanistan. American democracy as pressed on the Global South involves a rigid adherence to a market economy, globalization of trade, Western technology and values, an open society and multiculturalism, and an individualist focus on human rights that largely negates collective and national rights and undermines state sovereignty. These measures are pursued by both soft and military means under the rubric of the US international order. And that order is increasingly being undermined by both the rising power of China, Russia and the Global South and by a crisis within US democracy.

Although the regional and international dimensions of the struggles for democracy in the HOA are noted in the case studies of Ethiopia, Sudan and South Sudan, the following chapter 'Horn of Africa Relations in the Wake of US Decline' considers these dimensions holistically in a context where US power is in decline, China is a rising power and Russia has ended its post-Soviet subservience. This process began in the wake of US failures in the Iraq War, but considerably accelerated after the Russia–NATO proxy war in Ukraine began. Indicative of these changing power relations is that Middle Eastern states previously subject to the United States are increasingly becoming powers in their own right and are shaping the political trajectory of the HOA. The

---

2. Neoliberalism is here defined as 'the new political, economic, and social arrangements within society that emphasize market relations, re-tasking the role of the state, and individual responsibility' and 'the extension of competitive markets into all areas of life, including the economy, politics, and society' (Simon Springer, Kean Birch, and Julie MacLeavy, 2016).

United States and China are in the early stages of a big power competition, and while the United States characterizes this conflict as one between democracy and authoritarianism, the real contest is between efforts by the United States to maintain its global hegemony and the desire of China (and Russia) to establish a multipolar world. The primary focus of the United States and China as well as the Middle Eastern states is to project power in the Red Sea which links the Suez Canal and the Mediterranean to the Indian Ocean. This involves establishing naval bases, gaining commercial control of ports and building alliances with countries adjacent to the Red Sea. The United States has long dominated this area, but its economic role in the Middle East and by extension its political power in the region and the Horn are in decline, while China is becoming ever-more powerful in the economic, political and diplomatic spheres. This was graphically on display when China oversaw a peace agreement between the governments of Saudi Arabia and Iran, which the United States has long sought to either overthrow or isolate.

In this context Middle Eastern states have become increasingly active in Africa, particularly the adjacent HOA, where they have opposed a democratic transition in Sudan, and struggles for national self-determination by Tigrayans and Oromos in Ethiopia. Egypt, Saudi Arabia and the UAE played a role in displacing Sudan's Omar al-Bashir regime but sided with the military wing of the resulting transitional government and opposed demands of the street for a solely civilian government and a democratic transformation.

Turkiye, the UAE and Iran provided Ethiopia's Abiy Ahmed government with weaponry, particularly drones, which saved it from being overthrown in late 2021 by Tigrayan forces advancing on Addis Ababa. While pursuing their national interests in the HOA has sometimes involved China and Russia coming to the support of unsavoury regimes who happen to be at odds with the United States, their growing power in the region and opposition to Western hegemony is providing a small window for countries in the region to pursue alternative forms of development, governance and international alliances.

What follows are three case studies drawn from the HOA, in the first instance because this is my area of expertise, but also because the negative experience of these states with Western democracy is sufficiently diverse that the conclusions drawn can be generalized to much of the Global South. Ethiopia's post-1991 rulers rejected Western democracy but failed to construct an effective alternative means of accountable government and were replaced by Abiy Ahmed who espoused democracy but was soon more authoritarian than the country's previous rulers and moreover took the country into a horrific war. Meanwhile, Sudan has experienced repeated democratic popular uprisings that had widespread support, but to date they have failed to achieve sustainable democracy and instead on each occasion brought the military to power. In April 2023 factions of the security services began a violent conflict for power in the state. Lastly, the United States served as the 'midwife' of the world's newest independent state, South Sudan, but it has failed to realize Western and local hopes of achieving democracy and has become a kleptocratic dictatorial state suffering chronic war and instability.

The chapter 'Ethiopia and the Challenge of Democracy' focuses on the period from 1991 when the EPRDF assumed state power to 2019 when Prime Minister Abiy Ahmed dissolved the Front and established the Prosperity Party. Ethiopia had long been organized as an empire-state under an Amhara-centred feudal aristocracy which was overthrown by the military in 1974 after years of student and workers' agitation and regional revolts. The military unleashed a social revolution by eliminating the feudal class and nationalizing land, but was unwilling to share power, brutal, and did not recognize the rights of oppressed nations. Assisted by the Eritrean Peoples Liberation Front (EPLF), the military was overthrown by the EPRDF together with the Oromo Liberation Front (OLF) and other smaller groups, all calling for the end of Amhara domination and national self-determination.

The cornerstone of the EPRDF programme was its system of multinational federalism which was modelled after the early experience of the Soviet Union. However, while the Bolsheviks supported a class-based unity of workers and peasants that transcended their national identities, under the Front ethno-nationalism became an end in itself and this fostered increasing instability.

The EPRDF rejected the Western focus on individual rights and held that sovereignty resides – according to its constitution – with the 'nations, nationalities, and peoples of Ethiopia'. Further, the EPRDF maintained that liberal democracy was inappropriate for a country emerging from feudalism and that Ethiopia's endemic poverty necessitated a major role of the state in the economy. Contending that Ethiopia's poverty posed an existential threat to the country it constructed a developmental state which between 2004 and 2019 produced growth rates over 9 per cent, while poverty declined from 46 per cent in 1995 to 24 per cent in 2016 (Chowdhury and Sundaram, 30 August 2021). Although the EPRDF welcomed foreign capital, state-led development was a constant source of tensions with the West and the IMF. The EPRDF established a parliamentary form of governance, but most power resided with the EPRDF, and this too was a source of tension with the West and domestically.

The Front believed its system of federalism resolved the problem of national oppression and that together with rising living standards and developmentalism would gain it legitimacy when what was required was a democratization of the country. To be sure, the EPRDF's arguments against liberal democracy were sound, multinational federalism went far to ending national oppression, and raising the standard of living of Ethiopia's destitute peasantry represented important democratic advances, even if they are not recognized by the proponents of Western democracy. But the failure of the EPRDF to construct a system of accountable governance produced extreme forms of ethno-nationalism, the demise of the EPRDF and civil war in November 2020. The pitiless lesson of Ethiopia is that without popular acceptance the EPRDF's considerable achievements have been ground to dust in war.

Although having a markedly different trajectory than Ethiopia, as considered in 'Sudan, the United States, and the Propagation of Democracy', Sudan has also been unable to implement a sustainable system of democracy. Unlike Ethiopia,

Sudan was a model British colony and had a relatively well-developed civil society when it attained independence peacefully in 1956. But as was typical in colonial societies, the departing British handed over state power to a carefully nurtured elite drawn from traditional Muslim sectarian elites from the riverine core of Sudan to protect their interests.

This model proved disastrous, and Sudan has been ruled by dictatorships for most of its post-colonial history and the country has experienced multiple wars in the periphery, including the loss of one-third of its territory and people with the secession of South Sudan in 2011. Unlike Ethiopia, in Sudan Western democracy has been the demand of three uprisings and regional-based revolts. But these uprisings did not produce sustainable democracies and the failures of the 1986–9 democratic government gave rise to an Islamist-led coup government which held power until 2019. When the Islamist regime could no longer be saved, the military overthrew President al-Bashir to protect its interests, a military-civilian transitional government was formed and in October 2021 the military carried out another coup and ruled on its own. Although its rhetoric suggests otherwise, the United States has generally favoured Sudanese dictatorships, undermined the 1986–9 democratic government and supported a military-civilian transitional government in 2019 over a civil administration wanted by the people.

A major problem of the three post-uprising governments is that they were devoted to implementing a Western conception of democracy which gives primacy to elections and protection of political and individual rights. This produced endless discussions, jockeying for power and a focus on issues of concern to the political elites. But it gave short shrift to the demands of repressed minorities and regions and failed to improve the dire living conditions of most Sudanese. Hobbled by their divisions, the limitations of parliamentarianism and the opposition of vested interests, the democratic governments never carried out the needed structural changes, and soon the people became disillusioned with the politicians' games and that provided the opening for the next coup.

'South Sudan: Another Failed United States Democracy Project' provides a different example of the failure of Western democracy. Informed by post-Cold War fears that a 'failed state' was a threat to regional stability and the Responsibility to Protect doctrine, the second Clinton administration became increasingly engaged in the civil war in Sudan, despite the country's lack of strategic significance. Further propelling this engagement was the influence of a Democratic Party-linked lobby group mesmerized by the southern Sudanese rebel leader, Dr John Garang. Even though Garang had until recently presented as a Marxist-Leninist, was supported by the Soviet-backed Derg and his Sudan Peoples Liberation Army (SPLA) had an appalling record of human rights abuses, the lobbyists repackaged him as an African hero and a democrat fighting for the rights of oppressed southern Sudanese Africans victimized by northern Sudanese Arabs.

With Clinton's departure, the Bush administration took up Sudan's civil war, although this time the concern was with southern Sudanese Christians persecuted by northern Sudanese Muslims because evangelical Christians constituted a major part of Bush's constituency. Bush responded by supporting a regional-based, but Western-dominated, peace process. The resulting agreement committed the Government of Sudan and the SPLA to jointly carry out a democratic transformation if the southern Sudanese voted in a referendum for unity or for each party to construct democratic states should southern Sudanese vote to secede. However, the northern and southern Sudanese elites had no intention of overseeing a democratic transformation as made clear by the 2010 national elections which were widely viewed as fraudulent. Despite the critical role elections play for theorists of Western democracy and the importance of democracy for supporters of liberal peacemaking, the Western-led international community endorsed the election to ensure that the peace process was not derailed.

In the 2011 referendum southern Sudanese voted overwhelmingly to secede and the peace agreement served as the constitution for the six-year transitional period and the independent government. The United States shaped the resulting government and South Sudan was intended to become a model of Western democracy. But after Garang died in a helicopter crash in 2005, the SPLA and Government of South Sudan were led by Salva Kiir who was primarily concerned with institutionalizing the domination of his Dinka community and reaping the spoils of office. As explained below this led to growing inter-ethnic tensions and after Salva's US-trained and -equipped security services unleashed a genocidal attack on the Nuer led by his Vice-President, Dr. Riek Macher, in the capital city of Juba in December 2013, the country descended into civil war. By the end of 2021 the war had left half of South Sudan's estimated population of 12 million dependent on foreign food relief and 400,000 people had died. Not only had the country proved unable to realize its enormous economic potential but the Western model of democracy that it was bequeathed has failed.

In the 'Conclusion' I contend that the case studies of Ethiopia, Sudan and South Sudan make clear the failure of the US model of democracy and the pressing need for models that better address their needs and the people of the Global South. This can only be achieved by a fundamental break from Western subservience; in other words, democracy is unattainable without national sovereignty. Further, the rights of oppressed national and other minorities must be championed and mobilized in a unifying class struggle devoted to raising living standards and addressing economic and social injustices. The US liberal international order is in decline and along with it the systems of governance, institutions and values that have served as a global framework since the end of the Cold War and that provides an opportunity for the re-emergence of the Non-Alignment Movement and the kind of changes that until now had been impossible.

# Chapter 1

## RISE AND DECLINE OF US DEMOCRACY

The roots of Western democracy lie in the French and American revolutions, the spread of capitalism, and the growth of an increasingly militant working class unwilling to accept its marginalization. The mounting political consciousness of the working class, women, racialized minorities and others threatened stability and they had to be pacified through the expansion of the ballot and granting basic rights if capitalism was to survive. The need for stability and Western unity continued during the Cold War and the West was compelled to institute some controls over the market, increase social welfare measures and oversee a steady rise in living standards. But faced with a multifaceted crisis in the 1970s neoliberalism gave the market primacy in meeting social welfare needs, reformulated the state to better serve the interests of big capital and made capitalism a defining feature of democracy.

With the end of the Second World War and the start of the Cold War, a US-led international order was constructed to militarily confront the socialist Eastern Bloc, protect Western market economies, provide a legal regime and ideological framework for US global dominance, and promote a version of democracy based on capitalism. Pursued through the UN, IMF, World Bank, the World Trade Organization, treaties and economic agreements, the bounded orders (West versus Soviet) became a US liberal international order with the end of the Cold War. And within this context the United States set about propagating an American version of democracy that involved subservience to Washington and a notion of human rights shaped by neoliberalism. While the United States zealously protected its own national sovereignty, the international liberal order set about undermining national sovereignty by popularizing liberal peacemaking, the Responsibility to Protect doctrine, and endorsing the notion of failed states. Collectively these measures provided the legal or political basis for US-led military interventions and the imposition of sanctions for states unwilling to accept the US international order. Significantly the US international world order was pursued in opposition to and as an alternative to a UN-based system of international law. For many years after the Second World War this approach ensured the unipolar dominance of the United States, but a new era is emerging in which Russia, China and important sections of the Global South are refusing to accept this order.

Elections are held to be the centre-piece of US democracy by 82 per cent of Americans, but at the same time 31 per cent of the population does not believe they have free and fair elections according to the 2022 Democracy Perception Index (Latana, 2022).[1] Increasingly US elections are no longer considered a means to determine the general will of the people but instead simply a mechanism for the orderly circulation of elites, the preservation of the status quo and that these same elites lead the institutions of the liberal world order. Under the influence of neoliberalism human rights necessitate a market economy, while social and economic rights are usually dismissed as products of a failed Soviet socialism. But the orderly transfer of power among a broadly united elite is breaking down and the outcome of elections is no longer accepted by large number of citizens.

Added to this, in recent years successive US governments have pursued a Global War on Terror (GWOT), 'surveillance capitalism', foreign wars to fight 'terrorism' and propagate Western democracy, and censorship of unacceptable political views. Under the guise of national security, the result has been to undermine fundamental rights to free speech, assembly and privacy. In recent years this has involved the complementarity of interests between the security agencies, the mass media, big technology companies and the Democratic Party. This is threatening the viability and legitimacy of American democracy as well as producing growing alienation and dissent.

## US liberal international order

Crucial to US hegemony, warding off the threat of Eastern Bloc and domestic socialism, and establishing global hegemony were the construction of a US-led order or a rules-based order. An 'order' according to Mearsheimer is 'an organized group of international institutions that help govern the interactions among the member states [and] Great Powers create and manage orders' (John Mearsheimer, 1 April 2019). Great powers write the rules of the order to advance their own interests. Since the late 1940s this has involved a set of structured relationships based on political liberalism, economic liberalism and liberal internationalism under US leadership (David Lake, Lisa Martin, and Thomas Risse, 2021). The main instruments to achieving this were NATO, the World Bank, the IMF, General Agreement on Tariffs and Trade (GATT) which was absorbed into the World Trade Organization (WTO), a host of trade agreements and a selective acceptance of human rights accords.

Washington's new world order took form at Bretton Woods, New Hampshire, in July 1944 where forty-four Allied nations forged a new financial system led by the World Bank and at San Francisco in June 1945, where the UN Charter was drafted. The international order, however, was held together by NATO

---

1. The same study found that only 5 per cent of the Chinese believe they do not have free and fair elections.

whose task was to 'keep the Russians out, the Americans in, and the Germans down', according to its first Secretary General, Lord Ismay. While NATO's civil administration is run by Europeans, its military command represented by the Supreme Allied Commander Europe (SACEUR) stationed in Belgium has always been an American who also reports to the Pentagon. Moreover, constituent states must formally submit their ratification to Washington – not Brussels, the nominal headquarters of NATO. Because Western European countries were wary of its re-armament, NATO provided the cover to re-arm West Germany by embedding it in a larger military grouping, as well as playing an important role in controlling socialist and communist parties *within* member states.

NATO was the premier military alliance of the United States, but not the only one: the United States established pacts with countries and regions to contain the Soviet Union and China during the Cold War while the Five Eyes made up of the Anglo-Saxon states of the United States, Canada, UK, Australia and New Zealand was established during the Second World War and has continued to the present. It was supplemented in 2021 when Australia, UK and the United States (AUKUS) signed a security pact aimed at China, while the Quad made up of the United States, Japan, India and Australia was also established to contain China. In addition, the United States has 130,000 soldiers in eighty countries and could have as many as 1,000 military bases around the world (Alice Slater, 24 January 2018).

With the end of the Cold War and the easing of international tensions, it was widely assumed that there would be a peace dividend, but instead the stage was set for the unipolar dominance of the United States and the construction of the US liberal international order. The character of that order was made clear in the first decade of the post-Cold War era with a new age of militarism and imperialism as the United States carried out wars and 'humanitarian' interventions in Panama, the Persian Gulf, Somalia, Haiti, Bosnia, Columbia and Serbia while maintaining Cold War deployments in East Asia and the Pacific (Chalmers Johnson, 2004, p. 3).

Instead of dissolving when Communist Party of the Soviet Union General Secretary Mikhail Gorbachev agreed to the unity of East and West Germany and to disband the Warsaw Pact, NATO expanded. And this, despite the fact that the United States had no ideological enemy, faced a much-degraded Russian Federation anxious to be part of a European community, and had promised Gorbachev that NATO would not expand east. NATO rejected Gorbachev's proposal for unity from Lisbon to Vladivostok, characterized by a pan-European security system, free trade and 'intra-European relations founded on international law' (Tom Casier, 2018, p. 17). In March 1999, Poland, Hungary and the Czech Republic joined NATO making clear that a post-communist Russia was still viewed as the principal threat. In June 2008 Russian President Dmitri Medvedev advocated a new regional European Security Pact, based on the United Nations Charter (Oleg Shchedrov, 5 June 2008). But this appeal too was rejected by the West, which looked to NATO to achieve security and propagate a US liberal international order as an alternative to international law. *The New York Times* editorial board acknowledged that NATO was 'the core of an American-led liberal world order' (New York Times, 8 July 2018). Indeed, NATO is becoming global with military operations in Afghanistan, the bombing of Libya, proxy war in Ukraine and its aggressive position on Taiwan.

Complementing its military confrontation with the Eastern Bloc, the United States and its Western allies supported a human rights narrative that contrasted the human rights of the West with the supposed lack of human rights in the Eastern Bloc by discounting their emphasis on economic and social rights. The West, and particularly the United States, has been ambivalent about the United Nations Charter and the *Universal Declaration of Human Rights* (UDHR) of 1948 and has largely ignored the two UN Covenants on Civil and Political Rights, and on Economic, Social and Cultural Rights of 1966. This is ironic because a speech in 1944 by President Franklin Roosevelt which emphasized that 'the one supreme objective for the future' for all nations is security and that meant 'economic security, social security, moral security' provided an important stimulus for the UN Covenants (Cass Sunstein, 1 October 2004). Under US rendering, the UN Charter principles of sovereign equality, non-intervention, international cooperation and prohibition of violence have largely been rejected. Human rights in turn are separated from the governing principles of international law or the body of decisions, precedents, agreements and treaties under the umbrella of the *Charter of the United Nations* and the multiple institutions, policies and protocols attached to it.

Together the UN Covenants constitute an explicit inclusion of economic, social and cultural rights as human rights within the scope of international law and can be seen as a reproach to neoliberalism, not only because of the rights designated, but because to realize them involves state regulation of the market. These rights include but are not limited to the right to work, just and favourable conditions of work, the right to form and join trade unions, the right to an adequate standard of living, and the rights to food, adequate housing, health and education (Jeff King, 2003). The Covenants also make clear that 'all peoples have the right of self-determination. By virtue of that right they freely determine their political status and freely pursue their economic, social and cultural development'.

The United States agreed to the treaty on political rights in 1992 but has still not ratified the *International Covenant on Economic, Social and Cultural Rights* (Civil and Human Rights News, 10 December 2013), one of only a handful of countries which have refused. US policy since the Reagan administration has been to define human rights only as civil and political rights and to exclude economic, social and cultural rights. The United States has used the language of human rights but has sought to undermine broader interpretations of human rights and international law while simultaneously co-opting them to claimed rights to the global free movement of capital and maintaining the security of foreign investment (Iona Cable, 27 April 2021).

As well as its objections to parts of the UDHR and the Covenants, the United States refuses to accept the authority of the International Criminal Court (ICC) over Americans (even while it supported ICC efforts to prosecute Sudan's President

Omar al-Bashir).[2] It also does not generally allow its armed forces to be led by non-American UN officers, and only contributes about 1 per cent of the costs of UN peacekeeping missions (United Nations Peacekeeping). The United States also objected to international law when, for example, it was used to prosecute Chile's former dictator Augusto Pinochet who the United States helped bring to power (CNN, 12 April 1999). The United States went to the extreme of passing the American Servicemembers Protection Act of 2002 (otherwise known as the Hague Invasion Act) which authorizes the use of military force to liberate any American or citizen of a US-allied country held by the court, located in The Hague (Human Rights Watch, 3 August 2002). Further demonstrating its 'exceptional' character, the United States rejected the decision of the International Court of Justice which found that US actions in training and financing the Nicaraguan contras, their attack on Puerto Sandino and interference with maritime commerce constituted breaches of international law and the obligation not to violate national sovereignty (Martin Cleaver and Mark Tran, 28 June 1986).

The United States passed the 1948 *Convention on the Prevention and Punishment of Genocide* drafted in the aftermath of the Holocaust in 1988, but only after it lodged a reservation to protect itself from being brought before the court against its will for any alleged violation (Rebecca Hamilton, 17 August 2011). Under the US international order, the United States does not consider itself bound by international law, or to put it differently the United States refuses to be bound by any set of laws or organizations which it does not control.

Following the precepts of neoliberalism, the United States and many Western human rights organizations hold the market to be a precondition for human rights. Western leaders feared that post-colonial states would employ the human rights narrative and the emphasis on political equality to pursue economic equality and redistribute resources and sought to create a global order that would curtail these demands. They sought to entrench a notion of human rights based on 'the morals of the market' which involved individualistic and commercial values that prioritized the pursuit of self-interest above the development of common purposes (Jessica Whyte, 2019). This perspective was at odds with that of Marx who held that the freedom of human beings was to be achieved

---

2. Continuing a policy that began with the establishment of the ICC, US National Security Advisor, John Bolton, described the ICC as 'illegitimate' and threatened sanctions against its judges should the court proceed with any investigation into alleged war crimes by Americans in Afghanistan (BBC, 11 September 2018). Secretary of State, Mike Pompeo, announced diplomatic sanctions against the International Criminal Court. Members of the court investigating war crimes committed during the Afghanistan war would be denied entry to the United States, he said. Pompeo also imposed sanctions on International Criminal Court prosecutor Fatou Bensouda (Daphne Psaledakis and Michelle Nichols, 15 September 2020). As well as protecting its own citizens against charges by the ICC, the United States also protects Israel from charges related to abuses by its citizens in the Middle East.

through collective liberation and that the individual liberty championed by classical liberalism was selfish. This truncated understanding of human rights has figured prominently as a justification for its military interventions, such as that in Libya which was also supported by leading Western human rights organizations. According to Alfred de Zayas, a former UN independent expert on the Promotion of a Democratic and Equitable International Order, a human rights industry has been established to advance the geo-political interests of the West (Alfred de Zayas, 2022).

In the heady days around the end of the Cold War when President George H. W. Bush was engaged in talks with Mikhail Gorbachev, the vision of a new liberal democratic peaceful world under the leadership of the United States took form. Bush launched what he called the 'new world order' (George H. W. Bush, 11 September 1990) because 'there is no substitute for American leadership', or as President Clinton and Madeleine Albright liked to say, the United States is 'the indispensable nation' (Peter Jackson, 29 October 2021). This meant a rejection of international law, and in his State of the Union address on 28 January 2003, George Bush Junior declared that if the Security Council did not agree to military action against Iraq, he would act contrary to the prohibition on the use of violence of the UN Charter (Michael Welton, 2 May 2022). Indeed, the United States has always opposed a UN-based system of international law because that system rejects the use of force in foreign policy.

The expectation was that with the victories of the Western democracies in the Cold War there would be a new era of peace, and this encouraged a revival of the thesis by Immanuel Kant that democracy provided an antidote to war by fostering commerce which makes war unprofitable (George Smith, 20 June 2016). In *The Great Transformation*, Karl Polanyi followed a similar tract and held that peace and trade had become linked by way of monetary integration and this muted geo-political rivalries (Karl Polanyi, 1944). Francis Fukuyama took a step further and contended that the end of the Cold War would usher in a global liberal democracy and ensure world peace (Francis Fukuyama, 1989).

From those beliefs it was contended that there has never been a war between democracies, but Mearsheimer provided contrary examples, many cases of democracies waging wars in pursuit of democracy, and held that such theories could not provide an explanation of why democracies would not go to war with one another (John Mearsheimer, 2018, p. 195) Moreover, a thirty-two-year study into the association of democracy and conflict globally concluded that the spread of democracy does not reduce the level of conflict (D. Reiter, 2001).

Contrary to expectations the end of the Cold War did not usher in a world of peace and instead fuelled a growing number of internal conflicts. In response and inspired by the Western optimism of the period, the UN published *An Agenda for Peace: Preventive Diplomacy, Peace-Making and Peace Keeping* in 1992. The Agenda for Peace was informed by liberal principles and values and as a result peacekeeping became 'liberal peacekeeping' (Michael Barnett, 1997). However, in marked contrast to the recent past which stressed national sovereignty, the Agenda held that 'the time of absolute and exclusive sovereignty ... has passed'.

This declaration began a process of undermining state sovereignty and provided justification for Western interventions in the Global South.

The many failures of this approach led the UN to issue a *Supplement to an Agenda for Peace* in 1995 which called for more nuanced theorization and a wider frame of reference for internationally sponsored peacemaking missions. The Supplement attributed the increase in internal conflicts in Africa to the continent's global marginalization and called for deepening the continent's ties with the developed world. The Supplement also called for consideration of the 'root causes' of conflicts, but in practice the West refused to consider the possibility that capitalism or economic and political dependency, much less neoliberalism, could be root causes of conflicts. Problems continued, however, and in 2001 the Security Council further broadened the focus of peacemaking to include the promotion of democracy (UN, 2001). But none of these refinements overcame the political character of the process, or the fact that UN-orchestrated peacemaking was still directed at reproducing liberal Western states and societies in environments where such values and institutions had little resonance (John Young, 2012, p. 6). Indeed, as will be seen below US-led liberal peacemaking in Sudan and South Sudan did not result in any real understanding of the roots of the conflict, did not lead to a democratic transformation and often exacerbated conflicts.

The liberal peacemaking approach of the UN was embraced by the United States because it closely corresponded to US political and economic interests. It involves 'the promotion of democracy, market-based economic reforms and a range of other institutions associated with "modern" states as a driving force for building "peace"' (Newman, Paris, and Richmond, 2009, p. 3). Crucially liberal peacemaking involves elevating Western experience, values and ideals to the level of universality (Oliver Richmond, July 2008). Peacemaking and particularly peacekeeping has taken the form in the post-Cold War era of unilateral military action by major powers (typically the United States) in which the UN acts as a sanctioning mechanism (Phyllis Bennis, 1996). Bennis argues that any UN commitment to peacekeeping simply reflects the interests of the United States: 'In foreign policy analysis it must be taken for granted that any government's decision-making will be guided by the perceived interests of that government ... not by the broader, more evanescent sound bite concerns of internationalism or humanitarianism' (Phyllis Bennis, 1996, p. 84).

In the same vein, the UN endorsed the Responsibility to Protect (R2P) doctrine in 2009 which also undermined the principle of state sovereignty and provided a rationale for increased international (read Western) intervention. The atrocities committed in the 1990s in the Balkans and Rwanda, which the international community failed to prevent, and the NATO bombing of a sovereign Serbia for three months without a UN Security Council resolution served to undermine notions of international cooperation and of Western intervention premised on humanitarianism. Needing a stronger ideological basis, the Canadian government established the International Commission on Intervention and State Sovereignty (ICISS), which issued a report entitled 'The Responsibility to Protect' (ICISS, 2001). Inspired by Francis Deng, a Sudanese and subsequent South Sudanese national after South Sudan's secession, the report concluded that sovereignty is dependent upon the state's responsibility to its people and if that is not fulfilled then the contract between the government and its citizen is void and sovereignty is not legitimate.

This opened the door to external intervention, but the report refrained from identifying what would constitute just cause for preemptive humanitarian intervention, who other than a vague international community would decide that just cause requirements had been met, and who or which country or organization would carry out the intervention. Despite the multiple levels of confusion two years later President George Bush used the just cause rationale to justify the US invasion of Iraq (Dale Snauwaert, 2004). When the R2P doctrine was being debated in the UN, the then Nicaraguan President of the UN General Assembly, Miguel d'Escoto Brockmann, said a more accurate name for R2P would be the 'right to intervene' (Miguel d'Escoto Brockmann, 28 July 2009), and the targets for intervention have invariably been enemies of the West.

Parallel to this was the growing popularity among the Western foreign policy establishment of the notion of a failed state, or a state that has deteriorated to a point where it no longer assumed the responsibilities of a sovereign government or exerted control over its territory, and thus posed a threat to the citizens of the country and crucially neighbouring states and the international liberal order. Like R2P, the application of the term failed state was used to justify Western military interventions and state-building based on Western models (Susan Woodward, 2017). It was employed to legitimize the US invasion of Afghanistan and US peacemaking in Sudan. Having defined the problem as a dysfunctional state, the solution was held to lie in introducing Western practices of liberal market-oriented governance (John Young, 2012, p. 7). And if these measures failed to produce the desired results, there were sanctions, colour revolutions and ultimately invasions.

Buttressing the US international order, the ideological underpinning of Western interventions in the Global South was provided by modernization theory which emerged in the 1950s as the leading explanation of how the industrial societies of North America and Western Europe had developed and was presented as a model for the rest of the world. Ignoring the role of slavery and imperialism in the development of the West, the theory concentrated on overcoming internal obstacles to development to transform 'traditional' societies into modern capitalist countries, and the role that Western intervention and aid programmes could have in that process. Although forced to introduce representative institutions, they were not designed to guarantee democratic rights and freedoms but instead were employed to safeguard and protect the institutions that had secured foreign domination over the people of Africa (Crawford Young, 1994).

The most influential formulation of this theory was Walter Rostow's *The Stages of Economic Growth: A Non-Communist Manifesto* (Walter Rostow, 1960) which attempted to repel communist advances and informed a generation of US agencies and foreign development policies (Dianne Kunz, 1997, pp. 125–8). As its critics pointed out, modernization theory was ethnocentric, did not explain the development of countries like Japan which modernized without ending traditional practices and was foremost a mechanism to counter the growing appeal of socialist versions of development that were popular in this period. In the face of these criticisms, modernization theory retreated, but many of these ideas were repackaged in the 1980s as neoliberalism with a new emphasis on the centrality of markets in development.

In the post-war years the West opposed developing countries attempting to protect domestic industries against foreign competition and employed the language of human rights to argue for the right of free capital movement and this led to the establishment of the World Trade Organization in 1995 (World Trade Organization). Although protectionism to facilitate industrial development had been critical to the rapid industrialization of the Soviet Union and the United States in their early history, it was largely denied to developing countries because protectionism was considered a relic of a failed Soviet model of state-led development. Countries in the Global South were pressed to concentrate on their comparative advantage, which meant accepting their role as providers of raw materials in an international division of labour which reinforced their secondary position in the global economy.

One consequence of this trade regime – indeed a clear objective of the World Bank – has been to undermine food grain self-sufficiency in developing countries and thus provide markets for surplus food grains from the metropoles while turning land-use in the peripheries into centres for the export of cash crops. As a result of WTO- and IMF-imposed Structural Adjustment Programs, Africa was transformed from a net food exporter into a net food importer in the 1980s, and between 1980 and 2007 Africa's total net food imports grew at an average of 3.4 per cent per year in real terms (Anis Chowdhury and Jomo Sundaram, 14 October 2017). Making countries of the Global South dependent on food imports from the United States also means making them vulnerable to Western sanctions. As the late President of Burkina Faso, Thomas Sankara, succinctly put it, 'He who feeds you controls you.'

Further undermining the national sovereignty of developing countries, the World Bank and IMF became major proponents of 'good governance' as part of the war against corruption. In practice this served as another means for the West to oppose strong state regulation and support privatization. Since corruption was held to be rooted in the post-colonial state, the state or at least an activist state was attacked as a means to press for privatization and acceptance of governance-related conditionalities for the provision of aid (Charlie Kimber, 27 June 2005). Another venue for this attack was over the New Partnership for African Development ((NEPAD), 37th Session of the Heads of State, 2001) which rejected state-led or autonomous development. NEPAD proponents held that African governments were largely responsible for the continent's poor economic performance and their marginal role in the global economy, and this necessitated a commitment to good governance linked to economic liberalization while government intervention in the economy was associated with bad governance. African leaders committed to abide to Western stipulated codes of governance and adherence to neoliberalism in return for development assistance and loans.

The end of the Cold War with the West's victory over the Eastern Bloc was held by Western decision-makers as a global endorsement of American democracy. In his 1992 triumphalist study – *The End of History and the Last Man* – Francis Fukuyama claimed that capitalism and Western liberal democracy represented the endpoint of human history. Authoritarian regimes had outgrown their populations as education and politicization expanded and liberal democracy was the only conceivable future (Fukuyama, 1992, pp. 42–3). It was thus only a small step to Margaret Thatcher's contention that 'there is no alternative' or TINA (Claire Berlinski, 8 November 2011). In the wake of this victory the US-led West demanded that its system of economic organization, governance, values and ideology be embraced by states in the periphery, while socialism was to be relegated to history's dustbin. Following this reasoning Fukuyama has been a strong supporter of NATO and held that if 'the United States and the rest of the West' does not stop Russia, China and other non-democratic powers from doing as they wish and dominate the world, we could be facing the 'end of history' (Santiago Zabala and Claudio Gallo, 10 May 2022).

The establishment and development of the US international liberal order with its undermining of national sovereignty and the singular pursuit of US expansionist interests represented the final rejection of Westphalian principles. As Kissinger explained, those principles involved an acceptance of reality and rejection of any moral superiority and instead 'relied on a system of independent states refraining from interference in each other's domestic affairs and checking each other's ambitions through a general equilibrium of power' (Henry Kissinger, 2014).

## *Rise and decline of US elections*

Western theorists of democracy consider multi-party elections of all adults the essence of a democratic society, but such elections were not held until well into the twentieth century. Leaders of the American Revolution were all wealthy white men, some of them slave owners, and were not only opposed to the vote for Afro-Americans, women and indigenous people, but also the white working class. Even after the American Revolution most states retained property requirements that prevented working-class and poor people from voting on the grounds that to be trustworthy citizens needed an economic stake in the society. As a result, it is estimated that when George Washington won the first US presidential vote only 6 per cent of the population was eligible to vote (Northern California Citizenship Project, 2004). It was not until 1860 that more than 90 per cent of adult white men possessed the right to vote.

While the 13th Amendment banned slavery and all involuntary servitude, the 1868 14th Amendment declared that all male citizens over twenty-one years old should be able to vote and the 1870 15th Amendment affirmed the right to vote irrespective of race (Aaron Finch, 16 November 2021). However, the southern states suppressed the Black vote through intimidation and acts of violence, literacy tests, and the like until the civil rights movement in the 1960s and the passage of the Civil Rights Act and the Voting Rights Act, and even later there have been obstacles to Black and poor people voting. The struggle of women for the vote was not realized until the passing of the 19th Amendment in 1919. And indigenous Americans were not permitted to vote until the passing of the Snyder Act of 1924, and it still took over forty years for all fifty states to allow Native Americans to vote (Library of Congress).

The pivotal place that elections hold in the American understanding of democracy and even the understanding of democracy writ large is based to a considerable degree on Joseph Schumpeter's 1942 publication of *Capitalism, Socialism and Democracy*. Although a book about what Schumpeter considered the inevitability of socialism replacing capitalism, his refining of democracy became 'canonical in postwar American political science' (Gerry Mackie, 2009). Schumpeter challenges the classical doctrine of democracy which held that the people through their elected representatives realize the common good. He says there is usually no will of the people, nor common good, and when there is, autocracy is preferable. Schumpeter favoured the rule of knowledgeable elites in society, a view he shared with Max Weber who called for 'competitive elitism'. Voters do not control legislatures and are instead controlled by leaders who manufacture the will of the people, Schumpeter held.

Devoid of any ethical content democracy is merely an instrument for the orderly circulation of elites who compete for votes in elections. According to Schumpeter, 'Democracy does not mean and cannot mean that the people actually rule in any obvious sense of terms "people" and "rule". Democracy means only that the people have the opportunity of accepting or refusing the men who are to rule them' (Joseph Schumpeter, 1987, pp. 284–5). Democracy can only be representative democracy and that is expressed by 'the rule of the politician'. Nor are elections a contest between contesting ideological or political agendas and instead they are largely about removing political leaders that fail to perform. Schumpeter's work drew on that of classical elite theorists such as Mosca, Pareto and Michel who contended that in practice democracy is a system where the organized few rule over the unorganized majority. But his contribution was to emphasize the critical role that the process, and particularly elections, played in determining democracy.

Samuel Huntington, arguably the leading American political scientist of his generation, followed Schumpeter and held that free and fair elections are the essence of democracy and dismissed 'fuzzy norms' such as honesty, equal participation and power, and openness as being key to democracy (Samuel Huntington, 1991, p. 9). According to Huntington, the objective of elections is not to ascertain the concerns of the people, much less make governments accountable to the people, and instead they are held to ensure stability and the maintenance of the status quo. A political system is democratic 'to the extent that its most powerful collective decision-makers are selected through fair, honest, and periodic elections' (Huntington, 1991, p. 7).

There is an overwhelming emphasis on procedural definitions of democracy in the mainstream literature on democracy, particularly with respect to the non-Western world (Rita Abrahamsen, 2000, p. 68). Neither Weber, Schumpeter nor Huntington considered the limited influence of the citizenry in government a matter of concern, and indeed, Hochschild argues 'as democracies become more democratic, their decision-making processes become of lower quality in terms of cognitive processing of issues and candidate choice' (Jennifer Hochschild, June 2010). In light of these conditions and the assumption that the West exemplified democracy and served as a model for developing countries, there has been little interest in expanding democratic control beyond the focus on elections. The rejection of any normative understandings of democracy and 'what already exists provides the basis for the definition of democracy, while ideals of participation and self-fulfillment are regarded as irrelevant' (Rita Abrahamsen, 2000, p. 72).

One obvious problem with the emphasis on elections and procedures which Schumpeter and Huntington failed to address is that almost all countries in the contemporary world regularly hold elections, even elections that can be considered free and fair (or at least as free and fair as those conducted by the Western democracies), but by any normative understanding they cannot be considered democratic. For example, Narendra Modi of India, Rodrigo Duterte of the Philippines and Jair Bolsonaro of Brazil were invited by the Biden Administration to the first of two 'Summits for Democracy' on 9–10 December 2021, but their governments have been involved in the systemic abuse of human rights. Likewise, Israel was invited to the conference despite its oppression of Palestinians. As Professor John Keane noted, the guest list was a 'cynically drawn up, bureaucratically crafted, agency-structured invitation list that includes states that by any measure are falling way down the democracy rankings or aren't democracies at all' (Sydney Morning Herald, 11 December 2021).

The approach of Schumpeter and Huntington is premised on the conviction that democracy in the sense of collective decision-making is impossible and at best can serve as a safeguard against the concentration of political power (Stephen McBride, 2022, p. 39). Indeed, Huntington emphasizes the importance of free, open, and fair elections, high voter participation, stability, and institutionalization, while placing limits on political power (Samuel Huntington, 1991, p. 12). Such a perspective assumes a high degree of depoliticization in which the market together with technocrats and experts make most of the decision-making independent of official representatives.

As a result, 'the ballot box gives the illusion of freedom of political choice and popular sovereignty when all aspects of the citizen's life are surrendered to an institutional structure under the control of the financial elites whose interests the political class serves' (Cesran International, 2016). In 2007 Alan Greenspan, the former chair of the US Federal Reserve, came to a similar conclusion. When asked which candidate he was supporting in the forthcoming presidential election between Barack Obama and John McCain, he responded: 'We are fortunate that, thanks to globalisation, policy decisions in the US have been largely replaced by global market forces ... National security aside, it hardly makes any difference who will be the next president. The world is governed by market forces' (George Eaton, 16 June 2021).

Huntington's understanding of democracy makes no mention of equality or economic justice and does not even include universal suffrage or national self-determination. He proceeds from a world order based on *Pax Americana* but does not acknowledge that this regime was designed to preclude the emergence of autonomous democratic states and was foremost designed to construct a liberal international order and a network of client states for the United States during the Cold War. This leads to the kind of cynicism where even in cases where Western international observation missions have held elections to be free and fair, such as the 2006 victory of Hamas in the Gaza Strip, they are rejected by the West. Former President Jimmy Carter said that the 2006 Palestinian elections in which Hamas was declared the victor was the best-conducted election that The Carter Center had to date monitored,[3] but the West and Israel treated Hamas as a terrorist organization and endeavoured to isolate it internationally.

Schumpeter and Huntington held that elections were meant to confirm the status quo based on a broad unity of views between competing elites as exemplified by the Democratic and Republican Parties. But with the election of Donald Trump who held decidedly different views on the security state, foreign policy and particularly on the need for the United States to improve relations with Russia, that consensus broke down. In 2016 the Republican candidate for the presidency, Donald Trump, won the election, but the Democratic candidate, Hillary Clinton, challenged the result and claimed that Russian Federation President Vladimir Putin rigged the election in his favour.

While stories began circulating during the 2016 presidential campaign that Trump was beholden to Putin, they did not take hold because it was widely assumed, and certainly by the Democratic Party, that their candidate, Hillary Clinton, would win. However, when she unexpectedly lost, Clinton and the Democratic Party blamed their defeat on Russia hacking the email account of her campaign manager, John Podesta, which was then passed to Julian Assange where they were published in Wikileaks to benefit Trump's campaign (Ellen Nakashima and Shane Harris, 13 July 2018). The leaks revealed how the Democratic Party leadership and Clinton conspired to deprive Senator Bernie Sanders of the party's nomination for the presidency (Michael Sainato, 22 July 2016) and published eight speeches Clinton made to Wall Street bankers for $1.8 million in which contrary to her public persona as a voice of the middle class she made clear her sympathy for bankers (Dan Merica, CNN, 17 October 2016).

3. On 19 April immediately after the 11–18 April 2010 Sudanese national elections, former President Jimmy Carter as head of The Carter Center held a press conference in Khartoum attended by the author in which he said that the 2006 Gaza election won by Hamas was the best-conducted election of the 80+ elections his organization had observed. He also said that the Al Gore-George Bush presidential election of 2000 was a 'failed election'.

The evidence for the claim that Russia was behind the Democratic Party leaks was based on a report by a retired British spy, Christopher Steele, that Trump conspired with the Kremlin to win the 2016 election and that Russia had compromising information on him (Marshall Cohen, CNN, 18 November 2021), a charge that was endlessly repeated in the mainstream media. It wasn't until five years later that not only were the allegations proven to be false, but the funder of the 'Steele dossier' was found to be the Clinton's campaign in the words of CNN to 'dirty up Trump' (Marshall Cohen, CNN, 18 November 2021).

The allegations of Trump's collusion with Russia led to the formation of an investigation and hearings by former FBI Director, Special Counsel to the Congress, Robert Mueller. For twenty-two months the hearings dominated cable news and led to the awarding of Pulitzer Prizes to journalists of the *New York Times* and *Washington Post* for the propagation of claims that were largely made by unidentified intelligence agents. However, the Mueller report 'did not establish that members of the Trump Campaign conspired or coordinated with the Russian government' (BBC, 24 March 2019). Even after the publication of the Mueller report a Reuters/Ipsos survey found that 48 per cent of respondents said they believed that President Trump or someone from his campaign worked with Russia to influence the 2016 election (John Bowden, 27 March 2019), and that could have influenced Biden's victory in the 2020 presidential election.

The efforts to 'get Trump' have involved Russiagate, two failed impeachments, various other legal manoeuvres and an attempt to hold him responsible for a demonstration-cum-riot on 6 January 2020 at Capital Hill by Trump's followers protesting the outcome of the election. Although only one demonstrator was killed, the intelligence services and a sycophantic media labelled the riot an 'insurgency', thousands have been arrested and Biden said that it constituted 'the most significant test of our democracy since the civil war' (The Guardian, 17 July 2021). These efforts reached a peak when the former president and leading Republican candidate for the 2024 presidential elections was arrested for falsifying business records that directed hush money to two women before the 2016 presidential election (CNN, 4 April 2023).

Another example which has served to delegitimize American elections involves the intelligence services, media and the Democratic Party trying to influence the outcome of the 2020 presidential election between Trump and Joe Biden. Three weeks before the election on 14 October the *New York Post* revealed that it had material from the personal computer of Hunter Biden, son of Joe Biden, which (apart from the pornography and drug taking) suggested corruption by the elder Biden in Ukraine during his tenure as vice-president under Barack Obama (Emma-Jo Morris and Gabrielle Fonrouge, 14 October 2020). Within hours Twitter and Facebook restricted the publication and circulation of the *New York Post* story (The Guardian, 15 October 2020), which it was later revealed was done at the behest of the intelligence services (see below) and most of the media followed suit in suppressing the story.

Still days before the election on 20 October, a coalition of former intelligence officials including former director of national intelligence James Clapper, former

CIA directors Mike Hayden, Leon Panetta and John Brennan, and dozens of other former deputy directors and senior officials of American intelligence agencies released a letter claiming that the *New York Post* story involves 'Russia trying to influence how Americans vote' (Nick Visser, 20 October 2020). While the initial *New York Post* story received little attention, the claim that Russia was behind the laptop story was widely circulated and suggested that Russia was endeavouring to tarnish Joe Biden to improve the electoral prospects of Trump. Moreover, the letter was referred to by Biden during the 22 October debate with Trump and on other occasions to deflect accusations that he and his family were involved in influence-peddling. However, it was later learned that the FBI had a true copy of the material in the laptop since 2019 when they subpoenaed the files in connection with a money laundering investigation against Hunter and thus knew that it was genuine (Peter Van Buren, 31 December 2020).

It took the *New York Times* one and a half years to acknowledge that the computer in the possession of the *New York Post* was that of Hunter Biden and to authenticate thousands of the emails in the computer which among other things confirmed that Burisma Holdings, a Ukrainian energy company, paid the younger and unqualified Biden $50,000 a month to serve on its board. For this appointment Burisma expected Hunter to influence his father for the company's benefit, and he did arrange at least one meeting in April 2015 between his then vice president father and a Burisma executive (Jacob Sullum, 17 March 2020). Although Joe Biden has repeatedly said that he and his son never discussed Hunter Biden's business dealings, Hunter Biden's appointment to the Burisma board came at a time when his father as vice president was leading US policy on Ukraine and thus there was little doubt that the appointment was made to influence the elder Biden (Ryan Saavedra, 28 November 2019).

Instead of investigating such claims and others that were to emerge from the laptop that bank transactions revealed that Biden family members received more than $1 million from Chinese businessmen (Sophie Mann, 19 March 2023), the mainstream media continued to insist that any suggestion of the Bidens' corruption was 'Russian disinformation'. The mainstream media was so anxious that Trump not win a second term that it worked to suppress a story of considerable public interest. It was only after the Republicans became the majority in the House of Representatives after the November 2022 elections that it was announced that a House panel would examine the business links between Biden elder and his son (Kenneth Vogel, Katie Rogers and Glenn Thrush, 17 November 2022). In a manner reminiscent of the Steele dossier, former CIA Director, Mike Morell, told the House Judiciary Committee that he was asked by Secretary of State Antony Blinken, who at the time was a senior member of the Biden election campaign, to help discredit the laptop reporting and assist Biden's presidential campaign and he arranged for the statement of the intelligence officers (Harriet Alexander, 21 April 2023).

Whether sufficient numbers of the American public would have refrained from voting for Biden to turn the election in Trump's favour if they had been permitted to know about the material revealed in Hunter Biden's laptop cannot be conclusively known. However, a TIPP Insights survey found that 'two thirds of respondents said that the FBI and the intelligence community deliberately misled the public by urging Facebook and Twitter to stop spreading such stories [about Hunter Biden's computer], which the agency deemed foreign "disinformation"' (TIPP, 13 December 2022), while according to another poll conducted by Amac on the night of the presidential election, 36 per cent of Democratic Party voters said they knew nothing about the Hunter Biden laptop and 4.6 per cent of them said they would not have voted for Biden if they had known, enough to swing the election in Trump's favour (Amac, 12 November 2020).

## Propagation of Western democracy

There has always been a tension between capitalism and democracy, but the tension intensified with the advent of neoliberalism which further empowered the classes and corporations that controlled the market and reduced the capacity of the citizenry to influence government. Neoliberalism was less about the withdrawal of the state, as with the strengthening of institutional linkages between the state and capital. It also involved the reduction of the role of the state in meeting the welfare needs of the citizenry, transferring that role to the market, all the while maintaining that these developments constituted a positive reformulation of democracy. Citizens may not have understood the nuances of the theory, but they did understand that the regulatory capacity of the state was degraded, social and health services declined, big corporations became mega-corporations, unions were attacked and their standard of living often declined. Crucially the welfare of the citizenry became divorced from any understanding of democracy.

In the years immediately after the Second World War there was a wide agreement that to ensure the compatibility of capitalism and democracy or, to put it differently, to ensure that capitalism did not face a popular revolt, that restraints on the market had to be imposed. The response lay in Keynesian prescriptions which held that the state had an important role in guaranteeing full employment, carrying out a redistribution of national wealth, and expanding social, education and health provisions. And thus ensued three decades of what has been called 'the golden age of capitalism'.

But declining corporate profits, a series of oil crises, an increasingly militant working class and demands for reform coming from many sectors of society led to the rejection of Keynesian economics and the adoption of neoliberalism in the 1980s. Western states reduced their regulatory powers, and under a regime of unrestricted markets industrial production shifted to Asia and with it the loss of decently paid union jobs, and that produced growing economic polarization. The US Federal Reserve reported that the wealthiest 1 per cent of Americans controlled sixteen times more wealth than the bottom 50 per cent (Megan Leonhardt, 23 June 2022). Corresponding to the decline of the industrial sector, Western states led by the United States and UK have overseen the exponential growth of the financial sector and their economies have become dependent on credit expansion and imports. Since markets are held to be integral to democracy, these developments have been heralded as democratic advancements, but that is not how the losers in this process view them.

President Bush contended that 'successful societies privatize their economies and secure the rights of property', a policy pursued by the wholesale privatization of the post-war Iraqi economy by the United States, with the profitable sectors purchased by foreign and largely American capital to fulfil the US objective of controlling Middle Eastern oil. Bush compared his Middle East doctrine to Woodrow Wilson's 'Fourteen Points' and Franklin D. Roosevelt's 'Four Freedoms' (Lloyd E. Ambrosius, 8 May 2006). American presidents have historically cast their global ambitions as demonstrations of democratic benevolence. Critical to Bush's ambitions to democratize the Middle East was ignoring the fact that from the Shah of Iran to the despots of the Gulf, the United States had a long record of supporting authoritarian regimes as long as they bent to the will of the United States.

According to President Bush junior, 'The establishment of a free Iraq in the heart of the Middle East will be a watershed event in the global democratic revolution' and the military occupation of Iraq was only the first stage in a US crusade for democracy in the region that would continue 'for decades to come' (Bill Vann, 2003). This echoed claims by the Pentagon that toppling the Saddam Hussein regime would spread 'shock and awe' throughout the Middle East, bring about the collapse of regimes in Iran and Syria, and convince Palestinians to give up their resistance to Israeli rule. In the post-Cold War era US governments could generally count on the major international human rights organizations to endorse their interventions, demonize Saddam Hussein, Bashar al-Assad, Muammar Gaddafi and ignore Israeli apartheid (although that changed in 2021 when Human Rights Watch declared Israel an apartheid state and Amnesty International followed suit in 2022).

Despite Bush's rousing espousal of democracy in the Middle East, the project was always tempered by American security interests. After 9/11 counterterrorism became the primary US foreign policy concern and that provided the opening for the invasions of Afghanistan and Iraq. Enthusiasm for democracy was further dampened after the electoral victories of Hamas in Gaza, Hizbollah in Lebanon and the Muslim Brothers in Egypt. Huntington died in 2008 and thus was not able to give his views on the Arab and North African struggles against authoritarian regimes (the Arab Spring), but he opposed popular uprisings which he maintained were seldom successful and claimed that 'democracy can be created even if the people do not want it' (Huntington, 1991, p. 36). But the examples of Afghanistan and Iraq of the US top-down imposition of 'democracy' through elections produced corrupt unstable regimes under US-sanctioned elites with little legitimacy. Western failures at democracy promotion in Afghanistan and Iraq were unique only in the sense of how much time, energy and capital were put into the projects. One study determined that between the Second World War and 2004 the United States intervened in thirty-five countries and had a success rate of less than 3 per cent in facilitating the emergence of stable democracies (George Downes and Bruce Bueno de Mesquita, 2004), and these were 'democracies' as defined by the United States.

Complementary to Western efforts to impose its version of democracy and neoliberalism on peripheral states was a new push in the post-Cold War era to involve these states in counterterror regimes and ensure that their foreign policies conformed to the security objectives of the West. The concern with counterterrorism placed the West in the contradictory position of advocating democratic transformation on the one hand, while on the other reinforcing despotic states because they were held to be bulwarks in the GWOT. Moreover, while calling for shrinking the state, the GWOT necessitated that the state's security function be expanded and that governments purchase the latest weaponry from Western arms manufacturers. This approach became even more inconsistent when the United States backed Gulf monarchies and Turkiye supported competing *jihadi* groups in Iraq and Syria (New York Times, 13 June 2014). Meanwhile, the United States assisted jihadi groups in opposition to the Syrian and Libyan secular regimes, thus making clear that the United States placed a higher priority on fighting groups and states that challenged its hegemony than with any concern for secularism, democracy and even terrorism.

When key US ally in the Gulf, Saudi Arabia, was threatened by popular struggles, particularly those led by the Muslim Brothers, the kingdom responded by funding and supplying a host of jihadist movements. However, in Egypt the Saudis together with the United States supported General Abdel Fattah el-Sisi after he overthrew the democratically elected Muslim Brothers government of Mohamed Morsi and killed thousands of unarmed civilian supporters on the streets of Cairo. Backed up with billions of dollars from the UAE, Saudi Arabia and Kuwait they hoped to reverse the tide of the Arab Spring (David Butter, April 2020). After some initial confusion President Obama also supported el-Sisi, while Trump referred to him as his 'favourite dictator' (Jessica Campisi, 13 September 2019). Meanwhile, Israel welcomed el-Sisi because of his opposition to the Muslim Brothers who had founded Hamas, the ruling party in Gaza. el-Sisi implemented an austerity programme in response to the dictates of the international financial institutions (IFIs) which lowered the standard of living of the poor majority, rode rough shod over basic human and civil rights and conducted a sham presidential election in 2018. This caused embarrassment in the West, but not for long and led by the United States the West resumed supplying Egypt with the weaponry to fight its enemies (Middle East Eye, 3 September 2020), including the democratic opposition which joined the Muslim Brothers in el-Sisi's prisons.

It is easy to simply dismiss US propagation of democracy globally over many years as mere puffery that was turned off and on to meet the political needs of various Washington governments. That would not be mistaken, but it misses crucial points. Democracy (as defined in the restricted ways considered above) has become for US governments and decision-makers across the political spectrum a kind of state religion to which they are all devoted. The United States was founded by Puritans and other religious-minded and persecuted groups who viewed the country as the 'shining city on the hill', a land from which people escaped the corruption and degradation of the old world, and those ideas have never lost their resonance. Founding Father Thomas Jefferson wrote about an 'empire of liberty', while John Adams considered America as mankind's second chance of entering or achieving the paradise of Eden. However, the same Adams famously proclaimed 'America goes not abroad, in search of monsters to destroy' in a speech that has been quoted to oppose interference by the United States in the affairs of other nations (John Quincy Adams, 1821, p. 29).

Even President Woodrow Wilson, who wanted to make the world safe for democracy, was opposed to imposing democracy on other countries (David Hendrickson, 30 June 2022). Likewise, the charter of the United Nations that President Roosevelt shepherded to its birth in 1945 gave no powers in its chief policymaking institution, the Security Council, to change the governments of other states and instead its purpose was to ensure international peace and security (David Hendrickson, 30 June 2022). It is only with the advent of the Cold War and President Harry Truman that US policy explicitly endorsed regime change in the pursuit of democracy propagation. And this policy became even more explicit in the post-Cold War era when the first President Bush announced a 'new world order' in 1990 and Bush junior announced in 2002 what became known as the Bush Doctrine. The main components of this doctrine were stipulated in the government's *National Security Strategy* and highlighted preemption, military primacy, new multilateralism and the spread of democracy (Keir A. Lieber and Robert J. Lieber, December 2002).

In *The Four Ages of American Foreign Policy* Professor Michael Mandelbaum contends that the United States, more than other country, has tried to use foreign policy to promote the adoption of its political ideas beyond its borders. And those ideas have been principally democracy and peace among countries (Michael Mandelbaum, 1 June 2022). Mandelbaum concludes that the period between the end of the Cold War and 2015 (which he labels the United States as a 'hyperpower') was a failure precisely because of its attempt to propagate democracy internationally in parts of the world that lacked the necessary pre-conditions and that led to unnecessary wars in Iraq and Afghanistan and conflicts with Russia and China.

Propagating democracy had bipartisan support and was perhaps most graphically expressed by Secretary of State under Bill Clinton, Madeleine Albright, who justified the Iraqi war by saying, 'If we have to use force, it is because we are America; we are the indispensable nation. We stand tall and we see further than other countries into the future, and we see the danger here to all of us' (NBC-TV, 19 February 1998). The United States as the indispensable nation is associated with the notion of US exceptionalism which according to the Heritage Foundation is because, 'unlike any other nation, it [America] is dedicated to the principles of human liberty, grounded on the truths that all men are created equal and endowed with equal rights' (Matthew Spalding, 1 October 2010). And this belief in the inalienable rights of all individuals leads to the conviction that these rights must ultimately be realized over the entire world, and that the United States is destined to play the leading role in making that happen (John Mearsheimer, 2018).

Nor did US foreign policy failures, particularly in Vietnam, change the thinking of US governments when American democracy was rooted in a system of quasi-religious beliefs and could not be challenged on rational grounds. Indeed, the US defeat in Vietnam was not understood as due to the US being militarily and politically overwhelmed by the Vietnamese, but instead to anti-war civic activism in the United States. The response of American elites was not to see that activism as an inspiration for democracy since it helped end a tragedy, but instead to contend that the objectives of democracy could only be realized by democracy being contained.

This is aptly argued in a report by the Trilateral Commission, a highly influential body established by the American banker and philanthropist David Rockefeller. Examining the growth of political participation in the 1960s the chapter on the United States authored by Samuel Huntington concluded that the central problem facing US democracy stemmed from 'an excess of democracy' and he called for the restoration of 'the prestige and authority of central government institutions' (Trilateral Commission, 1975, p. 113). In other words, democracy had to be saved from itself by a reassertion of elite authority and this was to be accomplished with the advent of neoliberalism which fostered political passivity by weakening the role of the state (Chris Maisano, 2020). This is consistent with the Commission's task of promoting a consensus among the international ruling classes to manage their affairs.[4] The approach also ensured that the failed wars in Vietnam, Afghanistan, Iraq and even the unsuccessful efforts at democracy promotion in Sudan and South Sudan were nonetheless viewed as noble and civilizing projects, and their objectives were not to be challenged. Indeed, the failures were redeemed by the fact that they were struggles against authoritarian regimes in support of democracy.

## Decline of US democracy

Issues of contention in American democracy have been related to personalities, imagery, public relations, cultural presentation and the acquisition of identity blocks, while class as a mobilizing tool has lost its resonance when both leading parties support capitalism and foreign interventionism. Elections have typically been spectacles largely divorced from the interests of the people, a development encouraged by the decline of government decision-making and elite consensus around basic issues and the preservation of the American empire. This is not a matter of concern when, as Schumpeter and Huntington stress, the primary objective of democracy is to maintain stability and ensure the orderly circulation of elites. But in light of the controversies surrounding the 2016 and 2020 presidential elections the orderly circulation of elites is no longer assured and the status quo is increasingly being challenged.

---

4. Members of the Trilateral Commission include since 2021 US Secretary of State, Anthony Blinken, and US National Security Advisor, Jake Sullivan.

Although guaranteed by the First Amendment and held to be a cornerstone of liberal democracy, freedom of speech and freedom of the media have undergone increasing constraints in recent years. Although the ultra-rich have long used their resources to influence government decision-making, this took a major leap forward due to the 21 January 2010 Supreme Court decision which overruled a century of campaign finance law and held that corporations have a constitutional right to spend unlimited amounts of money to promote or defeat candidates. While *Public Citizen* called the decision 'a radical affront to American political culture and poses grave dangers to the integrity of our democracy' (Public Citizen, 3 February 2010), President Barack Obama noted that as a result of that decision 'ordinary Americans are shut out of the process' (Bruce Livesey, 2 November 2020). Added to this has been the crucial role of the corporate media, 90 per cent of which is controlled by six large corporations – Comcast, Walt Disney, AT&T, Paramount Global, Sony and Fox (Rebecca Strong, 18 April 2022), which almost always promote US foreign policy. However, cable news networks and broadcast television evening newscasts have had declining audiences for years (David Bauder, 27 December 2021), and this is widely attributed to distrust.

With most of the media serving the interests of the ruling elites there is usually little reason for overt government censorship. Where censorship is most evident is that carried out by the social media Technology giants – Facebook, Amazon, Apple, Microsoft, Alphabet and, until Elon Musk took over, by Twitter – and not officially by the government, even when the restrictions are pressed on the technology companies by elected politicians. This was graphically exposed by Matt Taibbi and Michael Shellenberger in a series of articles commissioned by Musk in early 2023 that came to be known as the 'Twitter Files' and showed how the previous owners of Twitter had cooperated with the intelligence services in free speech suppression (Twitter Files Archives).

These investigative reports made clear how government agencies and lawmakers interacted with Twitter over 'content moderation', which involved pressuring the social medial company to block posts not to the liking of the government, on a range of issues from Ukraine, the Middle East, the 6 January 2020 Capital Hill riots, Iran, Covid vaccines, etc., and smear those perceived to support Russia and China. Agencies of the US government restricted freedom of speech, controlled the narrative, and through the Twitter threads identified perceived enemies of the United States and the same thing was occurring in other areas of social media. However, instead of being embarrassed, the mainstream media either ignored the story or attacked the journalists, while the Democratic Party members of the House Judiciary Select Subcommittee reviewing the matter insulted the journalists and held that state censorship was necessary (Joshua Lee, 10 March 2023).

Apart from the direct suppression of free speech exposed by the Twitter Files, one of the most effective means to control dissenting voices as YouTube CEO Susan Wojcicki acknowledged is to boost 'authoritative' mainstream media sources and suppress alternative perspectives (Tom Parker, 8 April 2021). While many dissident views exist online, algorithms ensure that they are often difficult to find and may come with a warning. As a result, exponents of free speech and those exposing the underside of the US state such as Julian Assange, Chelsea Manning and Edward

Snowden are themselves denigrated, repressed, disappear off the internet and in the case of the former two are imprisoned.

In addition, free speech has been restricted by first considering views contrary to the accepted orthodoxy as 'hate speech' or 'disinformation' (with neither term defined), after which demands are made that the purveyors of these views are condemned, and their views must be prohibited. Once it is claimed that an issue is one of 'moral clarity', then the question is settled and does not allow for further discussion (Gary Morson, 14 March 2022). In such cases facts do not give rise to a narrative; the narrative determines the facts. The censorship is about control of the narrative and that became the state-directed task of the big technology companies. It is no longer about reporting the news but about managing the news and that involves taking on board a whole set of ideological assumptions. A fundamental rule is that anyone can post all the misinformation they want, but it must conform to the state's narrative, and this is achieved by a multitude of pressures as well as employing 'fact-checking' organizations to monitor and regulate information funded directly or indirectly by Western and US governments (Alan Macleod, 2 August 2022). Additionally, neoliberal billionaires like Bill Gates, Pierre Omidyar and George Soros are major funders of 'disinformation experts' who smear websites that propagate views that do not follow the state-approved narrative as being 'vectors of hate and disinformation' (Glen Greenwald, 12 April 2023).

The same combination of the Democratic Party, intelligence agencies, and much of big tech and the mass media has endeavoured to undermine leftist challenges to the system by the promotion of identity politics of race, gender and sexual orientation which denies the critical role of class in society and government decision-making. Fraser calls this development 'progressive neoliberalism' and holds that it replaced the more expansive, anti-hierarchical, egalitarian, class-sensitive and anti-capitalist understandings of emancipation that had flourished in the 1960s and 1970s (Nancy Fraser, 2017). According to Sohrab Ahmari this political re-alignment served to ideologically control the Western working class by masking concrete class and economic injustices with a thick fog of mystification (River Page, 2021). In contrast to an earlier era when the media was distrustful of the intelligence services, in the present era most of the media now serves as the hand maiden of the intelligence services and this has involved hiring many ex-intelligence officers as commentators. And this is the case even though, as former Secretary of State under Trump and former CIA Director Mike Pompeo said on a YouTube video that at the CIA, 'We lied. We cheated. We stole. It's – it was like – we had entire training courses. It reminds you of the glory of the American experiment' (Mike Pompeo, 25 April 2019).

The Democratic Party, the mainstream media and most academics are exponents of identity politics and focus exclusively on gender, race and 'white privilege', even though there is overwhelming statistical evidence that the best predictor of poverty and economic success in the United States is class (Robert Lynch, 18 March 2023). However, class is ignored by the politicians and media because it illustrates the contradiction at the core of capitalism and Western democracy. While previously civil rights and progressive activists struggled for equality and integration, present 'social warriors' are concerned with 'equity' and diversity which involves the privileging of minorities within oppressed groups, and its embrace by leading corporations in the West makes clear that it poses no threat to the existing societal balance of power.

At the global level the share of income of the poorest half of the world's people is about half what it was in 1820, inequality then expanded enormously during the height of colonial expansion, after which it declined until the introduction of neoliberalism in the 1980s (World Inequality Report, 2022). Neoliberalism produced a major increase in private wealth, a decline in publicly owned wealth, while deregulation encouraged global capital to employ cheap labour forces in the Global South and reduce the bargaining power of workers worldwide. The Inequality Report emphasizes that inequality is always a political choice and Western leaders made a conscious choice to enrich their already-wealthiest members and permit their weakest members to sink into greater poverty. Warren Buffet, financier and one of the richest men in the world, said, 'There's been class warfare going on for the last 20 years, and my class has won' (Greg Sargent, 2007). It was such conditions that led Nobel Economics prize winner Joseph Stiglitz to paraphrase Abraham Lincoln's famous definition of American democracy to instead take the form of government of the 1 per cent, by the 1 per cent, for the 1 per cent (Joseph Stiglitz, 31 March 2011).

The mystification of capitalist exploitation is deepened by the paltry number of American workers in unions (only 6 per cent in non-government employment), the failure of unions to keep wages up to the cost of living and the fact that unions are a minor part of the power structure with assets of $35.8 billion (Chris Bohner, Summer 2022). The result is that although Democratic Party operatives dominate the unions, the party had given up on the working class and as a result Trump carried the overall working-class (noncollege) vote by four points in the 2020 election (Catalist).

The embrace of neoliberalism by the social democratic parties of the UK and France, and the US Democratic Party has resulted in a loss of working-class membership and support, and the domination of these parties by a professional middle class (Thomas Piketty, March 2018). Piketty also found that high-education elites now vote for the 'left' (in the US the Democratic Party), while high-income/high-wealth elites still vote for the 'right' (the Republican Party) and this explains rising inequality and the lack of a democratic response to it (Thomas Piketty, March 2018, p. 63). By endorsing neoliberalism, the left effectively jettisoned its working-class supporters. According to a 2014 study by Princeton University what average citizens want has little or no influence on US policy and that 'America's claims to being a democratic society are [therefore] seriously threatened' and the US has become an 'oligarchy' (Martin Gilens and Benjamin Page, 9 April 2014).

The deterioration in living standards of many Western workers is a direct result of the decline of their power as represented by decreasing union membership with the advent of neoliberalism and has proceeded in conjunction with the financialization of the economy. Financialization involves profit making in the economy to increasingly occur through financial channels rather than through productive activities and this has led to the deindustrialization of much of the West. Indicative of this, the FIRE sector of the economy (finance, insurance, real estate, rental and leasing) constituted 22.3 per cent of Gross Domestic Product (GDP) of the United States in 2020 by industry while manufacturing was only 10.8 per cent (Statista). The big change in capitalism that led to financialization began during the Reagan administration and the influence of the economist Milton Friedman who argued that a corporation's only responsibility was to increase profits to shareholders (Michael Collins, 21 September 2018).

The exponential growth of the finance sector and decline of industrial employment was the result of a deliberate policy of the US slashing production costs of its multinationals which set up low-wage labour factories abroad, notably in China. This destructive process took place without any political debate in Western legislatures because it was not considered a political issue and its resolution would – as per the logic of neoliberalism – be determined by the market. The United States, however, mistakenly believed that it could induce China into embracing the liberal democratic order and American hegemony, and instead has belatedly concluded that China has become an existential threat (John Mearsheimer, November/December 2021).

The West claims that the threat posed by China is because of its 'authoritarianism', but the threat is posed by the superiority of its development model and the likelihood that China has surpassed or will soon surpass the West economically. Unlike the West, Chinese banks operate as public utilities to ensure that investments are for productive purposes, and this has led to the country becoming the manufacturing hub of the world. In the United States, however, the regulation of the banks is carried out by the Federal Reserve, effectively a committee of leading bankers which has overseen the decline of American manufacturing. As well as a multitude of supply chain issues that emerged during the Covid pandemic and produced shortages of consumer goods, the scaling down of US industrial capacity meant it was ill-equipped to confront Russia in the Ukraine, and as a result according to Vershinin the United States may no longer remain 'the arsenal of democracy' (Alex Vershinin, 17 June 2022). The displacement of a productive industrial elite with an unaccountable and parasitic class of rentier aristocrats poses a major and perhaps fatal threat to capitalism and Western democracy.

## Conclusion

The international order only became liberal and international with the end of the Cold War (Michael Barnett, 16 March 2021). This involved not only constructing the biggest and most expensive military in history, but also overseeing a set of laws, institutions, values, treaties and agreements that reinforced US power. To the extent that there have been divisions within the US ruling class over foreign interventions they have been between those who think the United States has the right to forcefully intervene without any outside constraint, and those who think the United States should seek the legitimacy of a multilateral organization, preferably the UN. But in practice this distinction can mean little. On 17 March 2011 the Security Council voted in favour of enforcing a no-fly zone in Libya and instituting sanctions against the Tripoli government because of human rights concerns (UN Security Council, 17 March 2011). The West used the resolution as a fig leaf to overthrow the Ghadaffi government and later it was found that many of the human rights allegations were false (Maximilian Forte, 31 August 2011).

But that hardly mattered because according to the Clinton administration's National Security Strategy document of 2000 the United States had the right to intervene in any country based on its 'vital interests' which included 'ensuring uninhibited access to key markets, energy supplies, and strategic resources' (GlobalSecurity.org., 2000). It also put to rest the idea that NATO was a 'purely defensive' pact. But the United States also learned a lesson and together with its European and Arab allies supported jihadi groups opposed to the Syrian regime and went on to occupy Syrian land and steal its oil production, without any multilateral approval. Such US foreign engagements also made clear its distain for national sovereignty and its willingness to use its overwhelming military power to challenge any states that challenge its hegemony.

For much of the post-Second World War period the overwhelming US military, economic and financial power has proved sufficient to maintain the liberal international order but the development of illiberal eastern European states, NATO's defeats in the greater Middle East, the global rise of China and Russia, internal contradictions, and what may prove most significant, the Western proxy war in Ukraine, are suffocating the ideal of a liberal international order and the prospects for the spread of Western democracy. According to Russian Foreign Minister Lavrov, about twenty countries have expressed an interest in joining BRICS and the Shanghai Conference (Ahmed Adel, 28 February 2023), both of which represent an alternative to US unipolarity. No doubt the increasing popularity of these organizations and the growing use of currencies other than the US dollar for trade (Lorimer Wilson, 6 February 2023) were because of the increasing use of sanctions, the confiscation in recent years of the Iranian and Venezuelan financial assets, particularly those of Russia in the wake of the Ukrainian war. Moreover, as the role of the US dollar in international trade declines, its status as the world's reserve currency is threatened and that will also reduce the effectiveness of sanctions in forcing countries to bend to the will of the United States. As explained by Senator Marco Rubio, 'We won't have to talk about sanctions in 5 years because there will be so many countries transacting in currencies other than the dollar that we won't have the ability to sanction them' (Ian Schwartz, 29 March 2023).

The crux of the problem lies with the United States claiming that its liberal international order trumps national sovereignty and Washington has the right to intervene in other countries according to a set of laws and principles of its own creation, thus undermining any notion of international law. That these views are also endorsed by its closest allies was made clear when former German Chancellor Angela Merkel and former French President Francois Hollande publicly acknowledged that although their governments proposed the plan which became the basis for the 2015 Minsk II agreement, laid down provisions for ending the

Ukraine civil war and provided rights for the besieged Russian-speaking population of the Donbass region, they had no intention of implementing the agreement. Indeed, despite her personal involvement and the fact that the agreement was endorsed unanimously by the UN Security Council, Merkel echoed Hollande and told *Die Zeit* newspaper that 'The 2014 Minsk Agreement was an attempt to give Ukraine time' to build up its armed forces so that in due time its military forces could re-take the Donbass (European Tribune, 25 December 2022).

Nonetheless, a multi-polar world is emerging, and this was acknowledged by the US Chairman of the Joint Chiefs of Staff, General Mark Milley, who said, 'We're entering into a tri-polar world with the US, Russia and China being all great powers' (RT, 3 November 2021). The United States, however, continues to fight ferociously to maintain its dominant position internationally and to press its systems of government, economic management and neoliberal values on the global community. Moeini sums it up: 'Liberalism can't live without aggressive universalism – the insistence that the whole world must operate according to norms perfected in the West and imposed on *panta ta ethnē* (all the nations), and that achieving global cultural homogeneity justifies all forms of interventionism' (Arta Moeini, 8 July 2022).

Trump rejected US exceptionalism and in response to Fox interviewer Bill O'Reilly calling Russian President Vladimir Putin, 'a killer' Trump said, 'There are a lot of killers. We have a lot of killers. You think our country is so innocent?' (Matt Ellentuck, 5 February 2017). He considered international trade deals bad for American workers, spoke disparagingly about NATO, opposed US democracy promotion, called the Iraq War 'a big, fat mistake' and promised 'to keep us out of endless war'. But in the biggest break from the US elite's consensus on national security, Trump condemned the militaristic US policy on Taiwan and the proxy war in Ukraine and famously said that under his presidency the Ukraine War would end peacefully in twenty-four hours (Daniel Stewart, 27 January 2023). Trump's presidency did not involve any significant break from the status quo and nor did he oppose neoliberalism, but it is these views (and not his supposed dictatorial tendencies or personal failings) that pose a threat to the security state and made him such an extreme object of revulsion for the US elites. It has also made him an unlikely voice of peace in an America where the Democratic Party, intelligence services, and most of the tech companies and media are avid proponents of war.

For the governments and people of the Global South, 'the power to define democracy resided with donors [and] democracy came to be associated primarily with elections and economic liberalism' (Rita Abrahamsen, 2000, p. 109). But the United States no longer passes the litmus test of Schumpeter and Huntington of peaceful and accepted elections as made clear by the continuing disputes over the outcomes of the 2016 and 2020 presidential victories of Donald Trump and Joe Biden. Moreover, the collusion between the Democratic Party, the intelligence agencies, the corporate media and big tech to fix elections revealed by Russiagate and the Hunter Biden's laptop affair makes clear the rot at the core of the American electoral system. And this rot has not gone unnoticed in the world. A November 2021 poll of seventeen advanced economies found that only 17 per cent considered the US democracy a good example for others to follow (Pew Research Center, 2021).

## Chapter 2

## SCRAMBLE FOR THE GREATER MIDDLE EAST IN THE WAKE OF US DECLINE

There is no region on the planet that has suffered more death, destruction and dislocation as a result of US imperial ambitions than the Middle East, and this has a marked effect on the adjacent HOA. Until recently the United States has largely been successful in its efforts to control the region's strategic energy resources, ensure that the energy trade was conducted in US dollars to ensure its status as the world reserve currency, and sell advanced weaponry to its client states. But to achieve these aims the United States has led two wars of choice against Iraq, a coalition of states against Libya to overthrow the government of Muammar Gaddafi, engaged in a failed effort involving neighbouring autocratic states and Islamist terrorist groups to overthrow the secular government of Bashar al-Assad, supported failed efforts by Saudi Arabia and the UAE to displace the Houthi regime in Yemen which has produced a major humanitarian crisis, and pursued debilitating sanctions against the government and people of Iran. The United States has also provided unwavering support to an Israel that has been described as practising 'apartheid'.

But US power and prestige is in decline, and this is producing another set of problems as wealthy and determined Middle Eastern states only recently under the sway of the United States are charting their own independent foreign policies. And nowhere is this being more evident than in the adjacent weak states of the HOA, and as a result the Horn is becoming part of one Greater Middle Eastern security unit. The states of the Middle East and the HOA have long had important geographic, religious, language and trade links, but with the United States no longer able to control what had been its client states, Middle Eastern governments are increasingly getting involved in the affairs of the countries of the Horn. This is exacerbating internal conflicts within the states of the Horn and involves pressing them to take sides in Middle East conflicts, aiding rebel movements in civil wars, and opposing democratic movements and developments that threaten their autocratic regimes. The Middle Eastern states have also been involved in a destabilizing competition for access to ports and naval bases on the HOA Red Sea coast.

US declining power in the Middle East, and by extension the HOA, is due to both its political and military failures in the region and a global reconfiguration of power that involves the rapidly growing economic influence of China and its corresponding increasing military and political capacity and the re-emergence of the Russian Federation as a serious participant on the world stage, particularly in the context of the Ukraine War. China has replaced the United States as the world's biggest importer of Middle Eastern oil, is the principal trading partner and source of investment for both the Middle East and the HOA and is the manufacturing hub of the world.

The rising status of China in the region was most graphically on display when it engineered a peace agreement between the governments of Saudi Arabia and Iran, which the United States has long sought to either overthrow or isolate. Meanwhile, Russia's power in the region is the result of its enormous oil reserves and status within OPEC+, export of grains, fertilizers, and weapons, effective diplomacy, and the prestige it has acquired in defending the al-Assad regime that the United States attempted to overthrow. Moreover, in the wake of the Russia–NATO proxy war in Ukraine, the demands of Russia and China for the end of US unipolarity and its international liberal world order and the establishment of a multipolar world have growing resonance in the region.

## An ascendent China

According to the IMF in 2016 China overtook the United States as the world's largest economy and in 2021 China accounted for 19 per cent of the global economy as opposed to the United States with 16 per cent and this gap is growing wider (International Monetary Fund, April 2022). This is also reflected in the Middle East where China is the biggest global importer of oil and source of investment. China's trade with Gulf Cooperation Council (GCC) states expanded from less than $10 billion in 2000 to nearly $150 billion in 2017 (Jonathan Fulton, 26 March 2019). After a peak of $69.03 billion in US direct investment in Africa, US investment dropped to $47.5 billion in 2020 (Ramzy Baroud, 30 December 2021). Meanwhile, China is the biggest trading nation and manufacturer in the world, Africa's largest trading partner since 2009, and it has major investments in the HOA. The Belt and Road Initiative which forty-six African states have signed represents China's framework for investment in the continent (CGTN Africa, 11 October 2021). Moreover, between 2007 and 2020 Chinese infrastructure financing for sub-Saharan Africa was 2.5 times as big as all other bilateral institutions combined (Economist, 20 May 2022). Although Chinese humanitarian assistance to the region is minor compared to the West, it has financed and carried out badly needed and costly infrastructural projects that are no longer pursued by the West.[1]

---

1. China's support of strategically significant infrastructural projects like the twinning of the Addis Ababa to Djibouti railway has a long history. In the 1970s China linked the port of Dar es Salaam in Tanzania with Kapiri Mposhi in Zambia to eliminate landlocked Zambia's economic dependence on Rhodesia and South Africa, both ruled by white-minority governments.

Chinese investment is welcomed by countries in the HOA (and elsewhere in the Global South) because it is not dependent upon political conditionalities. As yet, however, China does not have the political nor military power, the roots in the HOA, or the experience and diplomatic capacity of the United States, and additionally is limited by a powerful Western-dominated social media. However, in every sphere the distance between the two powers is narrowing to the benefit of China.

The Nixon administration executed an agreement with Saudi Arabia in which the kingdom agreed to conducts is oil trade in US dollars in exchange for US military support and hardware and as a result most oil importers and exporters fell in line (David Blackmon, 2 April 2023). But conditions have changed, and the United States is now the world's largest oil producer, the West is reducing fossil fuel consumption and China is the world's largest consumer of energy, most of which comes from the Persian Gulf and – in the wake of the Ukraine War – Russia. This is changing both the commercial relationship between Beijing and the Gulf and global geo-politics. In addition, the Gulf states want to tap into Beijing's investment capital as they transition from oil-producing states and to gain a counter-weight to their reliance on the United States.

Indicative of China's growing power was its diplomatic coup in brokering a peace agreement between long-time foes Iran and Saudi Arabia (the Joint Trilateral Statement) on 11 March 2023 in Beijing which analysts contend reflects a 'changing global order' (Mersiha Gadzo, 11 March 2023). Or as the CEO of the neo-con Foundation for the Defense of Democracies, Mark Dubowitz put it, 'Renewed Iran-Saudi ties as a result of Chinese mediation is a lose, lose, lose for American interests. It demonstrates that the Saudis don't trust Washington to have their back, that Iran sees an opportunity to peel away American allies to end its international isolation, and it establishes China as the majordomo of Middle Eastern power politics' (Foundation for the Defense of Democracies, 10 March 2023). This achievement comes a year after Xi Jinping's announcement in April 2022 of China's Global Security Initiative which made clear Beijing's intention of playing a leading role in foreign affairs (The Diplomat, 7 May 2022). Should the agreement hold, it will undermine US and Western sanctions designed to isolate Iran, improve the prospects of peace in Yemen, almost certainly lead to the decline of the US dollar in the international petroleum trade, and bring Iran and Saudi Arabia closer to joining the Chinese- and Russian-dominated Brazil, Russia, India, China and South Africa (BRICS) and the Shanghai Cooperation Organisation. Moreover and contrary to the claims by Albright and others that the United States is an 'indispensable nation' in the post-Cold War era, Trita Parsi of the Quincy Institute argued in a *New York Times* guest editorial that the Chinese success was due to the United States giving priority to war-making rather than diplomacy and peacemaking (New York Times, 22 March 2023). This development should also end the problem the conflict between Iran and Saudi Arabia has caused countries in the Horn and further the prospect of China replacing the United States as a peace-broker in the region.

While the West, particularly the United States and UK, have been the most adamant in pressing their version of democracy globally, in recent decades they have performed badly compared to 'authoritarian' China which has proven to be the most successful global example of economic development and improving the lives of millions of its poor. China also has a much better record than the West in protecting its people from the ravages of the Covid-19 pandemic. With 4.21 per cent of the world's population, the United States has suffered 16 per cent of the world's deaths, a death rate 719 times higher than China, its chief global competitor (Worldometer, 2021). Such comparisons are not lost on the Global South, including the HOA.

China's military strategy is largely focused on modernization and naval expansion with an emphasis on protecting its immediate periphery, which the United States is attempting to encircle and impose an embargo in the event of war (Tom Fowdy, 14 February 2022). Beijing seeks to ensure its energy supply lines remain intact in the event of conflict and that has involved establishing a military presence in the western Indian Ocean off the coast of the HOA through which its oil imports from the Gulf transit.

Although small compared to those of the United States and France, China's establishment in 2017 of its only foreign military base in Djibouti has multiple purposes: carrying out missions geared towards protecting strategic sea lanes, anti-piracy and counterterrorism operations, evacuating some of the estimated 100,000 Chinese nationals living in the HOA (of which 60,000 were in Ethiopia) in times of crisis, and with 24 per cent of EU imports coming from China, most of it by sea, Beijing has an interest in ensuring that they are secure (Mediterranean Defense, 27 March 2021). Another stimulus for establishing the base was China's problems in evacuating 36,000 nationals from Libya in 2011 when civil war broke out (Shaio Zerba, November 2014). China is also concerned with the heightened engagement in the HOA and the Red Sea of India, which has been a pillar of the US Indo-Pacific strategy and a major investor in the region.

China is very involved in investment, provision of infrastructure and services in Djibouti, holds 70 per cent of the country's debt (Tuvia Gering and Heath Sloane, 16 July 2021) and crucially twinned the rail links between Djibouti and Addis Ababa. Despite their mutual dependence, Djibouti has a protective treaty since independence in 1977 with France, mainly against Ethiopia and Somalia, which accounts for its relative stability (Macharia Munene, January-February 2022). Russia wanted to have a base in Djibouti, but the United States vetoed the idea.

While China has stressed that its Djibouti base is not part of any arms competition with the United States, it has also expressed the desire to 'break through the US maritime blockade, and protect China's oversea' interests (Sohu, 10 August 2018). Indeed, the Bab al-Mandab Strait is crucial to the ability of the United States to contain and deny China's access to its Maritime Silk Road and interfere with its access to energy supplies just as it did with Japan during the Second World War. Chinese concerns do not seem unreasonable when the leading candidate for the position of Secretary of Defence in the Biden cabinet and former Pentagon analyst, Michele Flournoy, proposed that the US Navy acquire the capacity to sink all Chinese shipping in the South China Sea within seventy-two hours in the event of war (Michele Flournoy, 18 June 2020).

Djibouti also hosts the biggest US base in Africa, Camp Lemonnier, as well as permanent naval bases for France and Italy. Its ports are also used by other Western states. Established in the wake of 9/11, Fort Lemonnier is used for tracking al-Qaeda, aiding the Emeriti and Saudi war on the Houthis, carrying out operations on 'extremists' in Somalia, and training Ethiopian, Somali, Ugandan and other forces. It also has naval refuelling facilities for United States and coalition ships, broadcasting facilities, and serves as a potential refuge for Americans fleeing conflicts in the HOA. In addition, the United States has 10,000 troops in Qatar, its largest base in the Middle East, 5,000 military personnel stationed in the UAE, and forces in Somalia, Oman, Bahrain and Saudi Arabia.

Headquartered in Stuttgart because it is associated with neo-colonialism, Africa Command (AFRICOM) is the US lead coordinator of diplomatic and other state functions in Africa, what the military calls a 'whole-of-government approach' which includes senior officials from the Departments of State, Homeland Security, Agriculture, Energy, Commerce, Justice and others (US Department of Defense, 7 February 2017). As well as a range of security tasks, AFRICOM is involved in development, public health and other humanitarian tasks that is now dwarfing the traditional focus on aid and diplomacy. In addition, AFRICOM is involved in training and supplying many African militaries, and the construction of African infrastructure that could be used by the United States in the event of conflict. The major impact of the US military presence in Africa is not in permanent infrastructure, but in Status of Forces Agreements negotiated with many African states which permit thousands of troops to arrive and depart from their airports and national military installations (known as 'lily pads'), which Schewe considers an 'imperial-scale military presence' (Eric Schewe, 11 April 2018).

The foremost concern of AFRICOM is with terrorism and specifically with failed states that could destabilize other areas and states; secondly, violence precipitated by non-traditional causes, such as migration, urbanization or refugee flows; thirdly, counterbalancing China's growing influence in the region, and lastly, securing access to oil and other natural resources (A. Carl LeVan, Fall, 2010). China's engagement in Africa is also premised on acquiring natural resources and gaining markets, but unlike US and European investors who focus on the short-term objectives its state-owned corporations have 'the objective of forming long-lasting relationships with the communities and governments with which they cooperate, assisted in part by their accessibility to very low cost of capital' (Hany Besada, 2013).

Another element of the emerging cold war between China and the United States is over the status of Taiwan and in 2020 Taipei established diplomatic relations with the secessionist region of Somaliland, which angered China (The Economist, 3 October 2020). As arguably the only democratic state in the HOA (and ironically it is not recognized internationally) Somaliland's government is trying to gain Washington's diplomatic recognition in return for using its port of Berbera to diversify away from neighbouring Djibouti because of its strong Chinese links (Jevans Nyabiage, 15 January 2022). To date, however, the United States and the international community have followed the lead of the African

Union in not recognizing Somaliland as an independent state and instead to consider it officially part of Somalia.

China's approach to regional governments is less judgmental than the United States and looks to enhance its position where the United States has demonstrated weakness. Thus, China backed the al-Bashir dictatorship but had no problem endorsing the successor transitional government; it was a strong supporter of the EPRDF and an equally strong supporter of the anti-EPRDF Abiy Ahmed government, and it has consistently supported the Salva Kiir dictatorship in South Sudan. In South Sudan, however, China has backed the Western-led Inter-Governmental Authority on Development (IGAD) peace process. China's biggest economic engagement in the HOA has been with Sudan and, after secession, the South Sudanese oil industry. Although developed by the US Chevron company and later by Canada's Talisman, US and Western sanctions precluded the role of their companies in Sudan, and as a result China (along with Malaysia and India) dominates the field. But that investment has had mixed results and South Sudan's civil war led to damaged pumping facilities and dramatically reduced oil production. Nonetheless, South Sudan is the third-largest oil exporter in sub-Saharan Africa and the state-owned China National Petroleum Corporation remains the country's biggest oil producer. In addition, Chinese corporations have major investments in telecommunications, transport infrastructure projects and mining, and as a result its investment in South Sudan dwarfs those of the United States and the EU.

China prioritizes development and investment as ends in themselves and to construct a global support network based on development and investment. This involves accepting the powers that be, irrespective of who they are or what their politics are, as long as they are receptive to positive engagement with China and do not recognize Taiwan – in other words, non-interference in the internal affairs of other countries, a popular principle in Africa.[2] As a victim of Western and Japanese imperialism, China became a prominent supporter of the non-aligned movement and aided a host of liberation movements in Africa. Beijing employs the rhetoric of Third World solidarity and South-South Cooperation, seeks to practise 'great power diplomacy with Chinese characteristics' and build a 'community of common destiny' (China.cn.org, 6 November 2019). While IMF structural adjustment policies are widely seen to have hampered Africa's development, China represents a positive alternative. China has offered Africa interest-free or low-interest loans with few or no conditions, unlike those of the IMF and World Bank that often have high interest and require expensive oversight

---

2. President Xi Jinping said, 'We follow a "five-no" approach in our relations with Africa: no interference in African countries' pursuit of development paths that fit their national conditions; no interference in African countries' internal affairs; no imposition of our will on Africa countries; no attachment of political strings to assistance to Africa; and no seeking of selfish political gains in investment and financing cooperation with Africa' (President Xi Jinping, 3 September 2019).

and compliance reviews. China is also sensitive to the economic predicaments facing Africa, offers practical solutions and frequently cancels debts (Ousman Murzik Kobo, March 2013). China is new to development finance, but it is now among the world's biggest development financiers and while OECD donor funding has declined relatively in recent years, China's contributions have significantly increased (Anis Chowdhury and Jomo Kwame Sundaram, 12 July 2022).

Although rapidly expanding, China's economic power, and particularly its welcome investment in infrastructure, it is not as yet making any effort to follow the United States and became a major military power and security provider in the Red Sea area. China's foremost concerns in the region are commercial and national security and thus it has an interest in stability. Until its success in brokering a peace agreement between Iran and Saudi Arabia, China has been reluctant to engage in mediation or other peacemaking efforts. But that may now change. The Stockholm International Peace Research Institute found that while global arms transfers from 2016 to 2020 levelled off compared to 2011–2015, arms imports in the volatile Middle East grew by 25 per cent (SIPRI, 15 March 2021). And despite not being a major arms exporter to the Middle East, according to SIPRI China increased its arms transfers to Saudi Arabia and the UAE by 386 per cent and 169 per cent, respectively, compared to 2011–2015. Some of that weaponry, notably drones exported to the UAE, were re-exported to Ethiopia and used very effectively in the Tigray War.

China sold weapons to both sides during the 1998–2000 Ethio-Eritrean War (Earl Conteh-Morgan, 19 April 2017). But when criticized for selling weapons to the al-Bashir regime which were used in its counter-insurgency operations in Darfur and led to calls by activists for a boycott of the 2008 Beijing Olympics, China used its influence with Sudan to facilitate the deployment of a joint AU–UN peacekeeping mission to Darfur in 2007 (Jesse Marks, 25 March 2022). Beijing offered restrained support for Sudan's transition to civilian governance in the aftermath of the 2019 coup (Laura Barber, 8 May 2020). China's most significant involvement with international peacekeeping has been the provision of troops to the UN peacekeeping mission in South Sudan. Although non-interference is one of Beijing's central foreign policy tenants, it is increasingly shaped by a significant degree of pragmatism, especially when interests and assets are at stake (Mordechai Chaziza, 8 May 2018).

China has used its growing economic power to get Djibouti, Egypt, Eritrea, Oman, Saudi Arabia, Somalia, South Sudan, Sudan, the UAE and Yemen sign a letter to the UN Human Rights Council supporting Beijing's policies in Xinjiang (USIP, April 2020). Beijing also employs soft power by providing funding for thousands of African officials, students and journalists to study and train in China and is opening Confucius Institutes throughout the HOA. However, China's growing economic engagement in the HOA has not been without drawbacks. In 2007 a rebel group seeking self-determination from Ethiopia attacked a Chinese gas/oil exploration base and killed nine Chinese employees, and in 2008 a Darfur rebel organization overran in Sudan's South Kordofan state a China National Petroleum Corporation (CNPC) operation, capturing nine Chinese employees, five of whom later died (David Shinn, 18 May 2021). But the biggest losses were incurred as a result of the South Sudan civil war.

For many years Emperor Haile-Selassie played a balancing act between Taiwan and the Peoples Republic of China without recognizing either country (David Shinn, May 2014). China's efforts to gain recognition were complicated by its provision of weapons to the rebel Eritrean Liberation Front (ELF) from the early 1960s (David Shinn, May 2014). Ethiopia and China also had different policies on Sudan, with Ethiopia supporting the SPLA while China backed the central government in Khartoum, which allowed the ELF to operate from Sudan. When Ethiopia finally recognized the PRC in 1970, it extracted a promise that Beijing would end its support for the ELF (David Shinn, May 2014).

Relations quickly deteriorated, however, after the Soviet-supported Derg came to power at the height of tensions between Moscow and Beijing. With the coming to power of the EPRDF in 1991 relations rapidly improved and China became Ethiopia's biggest source of investment and a major destination of its exports. Beijing supplied Ethiopia with military equipment, training, and relations were cemented with the signing of a military cooperation agreement in 2005 for training, exchange of technologies and joint peacekeeping missions (Aaron Tesfaye, 20 September 2019). The two countries also had robust party-to-party relations and strong relations between Ethiopia's Parliament and the China National People's Congress. Nonetheless, between 2011 and 2016 Ethiopia hosted a US drone base in Arba Minch used to attack terrorist groups in Somalia (BBC, 4 January 2016).

China's still weak position is reflected in its tendency to follow the old adage of befriending the enemies of its enemies. Thus, because of Abiy Ahmed's commitment to neoliberalism and liberal democracy, the United States and the West had good reason to think that Ethiopia could be weaned from its close relations with China developed under the EPRDF. In December 2019 Ethiopia received a $9 billion in financial aid from Western donors, the IMF and the World Bank (Simon Marks, 7 February 2020). This cash influx was considered not only a vote of confidence in Abiy and his Prosperity Party over the statist policies of the EPRDF, but a means to end Chinese economic dominance in the country.

However, after Western countries condemned Abiy's brutal war in Tigray, China saw an opening and embraced his government. Chinese Foreign Minister, Wang Yi, visited Addis Ababa in December 2021 and shortly after visited Eritrea whose relations with the West are poor and deteriorated further after Eritrean forces invaded Tigray in November 2020 (Eastafro, 12 January 2021). Along with Russia, China has played a crucial role in the Security Council blocking criticism of the Abiy Ahmed government for its humanitarian blockade of Tigray and efforts to press the government and the TPLF to start negotiations (William Worley, 21 June 2022). Although Chinese support provided the Abiy government with a measure of political space with which to manoeuvre in light of Western pressures, Ethiopia's foreign policy has primarily been directed to winning the favour of the still powerful West. The limitation of Western power, however, was expressed in the concern that if Abiy was pushed too hard the West could 'lose' Ethiopia to China and that also made clear that Abiy and Ethiopia were not without agency. This politics was played out in the UN Human Rights Council where despite Western lobbying all thirteen representatives from Africa in the forty-seven-member body opposed a resolution proposed by the European Union to discuss Addis Ababa's alleged war atrocities in Tigray region (Aggrey Mutambo, 14 December 2021). The vote can be explained in the first instance by the power of Ethiopia as the second largest country in Africa and host to the AU, but also concern with the Western emphasis and understanding of human rights and opposition to Western bullying.

Russia does not have the multifaceted economic outreach of China, but it has legitimacy because it was never a colonial power, the Soviet Union supported anti-colonial liberation movements in the Middle East and Africa, and Russia does not attempt to establish the neo-colonial relations that are the norm with the United States. As the second largest oil producer in the world Russia possesses political weight in the Middle East, and cooperation between Russia and Saudi Arabia has become a hallmark of the enlarged OPEC+ since 2016 (Baker Institute, 18 October 2022). Russia is also widely recognized for its diplomatic skills and its successful support of the al-Assad regime in Syria and naval base in the country. As a result, in March 2023, Russia appeared to be on the verge of ending the long and destructive feud between Turkiye and Syria (Bloomberg News, 15 March 2023). If successful this initiative will undermine US foreign policy in the region by bringing Russia and Turkiye, a NATO member, closer and make the illegal US occupation of Syria's oil fields untenable. In the wake of Syria moving to reconcile with Jordan, Saudi Arabia, Oman and the UAE, this also seriously undermines Washington-led Western effort to isolate and overthrow the Bashar al-Assad regime (Reuters, 19 March 2023) and two months later Syria rejoined the Arab League.

Russia has attempted to build on old Soviet ties, the sale of weaponry, grain and fertilizers, the provision of security services, and Russia's experience with mining, particularly through the semi-independent Wagner Group. Russia is anxious to expand into sub-Saharan Africa and in 2019 it held the first Russia–Africa Summit in Sochi, gathering representatives from all fifty-four African countries, with forty-three states being represented at the highest level, and in March 2023 Moscow hosted the 2nd International Parliamentary 'Russia–Africa' Conference with over forty official delegations to consider topics ranging from Russian-African cooperation to Western neo-colonialism (RT, 18 March 2023). Another Russia–Africa economic forum is to be held in St Petersburg in July 2023 which will serve as a platform for the development of Russian mining activities in Africa and most of the heads of state from the fifty-four African countries are expected to attend (Ben Aris, 16 April 2023). However, Grigory Lukyanov, a researcher at the Russian International Affairs Council, contends that the African embrace of Russia has less to do with any pro-Russian sentiments and instead because 'The anti-French, anti-British, anti-colonial agenda is once again dominant in Africa' (RT, 18 March 2023) and that is being stimulated by Western demands that African states follow its leadership in the Ukraine War.

Russia provided 49 per cent of the arms sold to Africa, far ahead of the United States in second place with 14 per cent in 2021 (Chtatou Mohamed and Kester Kenn Klomegah, 11 February 2022). Meanwhile, Russia donated more than 300 million Sputnik V doses to the African Union (AU) in 2021 (Chris Devonshire-Ellis,

2 December 2021). Russia also cancelled $20 billion in African debt and because of Western sanctions has provided some fertilizer stocks for free and Putin has promised that grain will also be provided for free to African states if sanctions on the transport of grain through Black Sea ports are not extended (Teller Report, 21 March 2023). Like China, Russia has little interest in the politics of the countries it is engaged with. During the Cold War the Eastern Bloc and China provided support for leftist anti-imperialist liberation movements operating from the peripheries, but today Russia and China typically support the status quo, particularly if the country in question has contentious relations with the West.

Sudan's al-Bashir attempted to end US opposition to his regime by offering cooperation during the GWOT and while not without some successes, Washington maintained its sanctions against the regime. As a result, in his final days in power al-Bashir turned to Russia, and the Wagner Group was employed in 2017 to train the Sudanese army. This relationship continued after the collapse of the regime and Wagner established two gold companies, Meroe Gold and M Invest (Mustapha Dalaa and Halime Afra Aksoy, 5 March 2021). The Wagner Group has also worked with a powerful Sudanese militia, the Rapid Support Forces (RSF), and has exchanged weapons for mining concessions in a pattern that Russia has followed elsewhere in Africa even while the RSF was beating and killing Sudanese demonstrators calling for the overthrow of the military (see below). In the UN Security Council Russia and China vetoed a draft resolution condemning Sudan's General al-Burhan's first coup in 2019 (Carole Landry, 4 June 2019).

The same approach is evident with respect to Ethiopia, where Russia's positive relations with the EPRDF government continued seamlessly with the anti-EPRDF Abiy government. Trade between Russia and Ethiopia is not significant, but Russia signed a military cooperation agreement with the Abiy Ahmed government in July 2021 (Ayyaantuu News, 12 July 2021), which can be interpreted as an endorsement of his war against the TPLF. Meanwhile, Eritrea's pariah status precluded US military engagement in spite of its strategic position on the Red Sea. American opposition to the regime[3] led Asmara to support Russia in UN votes on Ukraine, and according to Russian Foreign Minister, Sergey Lavrov, Moscow is ready to meet Eritrea's 'defense capabilities' (RT, 18 March 2023).

## Middle Eastern States in the Horn of Africa

During the Cold War the Americans and Soviets maintained a level of control over their regional client states and their conflicts because of fears that these conflicts could lead to a nuclear war, and this continued into the post-Cold War era, but with the decline of US power those constraints are weakening. As well as the US humiliating defeat in Afghanistan, the failure of the United States to overthrow

---

3. While the US Department of Defence has consistently pushed for links to Eritrea, the State Department cultivated close links with the TPLF/EPRDF and Prime Minister Meles Zenawi, and it resisted.

the Iranian and Syrian regimes, which were militarily supported by Russia and economically by China led to a major loss of American prestige in the region. In addition, incoming President Biden announced that the United States was ending support for the Saudi-UAE war in Yemen, pressed Saudi Arabia on the murder of Jamal Khashoggi, a journalist with the *Washington Post*, and called Saudi Arabia a 'pariah state' which angered Riyadh and led it to pursue a more independent foreign policy and strengthen ties with China and Russia. No doubt Saudi's Mohammed bin Salman and other Middle Eastern leaders have concluded that the United States is no longer able to dominate the Middle East and they have been striking out on their own and this has led to what is being called a 'new scramble for Africa'.

After the United States played the lead role in orchestrating the Sudan peace process and overseeing the secession of South Sudan in 2011, the American engagement increasingly declined, and into the vacuum former US client states became increasingly active. And those states – notably Saudi Arabia, the UAE and Egypt – are dedicated to ensuring that the democratic transformation demanded by Sudan's protestors are not realized (John Young, 2020a). These countries are equally adamant that the Muslim Brothers are eliminated in Sudan and throughout the region. While Abiy Ahmed has tried to project himself as a valiant defender of Ethiopian and African sovereignty in the face of claimed US subversion during the Tigray War, the most striking feature of US engagement in the country has been its impotence. The US void is being filled by regional states – notably Egypt, Turkiye, UAE, Saudi Arabia, to a lesser extent, Iran and China – which have provided crucial weaponry to the government and did not question Abiy's humanitarian blockade of Tigray.

The counterpart to the heightened engagement of Middle Eastern states in the HOA has been their efforts to draw countries in the Horn into their conflicts. The dispute between Qatar (and subsequently Turkiye) with Saudi Arabia and the UAE was not restricted to the Gulf and soon countries in the HOA were being pressed to take sides and this caused tensions. Sudan tried and failed to maintain good relations with both groups. al-Bashir welcomed Qatar's humanitarian aid and Turkiye's investment, but this angered the UAE and Saudi Arabia from whom the regime wanted financial support and their intercession with Washington to end its sanctions. These states were particularly upset at Turkish plans to develop Sudan's Red Sea port of Suakin, which they claimed would become a naval outpost only a short distance from Saudi Arabia (Sami Moubayed, 28 December 2017).

Ethiopia's relations with Egypt and the Gulf go back a millennium but involve considerable distrust; as an historically Christian dominated country with a large Muslim minority, Ethiopia felt threatened in a region dominated by Muslim states. In recent times Ethiopia had mixed relations with Qatar and did not have relations between 2008 and 2012 because of anger in Addis Ababa with Al-Jazeera's reporting on domestic disputes (Daniel Benaim, 9 April 2019). Since then, relations have improved based on Qatar's humanitarian contributions and its support of Ethiopia in its dispute with Egypt over the Renaissance Dam on the Nile. This followed from Qatar's conflict with the UAE and Saudi Arabia, which supported Egypt. Although Saudi Arabia is a major investor in Ethiopia, its support for Egypt dampened Riyadh-Addis Ababa relations. Eritrea alone took a clear position on the Gulf dispute and sided with the UAE and Saudi Arabia and in 2015 signed a thirty-year lease with the UAE and Saudi Arabia to establish a base in Assab (in violation of the UN arms embargo against Eritrea) which has been used to fight the Yemeni Houthis and subsequently the TPLF (Zeenat Hansrod, 25 December 2016). Although not announced, the UAE appears to have abandoned Assab in early 2021 as it pulled back from its active support for Saudi Arabia in Yemen, after which the facilities have presumably been handed over to the Eritrean military.

Although refusing to back the Saudi-led blockade of Qatar, al-Bashir severed ties with Iran and supported the Saudi and Emirati-led war in Yemen. While the Houthi rebellion did not pose any threat to Sudan's security or national interests, forces from Sudan, paid for by the UAE and Saudi Arabia, provided the largest foreign component of the anti-Houthi army (One World, 27 December 2019). Largely drawn from Janjaweed fighters with an infamous record of human rights abuses in Darfur (Human Rights Watch, 9 September 2015), the Rapid Support Force fighters led by Mohamed Hamdan Dagalo (otherwise known as Hemedti) since 2013 served as cannon fodder for the UAE and Saudi Arabia and thus kept fatalities within their own armed forces low. However, this engagement served to empower the RSF and cement relations between it and the Gulf states independent of Khartoum and that continued into the post-al-Bashir period. Since al-Bashir was overthrown Sudan's ties with Turkiye and Qatar, which are sympathetic to the Muslim Brotherhood, have weakened, while Saudi and Emirati ties have strengthened.

There has also been a destabilizing competition between Middle East powers for naval bases along the Red Sea. In his first meeting with Vladimir Putin in Sochi in November 2017 al-Bashir said, 'We are thankful to Russia for its position in the international arena, including Russia's position in the protection of Sudan. We are in need of protection from the aggressive acts of the United States' (AFP, 23 November 2017). al-Bashir went on to say, 'Sudan may become Russia's key to Africa' (President of Russia, 23 November 2017). This set the stage for Sudan granting port facilities to the Russian navy, a decision that was subsequently endorsed and pursued by the military wing of the post-al-Bashir transitional government, but which upset the civilian component of the government which has tried to win the favour of the United States. Russia wants to have access through Sudan to landlocked Central African Republic where the Wagner Group is involved in the mining industry. As a quid pro quo the Russian representative to the UN Security Council objected to calling the Sudan military takeover of 25 October 2021 a coup and insisted that protesters as well as the military were guilty of violence (Ephrem Kossaify, 28 October 2021).

In 2017 Turksom, Turkiye's most extensive military base abroad, was established in Somalia to provide a foothold in the HOA (Al-Jazeera, 1 October 2017). Turkiye and Qatar cooperated in the training of the Somali federal army of President Mohamed Abdullahi Farmajo (President 2017–2022) used to quell rebellions and strengthen Farmajo who was a close ally of Abiy Ahmed and Isaias Afwerki. In addition, Qatar paid for the training of Somali soldiers in Eritrea who were subsequently employed without the knowledge of their families in the Tigray invasion of November 2020 and others were sent to Libya (Abdi Sheikh, 28 January 2021). Still other Somali soldiers are being trained by Ethiopia and Uganda. The United States has also been involved in counter-insurgency training of Somali soldiers, although its primary interest appears to be concern of a political vacuum that could be filled by Russia and/or China. The United States has been involved in Somalia for almost twenty years and it operates several bases from which it launches drones, some of them armed largely against al-Shabaab, according to Nick Turse (The Intercept, 12 April 2023).

The UAE was quick to endorse the new neoliberal government of Abiy Ahmed by granting Ethiopia a $3 billion package of aid and investment in 2018 (Simon Marks, 7 February 2020). And the UAE together with Saudi Arabia brought President Isaias and Prime Minister Abiy together to sign a peace pact, which was later revealed as a war pact against the TPLF, but not before Abiy was awarded a Nobel Peace prize for his 'peacemaking'. Likewise, the UAE and Saudi Arabia rushed to the aid of Sudan's Transitional Military Council after the overthrow of al-Bashir, but what these states contended was a financial contribution to stability was viewed by the protesters as support for the military and an unwarranted involvement in the internal affairs of Sudan (John Young, 2020a).

The UAE built military bases and ports in both Assab Eritrea and Berbera Somalia, while in Djibouti the UAE established the port of Doraleh in a joint project with China (Zach Vertin, August 2019). Assab served as a forward base to launch airstrikes with Chinese drones against the Houthis and to funnel Sudanese and other foreign mercenaries onto the Arabian Peninsula before it was dismantled. The UAE's involvement was part of its strategy to build a security system across the Red Sea and the HOA. However, in September 2019 the UAE announced that its facilities at Berbera would only be used for civilian aircraft, presumably because of new strategic thinking over Yemen by UAE. Leader of a country of only 1 million people, UAE's Mohammad bin Zayed Al Nahyan had achieved this strategic position because of support by the United States with which it has closely cooperated. Control over the strait by the United States gives it leverage to potentially block China's Maritime Silk Road and this explains US support for the conflict in Yemen.

Internationalized by the West which opposed the influence of Muammar Gaddafi in the Middle East and Africa, the conflict in Libya divided the countries in the Middle East and Europe. The UAE, Saudi Arabia and Egypt supported the Libyan National Army of General Khalifa Haftar along with Russia and France, while the UN recognized the Government of National Accords in Tripoli supported by Turkiye. At the behest of the UAE, Sudan's Rapid Support Forces, an al-Bashir established Darfur-based militia, provided fighters for General Khalifa and facilitated the hiring of other Darfuri fighters for the conflict. al-Bashir created the RSF to protect himself because of suspicions as to the loyalty of his army and to crush rebellions in Sudan's peripheries, notably Darfur. But in the face of al-Bashir's financial and political concerns the RSF became important in gaining resources and support from the Gulf states. And to address EU efforts to stop potential refugees passing through north-western Sudan to Libya and across the Mediterranean to Europe it paid agencies of the Sudan government for the RSF to stop these would-be refugees (John Young, 2020a). The RSF did stop some refugees, but it also strengthened relations between RSF leader General Hemedti and Libyan warlord Khalifa Haftar in highly profitable smuggling operations, in addition to the supply of fighters to Haftar's war with the central government.

The most powerful military power in the Middle East is Israel and its involvement in the HOA has also proved destabilizing, Sudan being the primary example. Like the other countries in the Middle East, Israel has no interest in promoting democracy, but it does have an interest in eliminating or neutralizing its opponents in the region and strengthening its relations with the Arab autocracies and under President Trump and the Abrahams Accords it made considerable progress. Israel viewed the al-Bashir regime with disdain because of Sudan's long-standing support of the Palestinian cause and it conspired with Sudan's security chief, Salah Gosh, to engineer the overthrow of the Islamist regime (see below). And because coup General al-Burhan took the lead in setting Sudan on the road to diplomatic recognition, Israel had a vested interest in preserving the power of Sudan's military in the transitional government. Viewing Israel as an enemy of the Arabs and in an effort to win the favour of the United States, South Sudan was quick after independence to establish diplomatic relations with Tel Aviv. And this at a time when Israel was putting South Sudanese refugees trying to reach Europe in concentration camps (John Young, 2019, p. 61).

Notwithstanding the success of the US Abraham Accords in normalizing relations between the UAE, Bahrain, Morocco and Sudan with Israel, the people in the region and in the Muslim-inhabited areas of the HOA give no indication that they have changed their opposition to Israel. Moreover, as a result of a series of reconciliation processes and agreements among the Arab states and the formation of a hard right government under Benjamin Netanyahu in 2023 Israel is again facing regional isolation and the United States is witnessing the weakening of its major ally in the region (Hussein Aboubakr Mansour, 23 March 2023).

Regional actors were also involved in Sudan's military coup against al-Bashir, the military's decision to try and rule on its own and, when that initiative failed, to launch another coup on 25 October 2021 against the civilian wing of the transitional government headed by Abdalla Hamdok. According to Kholood Khair, 'It's clear that General Burhan must have gotten assurances, political and economic, from regional powers in Cairo and Abu Dhabi during his trips there' (Kholood Khair, 23 September 2021) while Jonas Horner, senior Sudan analyst at Crisis Group, said, 'Cairo appears to have been integral to Monday's coup' (Frank Andrews, 28 October 2021). Horner concluded that concern with Ethiopia's Renaissance Dam was the crucial factor for Egyptian involvement, but el-Sisi would also be fearful that the example of a popular uprising displacing the military in Sudan might encourage dissidents in Egypt.

Middle Eastern states have long been interested in Ethiopia as a source of investment, the most populous country in the HOA with 110 million people, the headquarters of the African Union and the Economic Commission of Africa, a major source of workers for the Gulf, and possessing a large internal market. The UAE provision of Chinese drones to destroy the TPLF's 3 November 2020 seizure of equipment of the Ethiopian National Defense Force in Tigray proved crucial in the army's quick take-over of Tigray in November/December 2020. Iran also supplied military equipment, including drones, to the Ethiopian army and, like Russia and China, welcomes positive relations with the biggest country in the HOA after the United States and al-Bashir's enemies in the Middle East pressured Sudan to break relations with Iran (John Young, 2020a). Moreover, Iran looks to Ethiopia as a key entry point to sell military equipment to the African market and having positive relations with a major country close to its security interests in the Arabian peninsula (Banafsheh Keynoush, 26 January 2022).

According to the Turkish Exporters Assembly, the export of Turkish arms and military aviation equipment to Ethiopia increased from $235,000 in January 2021 to $94.6 million in November 2021 (Vladimir Danilov, 24 December 2021), most of this being the supply of drones for the war in Tigray. This support was held to strengthen Turkiye's reputation in the African military and security market, encourage hope that Turkish construction companies could make a significant contribution to the reconstruction of infrastructure in the areas destroyed by the war, protect its large investments in the country and ensure that chaos in Ethiopia does not spread into neighbouring Somalia, the most important centre of Turkish influence in Africa (Abdolgader Mohamed Ali, 14 February 2022).

Middle Eastern engagement in the HOA is not restricted to security concerns and involves food deficient countries from the region acquiring farming land in Sudan and Ethiopia. This harkens back to the 1980s when Sudan was proclaimed 'the bread-basket of the Arab world', but that endeavour did not turn out well. In addition, Middle Eastern states are involved in various commercial investments and of late there is a growing interest of Gulf states in diversifying from their dependence on oil. All the Gulf states have made humanitarian contributions to the HOA, with Kuwait and Qatar standing out. Saudi Arabia also has an interest in the proselytization of its Wahhabi faith and this has caused divisions in Sudan and Ethiopia. Although denied by the UAE authorities, it is widely believed that Dubai is a centre for smuggled and unaccounted for African gold which fuels conflict, finances criminal and terrorist networks, and robs national treasuries. In Sudan it is estimated that 75 per cent of the gold mined in the country disappears on the black market and most or all of it ends up in Dubai (Simon Marks, Michael Kavanagh and Verity Radcliffe, 28 December 2021).

A common feature of these Middle Eastern states is that they are authoritarian and oppose democracy which they view as a contagious virus. For Egypt a democratic Sudan on its border is viewed as a threat and the UAE and Saudi Arabia also fear democracy, the Muslim Brothers and a return to the menacing days of the Arab Spring. All three countries are also concerned that a democratic government in Sudan could result in the loss of a valued participant in their support of Libya's General Khalifa Haftar, and for the latter two countries, Sudan's provision of soldiers to fight the Houthis in Yemen.

Beyond the region India has a major investment in South Sudan's oil industry, provided troops for the UN peacekeeping mission in the country, and in the UN New Delhi has repeatedly opposed any condemnations of Ethiopia for its human rights abuses during the Tigray (and later) Oromo wars (Yahoo! News, 26 August 2021). India is also concerned at the growing role of China in Africa, but this has not served to undermine its traditional close relations with Russia, which have grown stronger as a result of the Ukraine War. Indeed, despite Western sanctions India has become a major importer of Russian oil and refused US demands that it fall in line and condemn Russia in the UN for its invasion of Ukraine, another indication of declining US power.

The United States has been the ultimate guarantor of the security of the Gulf states, providing weaponry to all the countries in the region. The US dollar for the international trade in petroleum has been a bedrock of the US-dominated global economy, although with the advent of the Ukraine War and the increasingly positive relations between the oil producing states in the Gulf and Russia and China that is changing. What has been most noteworthy about US relations with its Middle Eastern client states is that with the exception of a brief period in the wake of 9/11 under President George Bush, the United States has never pressed them to end their authoritarianism and embrace democracy. This feature of US policy provided political space for these states but undermined the legitimacy of US democratic proselytizing globally.

Although its relations with the United States have become increasingly strained in recent years, Turkiye's membership in a US-led NATO, partnership in the GWOT, and control over the fate of millions of Syrian and other refugees on the border of Europe mean that the ties between the two countries are too important to risk an open break. But the purchase by Turkiye (and India) of Russian weaponry in open defiance of the United States makes clear that the Americans are not able to dominate these states as in the past. Moreover, in the wake of President Biden's announcement that the United States was stopping military support for the Saudi and Emirati anti-Houthi war, it was revealed in late December 2021 that there have been 'large-scale transfers of sensitive ballistic missile technology between China and Saudi Arabia' (Zachary Cohen, 23 December 2021). The United States has been adamant that its client states, including Israel, not import military equipment from Russia and China, and yet that is clearly occurring.

## Conclusion

The United States is losing peaceful economic competition with China, and unable to overcome that challenge it is increasingly relying on its overwhelming military power. The US pivot to Asia and its view that China (and in the wake of the Ukraine War, Russia) pose an existential threat to American hegemony mean a declining interest with developments in non-core areas like the HOA, and that is evident to all the parties in the greater region. Also evident is the failure or inability of the European Union to step into the gap and this is due to its many divisions over foreign policy which were evident in Libya when different European countries supported opposing sides of the conflict (Euractiv, 22 March 2011). EU foreign policy weakness is also due to a history of subservience to the United States and the latter's capacity to divide the Europeans. That same weakness was evident in Europe's poor performance in both the Sudan and South Sudan peace process even though the Europeans were footing most of the costs. Also indicative of declining EU, particularly French authority, in Africa was Mali's ejection of the French military from its peacekeeping mission in May 2022 because of concern that Paris was undermining its national sovereignty.

The countries in the Horn and Middle East recognize that the US role as their protector has ended and are taking foreign policy initiatives that would have been unimaginable even a decade ago, including developing ever-closer relations with China and Russia and rejecting pressure to normalize relations with Israel. The United States is responding to its declining capacity to compete economically with China in Africa and the HOA by increasing its military engagement through AFRICOM, but this agency and its programmes are widely viewed as another phase in Western neo-colonialism and constitute an extension of NATO. Meanwhile, in the wake of US failures in its response to the Covid pandemic and the West's inability to convince the Global South to accept sanctions against Russia after its invasion of Ukraine, China together with Russia are mobilizing support for the establishment of an alternative to the US international order.

In the greater Middle East, US client states have witnessed the failure of the United States to fulfil its plans to make Iraq a base for spreading democracy to the region and to overthrow the Iranian regime. They have observed the collapse of the US-backed Afghani regime, the success of Russia, Iran and Hezbollah in blocking efforts by the US-led Western and Gulf states to overthrow the al-Assad regime in Syria. Despite the support of the United States and other Western states, Saudi and UAE efforts to defeat the Houthi regime in Yemen have failed. States in the Middle East that had previously viewed the United States as a source of support and even survival have concluded that it is unreliable, increasingly weak and that the primary American security concern is no longer in the Middle East (and certainly not the HOA), and instead with China and Russia which the United States views as existential threats.

Although lacking the 'soft power' of the United States and some Western countries as well as generations of institutional linkages and a powerful supportive media, China and Russia are taking advantage of US global decline to advance their interests internationally. They have long condemned American hegemony and called for national sovereignty, but in the wake of the Ukraine War and the unwillingness of the Global South to fall in line with Western demands this appeal is getting traction. Indeed, at the height of the Ukraine War Saudi Arabia and the UAE aligned with Russia and refused Washington's entreaties (even after a visit by President Biden to the region in July 2022) to increase oil production to offset politically destabilizing rising prices at US gas pumps. This was followed by China's diplomacy in cementing a peace agreement between Iran and Saudi Arabia and Russia's efforts to end hostilities between Turkiye and Syria. These developments have also gone hand-in-hand with the increased use of local currencies at the expense of the US dollar in the energy trade. Together they serve to restructure power relations in the Middle East which have important implications for the HOA and will seriously undermine the authority of the United States and its Western allies in both regions.

Moreover, Russian and Chinese peacemaking in the region set them apart from the West which is encouraging conflicts and is opposed to a peaceful Middle East. A similar situation was evident when China proposed a ceasefire and peace process to end the conflict in the Ukraine and President Joe Biden promptly rejected it and held that the very idea of a Chinese peace initiative was 'irrational' (CNN, 24 February 2023). It speaks powerfully to the political and moral bankruptcy of the US international order that moves to peacefully resolve conflicts in the Middle East are held to pose a threat to its viability.

## Chapter 3

### ETHIOPIA AND THE CHALLENGE OF DEMOCRACY

In April 2018 Dr Abiy Ahmed was selected by the ruling EPRDF to serve as its leader and prime minister of Ethiopia, and in December 2019 he dissolved the EPRDF and formed the Prosperity Party. This ended almost three decades of EPRDF rule during which time the Front defeated the military Derg and brought peace to the country, implemented a system of national federalism that went far towards meeting popular demands for national self-determination, oversaw a dramatic improvement in the living standards of Ethiopia's poverty-stricken population, maintained the country's sovereignty and played a respected peacekeeping role in the HOA. However, while contending that Western liberal democracy was unsuitable for Ethiopia, the Front failed to construct viable alternative mechanisms of democratic governance. Meanwhile, Abiy proclaimed his commitment to liberal democracy and initially introduced major reforms, but very quickly was overseeing a regime more repressive than the one he replaced. And on 4 November 2020 Abiy together with the army of his comrade in arms, Eritrean President Isaias Afwerki, Amhara militias, drones from the United Arab Emirates, and a contingent of Somali soldiers launched a war against the region of Tigray and its ruling Tigray Peoples Liberation Front which had founded the EPRDF.

This study begins by briefly considering the Ethiopian Student Movement (ESM) which gave birth to the TPLF and other liberation movements that fought the military Derg and whose ideas shaped the country's politics until the advent of Abiy. The chapter will then turn to the EPRDF's three signature stratagems or policies: revolutionary democracy as an alternative to liberal democracy, national federalism as a response to the centrism and denial of the right of national self-determination of previous Ethiopian governments, and state-led development in opposition to the neoliberalism pressed by the West. These three policies can be recognized as core elements of the EPRDF's understanding of democracy and as such they are in marked opposition to the contrasting Western vision. Although achieving notable successes, the failure to make these three EPRDF priorities instruments for the country's democratization together with the autocratic rule of Meles Zenawi left the Front fatally weakened and produced growing opposition and the descent of the country into war. Ethiopian experience under the EPRDF demonstrates first that the model of Western democracy could not, and during the early period of the Abiy Ahmed rule did not, meet the needs of ordinary Ethiopians, and second that despite EPRDF successes in meeting popular demands for national self-determination and dramatically raising living standards, the failure of the Front to institute a viable system of democratic administration not only led to its collapse, but unrelenting war.

## Origins and development of the TPLF

Alone in Africa, Ethiopia was not colonized and thus passed from a traditional autocracy to state socialism under the military Derg, appropriately called 'garrison socialism' (John Markakis, 1987). Ideology took the form of divine right in the case of the Haile-Selassie regime and socialist developmentalism of the Derg. Both relied extensively on brute force to maintain power, and both were ultimately displaced by force, in the latter case by the EPRDF. As a result, and unlike other countries in Africa, Ethiopia did not have any experience with either political or economic liberalism and nor did liberal democracy figure in the legitimacy of the Haile-Selassie, Derg and EPRDF regimes. In addition, civil society was banned by the first two regimes and severely restricted by the EPRDF and that encouraged opposition to operate underground and take more radical forms. The foremost example of this was the Ethiopian Student Movement or ESM which proved crucial in bringing about the collapse of the imperial regime.

Ethiopia's long history cannot be summarized here, but it needs to be appreciated that Ethiopia as it is presently configured is not – despite claims – of ancient standing, but instead the product of imperial aggrandizement under Menelik II in the late nineteenth century of much of the highlands and lowlands south and west of his capital, Addis Ababa. Although held by the Europeans to be a savage, Menelik constructed his empire parallel to the European 'Scramble for Africa' and this empire was inherited by Emperor Haile-Selassie. Just like his European counterparts and Menelik, Haile-Selassie did not recognize either the individual or national rights of the people he ruled.

Eritrea followed a different trajectory. Although having links to Ethiopia and particularly Tigray since the Axumite civilization that dates back 3,000 years, it was captured by Italy in the late nineteenth century. The territory was then taken over by the British after the Italian defeat in the Second World War, but due to international arbitration Eritrea was handed over to Haile-Selassie after he promised to protect the cultural and national rights of the people. Behind that decision which flew in the face of the demands of Eritreans for independence, the US Ambassador to the UN, John Foster Dulles, said, 'From the point of view of justice, the opinions of the Eritrean people must receive consideration. Nevertheless, the strategic interest of the United States in the Red Sea basin and the considerations of security and world peace make it necessary that the country has to be linked with our ally Ethiopia' (Linda Heiden, 19 June 1979).

Although Haile-Selassie promised to protect the cultural, linguistic and political rights of the Eritreans, the emperor was caught in a dilemma: permitting Eritreans to have rights denied other Ethiopians would predictably lead them to demand similar rights, but to revoke the rights of Eritreans would likely produce a revolt. In the event, Haile-Selassie ended Eritrea's autonomy and thus he bears singular responsibility for the outbreak of the 1961 insurrection and three decades of war. The emperor assumed that the insurgency could be defeated, but he was mistaken and instead the Eritrean revolt served to inspire opposition to the regime in the Ethiopian heartland, particularly among the students.

In the 1960s the imperial regime faced growing internal opposition and was increasingly viewed as an anachronism, particularly after African states gained independence. Indicative of the mounting turmoil were regional revolts, workers' militancy and dissent in the military. But the brunt of the opposition in the 1960s and 1970s took form among university students, and their desire for Ethiopia's radical transformation laid the basis for the subsequent ideology and policies of a host of liberation movements, including the TPLF and EPRDF. Like other student movements internationally of the same era, the ESM was radicalized by opposition to US imperialism and the Vietnam War, as well as US support for the imperial regime and construction of the Kagnew listening station outside Asmara and naval facilities in Massawa which placed Ethiopia on the front lines in the Cold War (Briscoe Center for American History, 2015). The students were also angered at the presence in Ethiopia since the 1960s of an Israeli counter-insurgency unit to reinforce the authority of the imperial regime. In addition, the students were inspired by the failed coup of 1960 and noted the role of the United States in suppressing it. But they were particularly motivated by the struggle of the Eritrean liberation movements, and that would bring to the fore the national question.

The foremost objective of the ESM, to which all its components were dedicated, was the overthrow of the imperial regime and ending Ethiopia's backwardness. The students never seriously considered launching a liberal democratic revolution and this is not surprising because liberalism never had any basis in Ethiopia's feudal society. Instead, the students looked to Marxism-Leninism as a scientific formula that would end the old regime and usher in liberation. The students held that class represented the fundamental contradiction in Ethiopian society, but many, including the future members of the TPLF, increasingly considered the national issue of immediate concern, and thus they endorsed self-determination for the country's oppressed national minorities.[1] Particularly influential was Walelign Mekonnen's 'On the Question of Nationalities in Ethiopia' published in the student newspaper *Struggle* in November 1969. For the next five decades the national question and the subsidiary issues of who had and did not have the right to national self-determination up to and including secession, and how to balance the

---

1. Ethiopia is made up of eighty national groups, of which the largest are Oromo (34.4 per cent), Amhara (27 per cent), Somali (6.2 per cent) and Tigray (6.1 per cent) (World Population Review, 2022).

powers and rights of national governments with the central government would bedevil the country.

While all the heirs of the ESM were shaped by Marxism-Leninism, the TPLF and the Eritrean People's Liberation Front (EPLF) were the most committed and used the theory to develop their understanding of the national question (Leencho Lata, 2 November 2018). Although their devotion to the Marxist classics was unprecedented in Africa, TPLF veterans now acknowledge that their understanding was not deep. Most influential were the works of Lenin and Stalin and to a lesser extent Mao, Fidel and Che whose writings were widely available and devoted to the mechanics of gaining state power. TPLF leaders overlooked the brutality of Stalin and were impressed by his rapid industrialization of the Soviet Union, which they wanted to replicate in Ethiopia.

The Eritrean liberation movements, together with those who would establish the Oromo Liberation Front (OLF) and the Ogaden National Liberation Front (ONLF), held that Ethiopia constituted a colonial state, and the national issue could only be resolved by secession (Abdi M. Abdullahi, 2007). The TPLF accepted the right of Eritrea to secession because it had been a colony under Italy and later Ethiopia, and it further supported the right of self-determination for Ethiopia's oppressed nations (but not necessarily secession). Upon taking power in 1991 the EPRDF responded constructively to the demands of the EPLF by facilitating a referendum on the secession of Eritrea, not interfering with the referendum, and accepting the outcome. However, the TPLF rejected the OLF contention that feudal Ethiopia was a colonizing state and therefore Oromos did not have the automatic right of secession. The TPLF also insisted that the Ethiopian feudal state had been solely Amhara with a Shoan elite.

Largely devoid of any ideology except the need to overthrow the imperial regime, the Derg initially depended on the two main Ethiopian revolutionary movements – the Ethiopian People's Revolutionary Party (EPRP) and the All-Ethiopia Socialist Movement (MEISON) – and both espoused pan-Ethiopian nationalism and held class to be the central contradiction in Ethiopia (John Markakis, 1987, p. 244). The Derg attempted to mobilize on a class basis by giving land to the tiller which ended the feudal system and distributed land among the destitute peasantry including Muslims who had largely been precluded from holding land. But the Derg was unwilling to share power with either the EPRP or MEISON, and in the face of opposition it unleashed a brutal 'red terror' which saw thousands of the country's youths die on the streets of Addis Ababa and other Ethiopian cities. But the Derg's biggest failure was that it did not fully address the country's national contradictions and as a result it was challenged by multiple national-based revolts, in addition to the continuing Eritrean insurgency.

The TPLF accepted the primacy of class in Ethiopia, but the reality in Tigray was that there was effectively no working class or bourgeoisie, and the class structure was relatively fluid. The Tigrayan peasants had never been separated from their land, although most barely had enough land to ensure their survival, and thus the Derg did not win their support by its land reform. Instead, the people of Tigray were primarily motivated by nationalism and feared that the Derg would take the form of another repressive Shoan-Amhara regime. Tigrayans took enormous pride in their rich and ancient heritage and deeply resented their poverty which they attributed to Amhara rule since the death of the Tigrayan Emperor Yohannes IV in 1889.

Espousing the national cause was understood by the TPLF to be the most effective means to gain the allegiance of the peasants who made up the overwhelming majority of Tigray and were the most exploited group. But when the TPLF went to the field, it did not have an unambiguous position on self-determination of Tigray as was made clear with the publication in 1976 of *The TPLF Manifesto*, which entertained the colonial thesis and the possibility of Tigray seceding (John Young, 1998, pp. 99–100). However, this position was soon rejected even though the TPLF maintained the right of Tigray to secession if democracy could not be realized in the country.

Although the TPLF worked to improve the health, education and social conditions of Tigrayans, this was not based on liberal humanitarian sentiments because such values were largely absent in Ethiopia. Instead, improving the living conditions of the peasants was held to be necessary to bring them over to the revolution. Nor did the TPLF raise the banner of democracy even though by mobilizing the large majority of the population in struggle for their rights they were engaged in a democratic exercise, but not one that would be understood by Western liberal democrats. As a result of their involvement with the peasants the TPLF were increasingly influenced by Mao and the Chinese Communist Party and its focus on the peasantry, the mass line, self-reliance and protracted war. The TPLF leadership concluded that winning the support of the peasants would result from meeting their most basic welfare needs, advancing the position of women in Tigrayan society, overseeing the distribution of land made possible by the Derg's reforms, and although outnumbered and outgunned with time, they could militarily defeat the Derg (John Young, 1998).

Critical to the TPLF's success was its tutelage and then anti-Derg alliance with the EPLF even though relations were sometimes tense because of EPLF opposition to the TPLF's commitment to national self-determination. The EPLF was also opposed to the formation of the EPRDF coalition of national-based groups beginning with the Ethiopian Peoples' Democratic Movement (EPDM), later called Amhara Democratic Movement (ANDM) in 1989, the Oromo People's Democratic Organization (OPDO) in 1990 and the Southern Ethiopia Peoples' Democratic Front (SEPDF) in 1992. Essentially the EPRDF components adopted the politics and ideology of the TPLF and with it an armed struggle devoted to national self-determination and rooted in the national peasantries. But these components were never politically or militarily strong and did not have the legitimacy derived from the TPLF's years of struggle and its bond with the Tigrayan peasantry.

Representing the other five regions were parties that were either created or strongly influenced by the EPRDF after it took power in 1991: the Afar National Democratic Front (ANDF), the Hareri National League (HNL), the Gambela People's Democratic Movement (GPDM), the Ethiopian Somali People's Democratic Party (ESPDP) and the Benishangul-Gumuz People's Democratic

Unity Front (BGPDUF). The fact that all these parties were in the lowlands, while the EPRDF components were based in the highlands which served as the historical core of Ethiopia, tended to give them a second-class status that was never fully overcome during the EPRDF's rule.

Despite placing the peasants at the core of their programme, they did not figure in the TPLF leadership which was narrowly based among the petty-bourgeois intelligentsia and lower nobility. Nor were the peasants or even most of the TPLF fighters involved in the political, ideological and military debates that pre-occupied the leadership and were structured by Marxism-Leninism. Moreover, from the mid-1980s the ideological direction and strategy of the TPLF was determined by an even smaller group, the Marxist-Leninist League of Tigray (MLLT) first led by Abay Tsehai[2] and then Meles Zenawi, with Tewelde Wolde Mariam, deputy leader of the TPLF. The MLLT was not involved in administration but assumed a critical role in determining the political approach of the TPLF, while a military committee led by Generals Siye Abraha and Gebretsadkan Gebretensae designed the TPLF's military strategy (Gebretsadkan Gebretensae, 18 February 2002). Many TPLF veterans hold that the work by the MLLT was crucial to the defeat of the Derg. Parallel Marxist-Leninist elite groups were subsequently established in the other components of the EPRDF and at the centre.

Although the MLLT was widely known in Tigray, until recent years its existence was denied by the TPLF. The TPLF called itself a 'front' ostensibly because the organization included people of various political persuasions, but the reality was that it was a tightly run party ideologically guided by the interpretation of Marxism-Leninism provided by the MLLT. The TPLF leadership attempted to present itself internationally as non-sectarian by not formally endorsing any existing or previous leftist parties, and indeed criticizing both the Soviet Union and the People's Republic of China, but that was false, and the Marxist-Leninist character of the organization was evident to anyone who seriously studied it.

Despite operating through its mass organizations with a high degree of participation and equality, the Front's leadership was hierarchical, centralized and secretive, and there was no attempt to establish any system of representative decision-making (Sebhat Nega, 2 March 2020). This was in part due to concerns of security during the armed struggle but even after gaining state power decision-making in the TPLF and EPRDF remained highly centralized and opaque. While cultural elements were at play – Abyssinians were renowned for hierarchy and concealing emotions and objectives – these patterns of behaviour were also drawn from the work of Lenin on underground party work. Personality cults were strongly frowned upon and Meles Zenawi, for example, never had a popular following even in Tigray. All of which proved to be obstacles to gaining the support of non-Tigrayans. In Tigray, however, the TPLF was not challenged for its unintelligible decision-making because it was trusted, people feared disunity, and by the mid-

---

2. Abay was shot and killed in the first days of the November 2020 war while hiding in the mountains of Tigray.

1980s they had thrown their support behind the TPLF in a life and death war with the Derg. Tigrayans were by no means unique in being targeted by the Derg, but they stand out for their unity in struggle.

In its own terms the TPLF and EPRDF leaders were democratic, and this was foremost manifested in their commitment to serving the people, particularly the majority peasants, even if the structure of their movement and its objectives had little in common with Western democracy. TPLF fighters were the 'sons' and 'daughters' of the peasants and held in high esteem. Debate (along structured lines) was encouraged, formal titles abhorred and a high degree of social equality was practised, which was most striking with respect to gender relations given the patriarchal character of traditional Tigrayan society. Nonetheless, there was also a clear sense within the TPLF of the division between leaders and led. The Front's decision-making process was accepted by its constituents, but it had little in common with liberal democracy, and while the culture fostered by the TPLF during the armed struggle went some way in breaking down feudal values, the Front's efforts to build the widest possible unity placed marked limits on how far it was prepared to press its social reforms.

Although the peasants were encouraged to assume a major role in carrying out land reforms and leading local administrations, the TPLF set the parameters and oversaw the process, and peasants were not party to higher-level decision-making. Moreover, the land reform did not involve distribution of capital, particularly in the form of ploughs and bullocks for ploughing, which in Tigray was often the key marker of rural power and as a result a rich peasant could be employed by a poor peasant to do his ploughing. As with other changes introduced by the TPLF, land reform was held to be critical in winning support for the TPLF and the revolution (John Young, 1998, p. 186).

A similar pattern can be observed with respect to the TPLF approach to women. Although devoted to the advancement of women and girls, this commitment was not considered an end in itself but a means to break down feudal society and values and encourage women to play a needed role in the war under the banner of the TPLF. But when programmes such as the TPLF teaching women to plough in a traditional culture which did not permit women to assume that role or when growing numbers of women joined the TPLF as fighters, traditional elements in Tigrayan society voiced their concerted opposition and the TPLF backed down (John Young, 1998, pp. 180–1).

## Capitalism (reluctantly) embraced

Although EPRDF leaders rejected both Soviet and Chinese socialism, they nonetheless assumed they would come to power during the Cold War and find the needed political space to pursue their non-aligned socialist vision. But in the event, they came to power in 1991 in the wake of the collapse of the Eastern Bloc and the unipolar dominance of the United States and capitalism. Indicative of how ill-prepared they were for the situation, in 1990 Meles authored a book while in the field titled *The Question of Building an Independent National Economy in Ethiopia* (in Tigrigna and Amharigna) which examined and rejected the state-led development model of the Asian Tigers in favour of a socialist transformation. At this late stage Meles – and by extension the TPLF and EPRDF – viewed Albania, which rejected both the Soviet Union and China, as the only form of socialism in the world that could be endorsed, even though it never provided the EPRDF a model for governance or development. But assuming that the EPRDF would soon control the state and that global power was rapidly changing, Meles travelled to Europe and the United States in 1990. There he met government officials and representatives of various think tanks, including the Rand Corporation, and it was made clear to him that the EPRDF's commitment to Ethiopia's socialist transformation would not be accepted. Instead, the soon-to-be victors of the Cold War demanded that Ethiopia adhere to free markets, liberal democracy and multi-party elections, which would invariably bring the country under US domination.

It was against that background that the EPRDF held its first congress in the field in the same year, and Meles, who had largely laid down the ideological direction in the TPLF since the mid-1980s, put forward a revised and non-socialist strategy for their anticipated government. This proved a shock to the attendees and in the words of one TPLF cadre the programme was 'radically different' from that which the Front had stood for, while another said that it involved 'abandoning Marxism'. Meles, however, contended that the Front must 'put politics before ideology' if it was to survive in the new post-Cold War global era. TPLF leadership largely accepted the conclusion of Meles that the TPLF and EPRDF had to respond to the emerging configuration of international power, but they could not be suddenly transformed into liberal democrats and even the form and rhetoric of the change were not readily accepted by the cadres.

As a result, the shift from a commitment to socialist transformation to embracing capitalism was difficult, confused, and the Front did not acquire a firm ideological basis until a decade later with its endorsement of state-led development. Indeed, there was considerable resistance by TPLF cadres to abandoning the Front's political programme and Meles endeavoured to come up with a programme that would balance the deeply felt socialist sentiments of his comrades with the need to gain the tacit acceptance of the leaders of global capitalism. The TPLF/EPRDF leadership never entertained any 'third way' approach as espoused by social democrats, viewing it as a movement that could only develop in the industrialized world and not in an extremely undeveloped agrarian society like Ethiopia that unlike other parts of the colonized Global South had no experience with institutions and values of liberal democracy. In any case by 1990 social democracy had embraced neoliberalism. For Meles and the leaders of the EPRDF the choice was starkly between socialism and capitalism, and in the circumstances internationally they had no doubt that capitalism was the only way forward.

Meles concluded that Marxism-Leninism could not provide a model of governance, but the Front maintained its peasant focus and refused Western pressure to privatize land and key industries, especially telecommunications, which it was held would both derail their programme and undermine Ethiopian sovereignty. Nor was the Front prepared to jettison its Leninist party structure which had been the critical instrument upon which it rode to power, would carry out its development plans and was crucial to maintaining control in the countryside where its power was ultimately based. As a result, the transitional phase gave rise to tensions between officially rejecting socialism while maintaining a Leninist party organization and decision-making structure based on democratic centralism. This did not pose a major problem in the countryside where the EPRDF assumed a virtually hegemonic position and could employ coercion without constraint, but in the urban centres it was not readily accepted and the inhabitants' greater links to the outside world and growing familiarity with Western values made this contradiction increasingly difficult to manage.

### Revolutionary democracy versus liberal democracy

According to the West and the Bretton Woods agencies, along with a market economy, peripheral states must embrace liberal democracy. As well, the West insisted that developing countries must accept oversight and direction, a formula synonymous with neo-colonialism and hard to endorse for Ethiopians who alone in Africa successfully resisted Western colonialism. Indeed, the EPRDF was bluntly informed at the London conference days before it assumed power by then Assistant Undersecretary of State for African Affairs, Herman Cohen, 'no democracy, no cooperation' (UPI Archives, 8 June 1991). However, with a minuscule middle class and bourgeoisie in Ethiopia, a massive and poverty-stricken peasantry, and its origin in the Marxist-Leninist Ethiopian student movement, the EPRDF concluded that Western liberal democracy was not an appropriate model for Ethiopia. Moreover, the EPRDF came to power committed to a programme of national self-determination which the West did not acknowledge as a critical component of democracy. Indeed, there was little in the Western model of democracy that would address Ethiopia's daunting problems.

Under international pressure, however, the EPRDF agreed on a constitution, oversaw the establishment of a nominally parliamentary regime, held elections and proclaimed the rule of law. But in practice the Front opposed liberal democracy and held that revolutionary democracy and a vanguard party were needed to advance the interests of Ethiopia's impoverished peasants, oppressed nations and nationalities. EPRDF leaders reasoned that form rather than content was critical to gaining international legitimacy and despite the West's rhetoric about democracy in most states (including those in the West) power in the state resided with a minority that represented the dominant capitalist group in society.

In other words, the much-vaunted Western democracy was not what it claimed, and instead was directed by a powerful capitalist class that used the instruments of the state to place their interests above other groups in society, while parliaments and ideologues fostered the illusion of popular control. Because peripheral states rarely produced a large and powerful enough class of capitalists to hold state power on their own, their interests were supplemented or represented by other elite formations, backed up by a middle class and endorsed by a Western-dominated international state system. As Marxists the EPRDF held that the dominant class in society would also control the state and use the state to advance its class interests. And since the Front claimed to represent Ethiopia's peasants and marginalized nations, it intended to use the state to advance their interests. While establishing a parliamentary regime the EPRDF gave primacy to a separate set of Front-based institutions to pursue its objectives.

What set Ethiopia apart from the West (but not Africa or the Global South) was first, in the absence of a broad-based consensus among the country's political elite, elections could not provide an orderly means for the transfer of power as held by Schumpeter and Huntington because in Ethiopia they were held to be a zero-sum game. Second, the Front did not carry out a bourgeois revolution in the name of individual rights and private property, but a popular struggle for national rights and economic justice in which liberal values had no part, but broadly democratic collectivist values did. Third, Front power did not derive from the most advanced sections of society as did the ruling classes in the West, but from its mobilization of the peasantry as the leading group numerically in the country. Fourth, EPRDF legitimacy derived from its defeat of the hated Derg and subsequently from its economic and development achievements. And lastly, in its values and norms the peasantry was as far as could be imagined from the liberal ethos that dominated political life in the West.

As a result, the imposition of liberal democracy would be in opposition to the sentiments of most Ethiopians and thus undemocratic, although this was not a message that Western leaders and diplomats wanted to consider. And having committed their lives to the revolution and witnessed the death of comrades, friends and families in the war, EPRDF leaders and their followers were not prepared to be voted out of office in elections by people who had not undergone their sacrifices and objected to the Front's transformative vision.

Peasants were little affected by a far-off parliament while the system of land holding established by the Derg in the 1975 revolution was not fundamentally changed by the EPRDF. Apart from the disruption caused by the Ethio-Eritrean War of 1998–2000, the big change of its early years in power was eliminating the forced government purchases at fixed prices of agricultural goods which were bitterly resented by the peasantry. In addition, the government laid the basis for a rural market economy and devoted considerable resources to constructing highways, clinics and schools. The EPRDF exercised extensive control in rural Ethiopia because it resisted IMF demands to permit a market in land and that meant that the peasants remained dependent on Front-controlled local administrations. Unlike the situation in the urban centres where its control was never strong, in the countryside the EPRDF made it virtually impossible for other parties to mobilize and befitting its Marxist origins held that the Front alone represented the interests of the peasants and therefore other parties by definition lacked legitimacy.

Little political freedom was permitted in urban Ethiopia either, but criticisms of the government and lively public debates were widespread, even if they did not take place in the country's parliament which was overwhelmingly made up of EPRDF members and could only be expressed in a truncated form in the private media. This served as a safety valve for urban dissent, but it involved citizens talking to citizens and not citizens talking to their government and was not sustainable. Increasingly Ethiopia was becoming bifurcated with a rural majority singularly focused on development under the Marxist-Leninist-influenced EPRDF and a growing urban population, disaffected, marginalized and increasingly influenced by globalist values.

In Meles' search for a middle ground, he proclaimed the centrality of revolutionary democracy which was inspired by Lenin's Two Tactics of Social-Democracy in the Democratic Revolution (Vladimir Lenin, 1905). Lenin argued the necessity of struggling to establish a revolutionary democratic dictatorship of the proletariat and peasantry, whose organ was to be a provisional revolutionary government that would arise with the victory of the bourgeois democratic revolution. It was thus a strategy for advancing the bourgeois revolution to a socialist revolution, but there had not been a bourgeois democratic revolution in Ethiopia. And Meles' intent was not to advance to socialism but instead that revolutionary democracy usher in capitalism, albeit after the development of the productive forces. However, Lenin's contention that revolutionary democracy expressed group or collective rights and focused on development which benefitted the oppressed closely meshed with EPRDF convictions. The pursuit of these objectives was to be carried out through the agency of a vanguard party, democratic centralism and mass associations to ensure that the interests of the peasantry and the oppressed nations remained foremost. Revolutionary democracy was thus not a strategy but a 'tactically crafted' compromise to win the support of Meles' sceptical comrades on the one hand and gain the tacit acceptance of the West on the other (Gebru Asrat, 9 November 2018).

According to Meles, revolutionary democracy did not accept surrendering or even sharing power with the nascent bourgeoisie or urban middle class that was taking form due to the Front's success in developing the economy. But this was disingenuous and until the EPRDF found its ideological bearings by embracing state-led development, it carried out a programme of privatization in which the prime beneficiaries were an emerging bourgeoisie, albeit a bourgeoisie frequently linked to the regional ruling party or the EPRDF. The Front also established affiliated economic trusts that expanded middle-class employment and contributed to the development of a class whose interests were distinguished from those of workers and peasants.

The Front's virtual monopoly of power was justified on the grounds that it was protecting the interests of the peasant majority whose livelihood would be threatened if liberal democracy was embraced because that would inevitably produce rent seeking and compromise the rapid and balanced economic development the Front was committed to achieving. Moreover, an open multiparty liberal democracy would make it virtually impossible to prevent the diversion of rents into political patronage (Christopher Clapham, 2018). Revolutionary democracy went hand-in-hand with democratic centralism and the EPRDF as a vanguard party, even if this term was quietly dropped after the Front came to power because of its association with the Soviet Union. While a defence could be made of such instruments during times of armed struggle, it became more difficult when the war was over, and the Front had officially committed to a system of parliamentary rule. Whatever linguistic gymnastics were employed, the EPRDF largely remained a Leninist party and revolutionary democracy became a bedrock belief of the cadres. At the same time Meles' success in winning the EPRDF's endorsement of capitalism led the West to see him as a politically malleable leader who could be pushed to fully endorse capitalism together with liberal democracy.

Crucial to gaining tacit US acceptance of the EPRDF system of governance, according to an appealing argument of Leenco Lata, a former OLF leader, was a paper submitted by the renowned (and by no means leftist) American political scientist, Samuel Huntington (Samuel Huntington, 1993). At a time when his compatriot, Francis Fukuyama, contended that liberal democracy represented the endpoint in human history and Huntington advocated an American-led global programme of democratization (see above), he was prepared to accept the EPRDF design for rural Ethiopia so long as the Front permitted the emergence of a liberal regime in urban Ethiopia. Leenco argues this provided a 'life-line' grasped by the EPRDF since it meant that the Front could maintain its hegemony and Marxist-Leninist structures in the countryside in exchange for accepting basic human rights in the urban centres, a trade-off that made even more sense because the Front did not have the ability to exert the same level of control in the towns that it had in the rural areas (Leenco Lata, 2 November 2018).

However, for many critics of the EPRDF, revolutionary democracy was simply a rationale for suppressing human rights, overseeing parliaments that were overwhelmingly made up of Front members, a means to justify rule by a narrow elite and an instrument to attack external critics as supporters of neoliberalism. As a result, according to one critic it was 'neither revolutionary nor democratic' (Jean-Nicholas Bach, 2012). While there was some truth to these arguments, they invariably followed Thatcher's contention that there is no alternative to liberal democracy and did not address the concerns of the EPRDF that liberal democracy was a mere façade for the class rule of a minority and one that had scant regard for the interests of the groups that the EPRDF claimed to represent. Indeed, it can also be argued that liberal democracy may be liberal but in its rejection of equality and insistence on international oversight of financial institutions ultimately dictated by the United States it is not democratic and opposes national sovereignty in peripheral states.

Nonetheless, EPRDF opposition to liberal democracy would have carried more weight if it had been, first, more transparent in its decision-making and, second, willing to share power with groups of a similar political persuasion, and the OLF was the obvious candidate. Formulating Ethiopia's national constitution was a key opportunity in which to directly engage the people in a non-manipulative manner, distinguish the EPRDF from its predecessors and make a major contribution to building a democratic culture. Instead, constitution-making followed the pattern of the decision-making of the TPLF and EPRDF which was largely restricted to a minority and that served to deepen the distrust of the OLF.

Revolutionary democracy was not in principle opposed to human rights, just that human rights are not – pace neoliberalism – restricted to concern with individuals and viewed within the context of a market economy, but also include economic and civil rights. Moreover, the TPLF introduced an effective and very popular system of local accountability known as *gim gima*, which was widely practised and during the armed struggle was held to be crucial to ensuring the Front leadership did not follow the common path of many revolutionary parties that became increasingly focused on accumulating power and wealth upon gaining state power and lost their links to the masses (John Young, 1998, pp. 143–4). During the armed struggle, leaders, policies and ordinary cadres were made accountable at widely attended public gim gima sessions, and this not only led to revisions in policies, but even to the dismissal of elected leaders, and proved particularly effective at identifying the corruption of public officials and improving administration. Nor did these sessions only identify the failings of lower-level officials and after being introduced into other parts of Ethiopia post-1991 they led to the dismissal of dozens of the most senior leaders in regional governments. Gim gima was introduced into the schools in Tigray where it was very popular. Gim gima proved crucial in challenging the feudal hierarchical values of old Ethiopia, bridging the gap between leaders and citizens, and building a democratic culture.

But in the face of opposition by the federal civil service and other parts of the country it was largely reduced to serving as an instrument to assess performance and maintain Front discipline and ideological unity. Nor was such a grassroots decision-making institution that suggested Maoist origins popular in the West where elite-dominated parliaments, laws and courts were held to have the sole responsibility for public decision-making. As a result, no attempt was made to give gim gima a legal basis or ensure it adjust to the changing conditions of administering the state. The outcome of assessments was increasingly determined by political loyalty which undermined their effectiveness and foreclosed consideration of alternatives, the more so because decisions were largely made at the top where local level input was not always welcomed. What had been a crucial tool to learn from mistakes became an instrument to maintain the status quo. As one senior TPLF cadre noted, party members were sympathetic to gim gima and personal criticism during the armed struggle because they had little to lose materially, but after victory careers and social standing could be threatened and as a result this potentially revolutionary tool became formalistic and an instrument of management (Medhane Tadesse and John Young 2003). Significantly gim gima was again given a leading role by the TPLF and its military wing, the Tigray Defense Force (TDF), during the November 2020 war. While not immune to human rights abuses, gim gima represented a critical means by which the organs of government could be made accountable to the people and as such represented a democratic institution that responded directly to the needs of a pre-industrial society and was understood and popular with the peasants.

The EPRDF looked to the organization of the peasantry and state control of land and key industries as the basis of its power and to carry out its development programme. The TPLF officially ascribed to the leadership of the nascent working class – 'class in content but nationalist in form' was the Front's slogan, but this meant little in practical terms, either during the armed struggle or after coming to power. On the surface this is surprising given the ideology of the TPLF/EPRDF but can in part be explained by their primary focus on the peasantry, the Fronts' alienation from the working class after long years in the countryside, its small size in Ethiopia and even smaller size in Tigray, and perhaps concern that developing a militant trade union-based working class could undermine efforts to attract foreign investment and industrialize the country.

However, forcefully espousing working-class interests would have increased the EPRDF's democratic bone fides and diluted the extreme forms of ethno-nationalism that would emerge. Indeed, it was precisely because of fears of nationalist extremism that the Bolsheviks, upon which the EPRDF modelled its system of national federalism, made clear its opposition to insurgent nationalism as expressed in the slogan – 'national in form, but socialist in content' (John Young, 2021). Upon coming to power in a context where Ethiopia had virtually no industrial base and thus a small and weak trade union movement and the EPRDF focus was on the majority peasantry its neglect of the working class was understandable, but its own policies and industrialization were giving birth to a working class, and it proved negligent in not bringing to the fore the interests of that class.

The TPLF/EPRDF position on the peasantry was also strange for Marxist-imbued organizations because although there had been internal debates over the issue of peasant classes during the armed struggle (John Young, 1998, pp. 137–8), the TPLF never formally aligned with the poor and middle peasants and instead viewed the peasantry as an undifferentiated mass. To be sure, the class structure of the peasantry in Tigray was very fluid, but revolutionaries in the Soviet Union, China and Southeast Asia went to great lengths to classify the social composition of the peasantry and Marx specifically rejected the contention that peasants constituted a class (Karl Marx, 1851). Indirectly, however, through prioritizing investment in agriculture, rural infrastructure, education and health, the poor were the primary focus of EPRDF programmes, and this set its rural programme apart from those pursued by liberal reformist governments. But the EPRDF approach had little in common with the transformation of the peasantry and rapid industrialization usually called for by Marxists.

As class differentiation developed among the peasantry due to EPRDF policies, Meles considered the *kulaks* or rich peasants as natural leaders to serve as models for others because of their successes, particularly with technology, an astounding conclusion for a leader steeped in Marxism. The EPRDF discounted fears that the emergence of the rich peasants as a class would oppose them because they were constrained by the government's land-holding restrictions. This approach, however, does not fit easily with a concern for social justice and equality and suggests the deprecation of class in the EPRDF approach to revolution, development and crucially to democracy. It does, however, follow from a TPLF concern to maintain the widest possible alliance and this meant that while every effort was made by the Front to oversee the most equitable land distribution, capital in the form of bullocks and equipment, which often better distinguished poor from rich peasants, was not distributed. Nor is it necessarily true that rich peasants could not access land, even if they could not expand their ownership, and there are examples of how they gained access to the land of indebted peasants, thus reproducing class struggles at the local level (Rene Lefort, 2018).

## National federalism

In response to the national crisis which threatened disintegration of the country, the EPRDF implemented a system of national federalism shaped by early Bolshevik experience (John Young, 2021). Most influential for the TPLF, which one cadre said was read 'dozens of times', was Joseph Stalin's *Marxism and the National Question* published in 1913 (Joseph Stalin, 1913). Stalin defined the nation as 'a historically constituted, stable community of people, formed on the basis of a common language, territory, economic life, and psychological make-up manifested in a common culture' (Joseph Stalin, 1913, p. 10). Following Marx, Stalin held that nations developed in the context of the decline of feudalism and the rise of capitalism.

Based on this understanding the TPLF first mobilized its own people and set about constructing an alliance of nation-based liberation movements which led to the formation of the EPRDF, and in turn served as a model for the future system of national federalism. In so doing the Front had to confront two opposing groups. First, an Amhara-centric pan-Ethiopian nationalism led by a largely displaced Amhara elite which fiercely resented the EPRDF's attempt to de-centre the state and reduce the power it had held for hundreds of years, with the exception of the seventeen-year rule of the Tigrayan Emperor Yohannes in the mid-nineteenth century. Second, Oromos led by the OLF whose position wavered between contending that Oromia constituted a case of colonialism and demanded secession, and others who accepted a united Ethiopia if the EPRDF granted Oromos a high degree of autonomy but doubted the Front would keep its commitment.

Beyond Ethiopia, most Western academics have opposed national federalism and thus began what I have previously called 'a dialogue of the deaf' (John Young, 2021). Western analysis has typically been informed a belief in the superiority of the Western nation-state and support for models of federalism designed to suppress the kind of national consciousness EPRDF policies produced. Meanwhile, in the post-Cold War era the TPLF was reluctant to acknowledge the origins of national federalism in the writings and practice of the Bolsheviks. The TPLF, however, was not alone in looking to the experience of the Bolsheviks in overthrowing a regime that appeared remarkably like that of Ethiopia and as a result was widely studied by members of the Ethiopian Student Movement.

And just as the Bolsheviks gained the support of Russia's minorities in its civil war by proclaiming the right of national self-determination up to and including secession, so the EPRDF believed that it would not only meet the demands of Ethiopia's oppressed minorities by ending Amhara domination and establishing powerful local and national-based governments, but also win their political allegiance. In the event the EPRDF achieved a measure of success in overcoming centuries of ethnocratic rule, fostered the emergence of long-suppressed cultures and placed a measure of power in national leaderships, but as the history makes clear, the Front failed to win the support of these same nations.

One important factor explaining this failure was that due to the negative baggage from the past between Tigrayans and Oromos, Ethiopia's largest nation, and between the TPLF and OLF during the anti-Derg armed struggle trust was lacking. In 1980 the TPLF proposed a tactical alliance with the OLF, but both parties understood that unlike a strategic alliance, under this formula the two Fronts shared a common objective to overthrow the Derg, but once this objective was achieved, they would turn on one another (Leenco Lata, 27 February 2018). TPLF cadres looked down on the OLF because although it launched its armed struggle at approximately the same time as the TPLF and had a potentially much larger basis of support, by 1991 it had liberated very little territory while the TPLF had liberated its entire region by 1989. To the TPLF leadership, the OLF had failed to live up to its military potential, and in a martial Ethiopia, military achievements were a key marker of success. Although the two Fronts shared similar objectives, they distrusted one another and the TPLF concluded that it could not fully control the OLF which derived from a much larger community than Tigray. As a result, the TPLF established an alternative organization, the Oromo Peoples Democratic Organization, drawn from captured Derg soldiers and made it a component of the EPRDF.

With the Derg's defeat imminent, the various liberation movements met in London, but could not reach an agreement and the Derg was overthrown before their meeting was completed. Leenco Lata, who attended those talks, said that there 'was not a matter of differing political agendas as such [between the TPLF and OLF] but the OLF's fear that the TPLF aspires to forge hierarchical relations with the Oromos' (Leenco Lata, 13 March 2018). TPLF cadres interviewed for this research agreed that the conflict between the Fronts was little more than a power struggle, particularly after the OLF abandoned its commitment to the secession of Oromia. The OLF wanted to control Oromia and for the EPRDF to drop its support of the OPDO, and when this was refused the OLF prepared for war. In the event, the OLF left the transitional government in which it held four cabinet positions and engaged in a brief war with the government, which the EPRDF army, reformulated as the national army, conclusively won. During the same period the EPRDF banned the Ogaden National Liberation Front in the Somali region because it feared that the ONLF was organized and controlled by the Somali government and thus was a movement in favour of Somali unification, a sensitive issue after the 1977–8 Ethiopia-Somali War.

The defeat of the OLF settled the issue for the EPRDF leadership, even though the OLF continued a militarily ineffective insurgency. But the EPRDF was not successful in politically undermining the OLF's considerable following in Oromia which remained undeterred by the government's military victory and was widely held as the upholder of Oromo nationalism. If the EPRDF had reached an agreement with the OLF, it would have gone far to gaining legitimacy among Oromo who never accepted the OPDO, and this would have been crucial in gaining majority support in the country and establishing a democratic basis for government. The EPRDF had the power to ignore the OLF, but as would become apparent it paid a high political price, and indeed, it can be argued that there is a direct line between the failure of the TPLF and OLF to develop a strategic alliance and the displacement in 2018 of the EPRDF government. Recognizing that they had more in common than what divided them, in August 2021 it was announced that the Oromo Liberation Army, that had been the armed wing of the OLF,[3] signed a strategic agreement with the TPLF to overthrow the government of Abiy Ahmed (Tesfa-Alem Tekle, 13 August 2021), although there was some doubt that the OLA entirely represented the OLF.

The EPRDF's system of national federalism was an advance over that of the Derg since it acknowledged the political rights of the country's nations, up to and including secession, and permitted national elites to hold power at the regional level, albeit as components or allies of the Front. Crucially it rejected the nation-state model that underpins Western states and was bequeathed to Europe's colonies. The EPRDF concluded that this model has generally failed to meet the needs of Ethiopians because it involves ignoring contesting national interests and imposing what is often an entirely artificial national identity. Instead, the EPRDF boldly attempted to build national unity by fully acknowledging Ethiopia's diversity and constructing a state of an entirely different character than elsewhere in the world. Although this experiment appears to have withered, Abiy's attempt to re-centralize power is proving even more problematic.

The starting point is the constitution's definition of the nation which closely followed that of the Bolsheviks and granted full social and political rights to national minorities. But some of the opposition movements contended that in practice the EPRDF system was largely restricted to the cultural sphere and the right to secession was only theoretical. Indeed, there has been considerable focus on language, culture and raising the status of long-marginalized people. Moreover, while a reading of the Ethiopian constitution suggests that the regions are dominant, the centre became increasingly powerful. With the exception of Addis Ababa, all the regions have been dependent on the central government for most of their budgets (Assefa Fiseha, 2019b). While the constitution gives the regions the

---

3. The association between the OLA and OLF ended after the OLF signed a peace deal in Eritrea with the federal government and agreed to disarm in May 2019. The OLF then became a legally registered political party, while OLA was designated a terrorist organization, along with the TPLF by Ethiopia's parliament in May 2021 (Ermias Tasfaye, 8 July 2022). Many Amhara, however, believe this disassociation is no more than a temporary fiction.

authority to tax land, this has never been done to avoid adding to the burden of a still largely destitute peasantry.

A further basis for centralization is the constitution's Article 89 which makes clear that development is primarily the prerogative of the federal government and that 'government has the duty to hold, on behalf of the People, land and other natural resources and to deploy them for their common benefit and development' (Ethiopia Constitution, 1994). Although not critical in the early years of EPRDF rule before state-led development became the national policy, this provision led to the flow of power to the centre and growing resentment in the regions. As a result, the 'focus on centrally designed state led development compromised the autonomy of the states in a context of growing ethno-nationalism unleashed by self-rule' (Assefa Fiseha, 2018). The expansion of Addis Ababa airport, the extension of the capital into Oromo farming lands, the federal government's leasing of land to commercial investors and the construction of mega hydro-electrical projects caused regional tensions and were linked to state-led development.

The tension between national federalism and the developmental state was not intrinsic or inevitable and the economic objectives of the latter are not opposed to the advances that are the focus of the former. Instead, the problem is a product of the inability to achieve the right balance between the two and the failure to appreciate that class advancement was the critical link between the objectives of both policies. Just as the EPRDF had not been entirely successful at getting the right balance between the central and regional governments, a study of pre-2020 war Tigray was highly critical of government structures below the region, which apart from the education sector were weak and lacked autonomy (Assefa Fiseha, 2019a, p. 29).

The EPRDF's establishment of national states and fostering national identities as ends in themselves contradicted Bolshevik practice (Stalin, 1913). The early Bolsheviks placed national struggles within the broader context of class struggles and held that without giving primacy to class struggle national-based elites espousing nationalism would emerge and undermine the fundamental objective of socialism. For the Bolsheviks, nationalism was 'a bourgeois masking ideology' and they made a distinction between opposing national oppression which they championed and supporting nationalism which they opposed, a very different position than that of the EPRDF.

Another problem with national federalism arose as a result of the increasing demands of nations and nationalities for the protection of their cultures and languages and for power under a system which equated political power with ethnicity (Sarah Vaughan, 2003). While the EPRDF initially encouraged national aspirations, when this increasingly led to what were held to be a proliferation of regional states, the Front began applying constraints on the emergence of political units not considered viable. There were also problems in establishing mechanisms for the protection of minorities within national regions, particularly when this involved denying political rights to people not recognized as indigenous to the region. Again, an emphasis on class unity might have gone a long way to reducing this problem, but it was never considered.

Nonetheless, Ethiopian national federalism was sufficiently radical that Amhara ideologues claimed its provisions and particularly Article 39 – which holds that 'every nation, nationality and people in Ethiopia have the unconditional right to self-determination, including the right to secession' – would bring about the disintegration of Ethiopia. Indeed, the rhetoric of the Amhara opposition until the outbreak of the 1998–2000 Ethio-Eritrean War was that the TPLF-led EPRDF in cooperation with Eritrea was dedicated to the destruction of Ethiopia. Even with its weaknesses, the EPRDF's commitment to national self-determination and national federalism ensured that the Ethiopian national components did not fly apart after the overthrow of the Derg. Indeed, while national federalism may have appeared radical from a global perspective, in the context of Ethiopia the system was moderate and a compromise among competing groups, most of which favoured a radical devolution of state power.

Although undermined by the developmental state, national federalism ended centuries in which non-Amhara peoples and cultures had been denigrated, fostered local economies and put indigenous people rather than outsiders in positions of government. Even before the advent of the November 2020 Tigray War it was clear that national federalism needed to be revitalized, the regional states strengthened and that all parties that held power at the regional level should be made full members of the EPRDF. Moreover, although Tigray has been denied the right to peacefully secede from Ethiopia due to the November 2020 war, the fact that the right is affirmed in the constitution provides legitimacy for its armed struggle and that of the OLA against the central government and may yet prove to be an instrument in addressing demands for secession.

Although 2023 witnessed the apparent end of the Tigray war, Abiy's centralization project was challenged by the outbreak of an insurgency in the Amhara region and continuing insurgencies in Oromia, Benishangul-Gumuz, and Gambella, and endemic violence in the Somali region. All of which suggests that while the EPRDF decentring the state to national units was not entirely successful, recentring the state is likely to produce catastrophic results.

## State-led development

The EPRDF officially ended its commitment to socialist transformation upon coming to power, but what it favoured remained unclear for some years and instead the focus was on ensuring security, establishing its central and regional governments, increasing agricultural production, revitalizing the rural economy, constructing infrastructure and expanding government services. Complicating matters, the West gave the incoming EPRDF no time to get its ideological house in order before insisting that it privatize land and state assets, move to a full-fledged market economy and commit to these changes before the IMF would provide a desperately needed bridging loan, a demand condemned by the Nobel

Prize-winning economist Joseph Stiglitz (Joseph Stiglitz, 2002). In the event, the EPRDF refused to bend and was not given the loan, but it soon formally adopted a stabilization and structural adjustment programme supported by the IMF and the World Bank in 1991/2. Although the IMF would subsequently temper its demands because of the EPRDF's economic successes, it never stopped pressing the government to expand the scope of the market and reduce the role of the state in the economy.

In 1990 Meles was still committed to socialism, and part of his critique of the approach of the Asian Tigers was that they depended on US support in the context of the Cold War, which was not a possibility for the EPRDF. Thus, South Korea competed with North Korea, and Taiwan with China, and both were dependent on the United States while Ethiopia could not expect political or economic support from that quarter. In 2001, however, Meles revisited his earlier rejection of state-led development and – conveniently – found that the United States was not crucial to the economic success of these countries, and instead that the South Korean and Taiwanese states acquired most of their financial resources initially internally and later on the international financial markets.

The Tigers were authoritarian, hierarchical, centralized, highly organized, nationalist, fanatically anti-communist, militarist and willing to use state repression to meet their goals, and in the context of the Cold War the United States did not object. Unlike Ethiopia the Asian Tiger states were small in area and population and had coastal access which was crucial for their emphasis on exports. Moreover, the Tigers were largely ethnically homogeneous and emphasized nationalism while Ethiopia was very heterogeneous and the EPRDF was opposed to an Ethiopian nationalism traditionally associated with the Amhara. Meanwhile, Ethiopia evolved from an authoritarian past in which the perpetual goal of governments was to overcome regional power centres and centralize. By the standards of the Global South, Ethiopia was highly organized with a functioning bureaucracy and the EPRDF was widely deemed as competent with low levels of corruption. As a result, Ethiopia was able to mobilize considerable international development assistance.

The Asian Tigers began their developmental assent as militarized dictatorships and there was no tension between their organization, class basis in a national bourgeoisie, and becoming fully developed capitalist states within the security embrace of the United States. In contrast the EPRDF came from a socialist background and was rooted in a pre-capitalist welfare seeking peasantry who resisted the Derg's regulation of their product but opposed a market in land. The EPRDF thus adopted state-led development and import substitution which had been the model of industrialization by Britain, the United States, Germany and Japan, but after the Western adoption of neoliberalism and rejection of Keynesian economics this approach was denied to the Global South.

In the immediate post-Cold War era when Western triumphalism was at its peak, Ethiopia could not look to the West or the International Financial Institutions to support state-led development. In any case the West steadily reduced its engagement in Africa and did not have the investment capital for the expensive infrastructural projects wanted by the EPRDF. China, however, was willing, and after 1995 it began to export investment capital as part of its 'Go Out Strategy' (Edson Ziso, 2018, p. 104). Moreover, the ever-increasing demand for investment capital to fund infrastructural projects and raise education and health standards could not come from exports (unlike the Asian Tigers) since Ethiopia had few, and as a result the country ran increasingly large balance of payments deficits largely covered by loans from China.

The EPRDF hoped that its signature development project, the massive Great Ethiopian Renaissance Dam (GERD) on the Blue Nile, would in time overcome this problem and Ethiopia would export hydro-electricity to neighbouring countries. Crucially GERD was financed by internal sources so as not to permit foreign donors and IFIs to use debt to hold Ethiopia to ransom and undermine Ethiopia's national sovereignty.

By committing to state-led development the Front escaped the ideological dead-end its inability to carry out a socialist transformation had produced, and according to one observer, Meles found the 'magic formula' which would produce unlimited economic growth. However, the fight against the rent seeking that this programme produced was not entirely successful and corruption proved to be a problem in state-owned industries like fertilizer and sugar (John Markakis, 2021), the mega projects favoured by the government such as the Renaissance Dam, and the production of military hardware.

Critics referred to state-led development as 'developmental authoritarianism' which ignored human rights and thwarted civil society development. To some extent that proved to be the case and it undermined progress towards a wider popular base in the state or individual freedom, but these Western values had little resonance with Meles and the EPRDF which were pre-occupied with economic development and raising the living standards of a destitute population. This concern – even obsession – with development and encouraging an entrepreneurial culture led to members of the political and military elite taking up roles in business (particularly the EPRDF affiliates) blurring of lines between the political and economic spheres and this led to allegations of corruption. Even when there was little evidence of actual corruption, the leading role of the state and the Front in economic development and the absence of any capitalist equivalent to socialist morality led to tensions between the pursuit of private and public interests.

The EPRDF expected that developmentalism, economic justice and rapidly increasing living standards would gain it the support of Ethiopians. The focus on development was justified by the need to rapidly overcome Ethiopia's devastating poverty and highlighted economic justice over its poor human rights record, a trade-off rejected by the West which refused to entertain the notion that economic justice was a critical component of democracy, or that its conception of human rights could be challenged. But the narrow economistic thinking of Meles and his advisors that virtually ignored political developments proved to be not only short-sighted but undermined the regime. It is also strange that a Meles who had been propelled to power on the basis of Tigrayan nationalism could not understand that his policies were generating a widespread and destabilizing ethno-nationalism.

A critical task of revolutionary parties is the creation of alternative institutions to those of the state (Jeffrey Migdal, 1974), and during the armed struggle in Tigray the TPLF closely followed that dictum. But its system of governance in Tigray developed in an environment of considerable trust that took many years to take root. Even in the Tigrayan heartland, however, administration remained opaque. Beyond Tigray the TPLF looked to military power and its ethno-nationalist allies in the EPRDF as a basis for its power and policy implementation, not trust based on support for its programme and governance and popular engagement. Reliance on hard versus soft power undermined the Front's relationship with the non-Tigrayan-oppressed people of Ethiopia who should have been its natural constituency. As a result, even though TPLF dominance of the EPRDF and the government steadily declined, anti-TPLF sloganeering proved to be the most effective mobilizing tool of the opposition.

While the Front acceded to a largely open economy and welcomed foreign investment and the repatriation of some profits, it only permitted a market in land in the urban centres and what were held (not always correctly) to be the under-populated lowlands. Indeed, betraying their origins in a peasant society, Meles and his advisors frequently and conveniently ignored the livelihoods of Ethiopia's pastoralists. Meanwhile, the state retained key enterprises (notably telecommunications), restricted international ownership of banks, and looked to state-led development and planning to overcome Ethiopia's extreme poverty. These were 'red lines' that could not be passed according to Meles, as much because they were inconsistent with autonomous development and the pressing needs of the poor, and because there were limits as to how far his compatriots in the EPRDF could compromise with his rightward thrust. Indeed, Meles's successor, Hailemariam Desalegn, tried to move beyond these 'red lines' but found it impossible.

However, the government slogan of 'building one political and economic community' summed up a shift from devolved ethno-nationalist authority to centralization and was at odds with the TPLF and EPRDF commitment to national federalism (Assefa Fiseha, 2019b). The thrust towards centralization produced resistance from those involved in the emerging regional economies and this opposition became increasingly politicized, particularly in a context where there were no countervailing measures to contain conflicts between regions and demands by ethnic communities for their own political institutions. Instead of poverty being an existential threat, the centralization of authority and the resentment this caused became a major hazard for the government and the viability of the EPRDF created state. The economic success of the developmental state cannot be denied, but it could only make sustained headway if it had popular support, and Meles and his advisors failed to understand this. Under the Meles' centred technocratic elite that dominated the administration, there was little place for consultative endeavours or ideological debate. The government's priority was to end poverty and backwardness and the means was the plan and its implementation and other concerns were placed on the back burner, according to one of Meles' key advisors, Bereket Simon (Bereket Simon, 10 November 2018).

## Meles: The making of an autocrat

Although exaggerated by its critics the TPLF clearly played a leading role in the EPRDF; what is more significant, however, is the centrality of the role of Meles Zenawi in both Fronts and the national government, and he was not a democrat in either the Western or Marxist sense. While the early years of the EPRDF were characterized by collegial leadership and open debate, albeit with the more politically developed TPLF assuming the major role, in 2001 Meles Zenawi purged the TPLF and the EPRDF, centralizing power in the Prime Minister's Office, and his death in 2012 left the Fronts directionless and incapable of confronting the mounting challenges.

Meles became an early member of the TPLF where he proved to be a poor military commander and at one point was punished for cowardice in battle before it was decided to assign him to the Front's Political Department, which had little status when the Front was pre-occupied with the armed struggle. Meles, however, proved to be an adept ideologue, rising quickly in the leadership, both in the Marxist-Leninist League of Tigray where he became chairman in 1984, and in 1989 Sebhat Nega requested that his position of secretary general of the TPLF be turned over to him (John Young, 1998, pp. 139–40).

Although ambitious, Meles was constrained by the institutional structure of the TPLF where politics and not personalities dominated and collegial decision-making prevailed. Crucial here was the relationship between Tewolde Wolde Mariam and Meles which one cadre described as 'the soul of the party' and another held that Tewolde provided the sober and constraining break on Meles' sharp intelligence. But that did not stop the Front leadership dividing over whether Eritrea would attack Ethiopia in the lead up to the 1998–2000 Ethio-Eritrean War and Meles led the camp that held that Isaias would not be that stupid. He then compounded his mistake in the eyes of many by favouring international conciliation efforts in opposition to the majority of the TPLF and EPRDF leadership and the military which wanted to take the war deep into Eritrea and overthrow the regime which had long been a thorn in the EPRDF's side.

While what became the Siye-Tewolde faction accused Meles of being a traitor, he accused his detractors of losing their links with the masses (Medhane Tadesse and John Young, 2003) and as a result the EPRDF failed to politically benefit from its military victory over Eritrea. This was a major self-delivered blow: Amhara chauvinists regularly accused the TPLF of complicity with their Eritrean 'cousins', but the war and the government's resounding victory over Isaias' army proved this to be false. This was the one big chance the EPRDF had of changing the political optics in Ethiopia and again Meles failed to understand the politics and instead put his intellectualizing and personal interests above those of the Front.

Further, Meles broke ranks and began an attack on his opponents in the TPLF and EPRDF with a long text based on Marx's Bonapartist thesis in which counter-revolutionary military officers seized power from revolutionaries and used selective reforms to co-opt the radicalism of the popular classes (Karl Marx, 1852). In peripheral societies Bonapartism is sometimes used to describe weak social class formations which permit military dictatorships to overcome political conflicts where no single social class is strong enough to dominate other classes. According to Meles, his Front detractors were 'rotten Bonapartists' who entertained anti-democratic tendencies, corrupt practices and aspired to promote themselves to the level of a ruling class (Paul Milkias, 2003). He then went on to dismiss twelve members of the TPLF Central Committee including Tewolde Wolde Mariam, Gebru Asrat, chairman of the Tigray Regional Government and Siye Abraha (who was also accused of racketeering). Meles denied his critics the opportunity to speak and even ignored the Front's Audit Committee which ruled against his measures.

With insufficient support in the TPLF, Meles turned to other components of the EPRDF, particularly the Amhara National Democratic Movement, to defeat the TPLF dissidents. Meanwhile, Dr Negasso Gidado, executive committee member of the OPDO and the Council of the EPRDF, as well as president of the Federal Government of Ethiopia, complained about Meles' 'high-handedness' and of passing legislation without the president's required signature. But Meles won over the OPDO leadership and Negasso was dismissed from its leadership, as was Kuma Demeksa, the president of Oromia on the grounds that he supported the dissidents (Negasso Gidada, 2017). Abate Kisho, leader of the Southern Ethiopia People's Democratic Front, faced the same fate after he condemned the 'unlawfulness' of the expulsion of the TPLF 'dissenters'.

While there is little doubt of corruption among some in the EPRDF leadership, including the family of Siye Abraha who was jailed, Meles used corruption to remove opponents while ignoring allegations of the transgressions of his supporters and even family members, including his brother Nikodimos (who started out poor but became one of the most wealthy people in the country) and his wife, Azeb [Lemlem] Gola, who headed Mega Corporation and served on the TPLF Politburo until mid-2018 when she was removed. While Meles demonstrated some tolerance for corruption by his political allies, he was not personally corrupt.

To protect himself Meles instructed the army not to take action until it received orders directly from the prime minister and commander in chief of the armed forces, in other words, himself. After voicing his unhappiness at Meles trying to make the army his political tool, Lt-General Tsadkan Gebretensae, the army chief of staff, who along with Samora Yunis were credited with playing the lead role in defeating Eritrea in the 1998–2000 war, was dismissed (after which Samora was appointed chief of staff), placed under house arrest and subsequently accused of corruption. Meles explained to his close colleagues that they must be loyal to the state, he represented the state, and anything less than devotion to him amounted to disloyalty to the state and they would be dismissed. It was the classic expression of dictators throughout the ages. With virtually all internal opposition eliminated or marginalized, Meles and his allies used the state and party media to discredit opponents.

As well as marginalizing his critics Meles' purge ended the collegial leadership that had been the pride of the Front, and by the end of his life there was an attempt, apparently orchestrated by his wife but some claim with his endorsement, to build a personality cult which had been abhorrent in the political culture of the TPLF. (An expression of this phenomenon is the massive picture of Meles placed on a hilltop outside Mekelle.) These expulsions made it possible for Meles to expand the country's military cooperation with the United States and brought it increasingly into the US and Western security network. Meles' power grab also served as the death knell of gim gima as an instrument to ensure the accountability of the leadership since Meles had forestalled any evaluation of his conduct. As a harbinger of the changes that would be introduced by Abiy Ahmed seventeen years later, the Meles-dominated EPRDF included the national bourgeoisie in its coalition of peasants, workers and the revolutionary intelligentsia and ruled that the country would be integrated into the global economy (Renewal, November 2001).

Not coincidentally in 2000 the Chinese Communist Party permitted capitalists to join the ruling party because it was held that they and not the working class represented the most advanced productive forces in China (Bruce Dickson, 2003), but they were never permitted to play a leading role in the party while in Meles' Ethiopia that was not a concern. China's move followed Deng Xiaoping's contention that the country needed to make peace with a capitalist world that would likely remain dominant for the foreseeable future and that the primary objective of the CCP must be to develop the forces of production and raise the livelihood of the people. This approach has continued to the present under President Xi Jinping, but unlike the EPRDF which rejected socialism, the CCP maintained this shift was necessary at 'this stage' and that socialism remained the ultimate objective of the party.

The purge of those in the Fronts identified as 'hard-liners', together with the resolutions passed, constituted a marked shift to the right and was strongly endorsed by the West, some of whose ambassadors in Addis Ababa publicly endorsed the 'reforms' and Meles' consolidation of power. Meanwhile, with cadres given the choice of either supporting the leader or being purged, inter-party debate declined, opportunism flourished and they learned to keep quiet. Meles was no longer the first among equals, but a giant who stood over the party and had complete control of its ideology, politics and direction of government policy. He had become, in Clapham's words, the 'philosopher king of the EPRDF' (Christopher Clapham, 2017, p. 69). With uncontested power Meles now largely operated outside the control of the institutions of the TPLF, the EPRDF and the government of Ethiopia. The revolutionary culture of the TPLF and the EPRDF died with these purges and the Fronts were reduced to instruments to mobilize support for and help implement policies of the philosopher king. Meanwhile, after his initial purges of the EPRDF, in the wake of the shock of the 2005 election Meles oversaw the quadrupling of Front membership between 2005 and 2008 from approximately 760,000 to more than 4 million members (Human Rights Watch, 24 March 2010).

During the armed struggle the TPLF had a small support base among young idealistic Westerners (particularly those working with the Relief Society of Tigray or REST) but with the EPRDF in power, it needed to have a foreign basis of support among powerful members of the international community. Despite the EPRDF's rocky start in relations with the West after coming to power in 1991, Meles' gained the support of key international actors of liberal persuasion. In particular, Meles won the admiration of Tony Blair who saw him as a devotee of his 'Third Way' and appointed him to his Commission for Africa in 2004, a short-lived body that promoted development and democracy, largely by increasing Western-backed loans to the continent (World Leaders Forum, September 2010). However, the Commission did little to change the relationship between the developed West and the underdeveloped countries of Africa, and thus Meles' participation served to give legitimacy to prevailing inequitable international relations. Such personal support helped make Ethiopia a major destination of international loans as well as the biggest recipient of UK development assistance. And after the haughty Blair was forced to step down because of anger over taking the UK into the Iraq War, Meles referred to him as 'a great friend for Africa' (Reuters, 16 May 2007).

Meanwhile, Bill Clinton saw Meles as part of a 'new generation' and considered him, together with Yoweri Museveni in Uganda, Paul Kagame in Rwanda and Isaias Afwerki in Eritrea as representing an 'African Renaissance' (Brett Schaefer, 10 May 2000). George Bush and Tony Blair brought together a group of African leaders to represent Africa's regional interest in the G8 gathering in Gleneagles England in July 2005 under the slogan of 'Make Poverty History', with Meles representing East Africa and the HOA. Further elevating his status in the West, he was awarded the Norwegian Green Revolution prize and awards for lifting much of Ethiopia out of poverty and hunger (Stephen Chan, 21 August 2012).

Meles went on to win further accolades from the international community, serving as chairman of the OAU from June 1995 to June 1996, chair of the African Heads of State and Government on Climate Change in 2009 and co-chairperson of the Global Coalition for Africa which brought together senior African policymakers and their partners to deepen dialogue and build consensus on Africa's priority development issues. In 2007 the African Union elected Meles to chair the executive committee of the NEPAD (the New Partnership for Africa's Development), a neoliberal initiative described above whose objectives were in contradiction to everything the EPRDF stood for. As one TPLF informant for this research said, 'After conquering Ethiopia, Meles now had ambitions to become king of Africa.'

Meles also gained Western support by presenting Ethiopia as a force for security, both domestically and in the region and the Ethiopian army played a major regional peacekeeping role in Sudan, South Sudan, Rwanda, Burundi and Liberia. But with US support 'peacekeeping' also involved Ethiopia invading Somalia in December 2006 to overthrow al-Shabaab (literally 'the Youth' which was falsely claimed to be linked to al-Qaeda) and led to the displacement of hundreds of thousands of Somalis. From 2007 to the present (mid-2023) US engagement in Somalia included airstrikes and detaining and torturing suspected terror suspects as part of the GWOT focus on al-Shabaab (Kelley Beaucar Vlahos, 18 August 2022). Meles' stance against Islamist extremism in Somalia made him a valuable partner of the West and Ethiopia joined Bush's 'coalition of the willing' in the war against Iraq, also a strange role for a champion of anti-imperialism.

Meles received further recognition by associating with Western celebrities like Bono and Bob Geldof (although the latter was subsequently banned from Ethiopia after criticizing Meles in the wake of the 2005 election violence), and he especially liked being feted by Western academics like Joseph Stiglitz, Jeffrey Sachs and Alex de Waal. He attended high-profile forums, received favourable coverage on the BBC and CNN, and was held internationally to be a representative of the developing world and its demands for justice in an inequitable global system.

Meles' international stature, however, was tarnished by the brutal suppression of dissent after the EPRDF suffered major losses in the 2005 elections. The Carter Center, which was one of the official observation missions, concluded that 'despite the positive developments in the pre-election period, the 2005 electoral process did not fulfil Ethiopia's obligations to ensure political rights and freedoms necessary for genuinely democratic elections' (The Carter Center, 2009). Assuming that the ideological issues had been resolved and the Front was secure, Meles permitted the most open election in Ethiopian history, which to the shock of Ethiopians saw opposition politicians openly attacking the country's leaders in the national media. But when it became clear that the opposition might displace the EPRDF, and indeed had won overwhelmingly in Addis Ababa, the security services were unleashed, and according to the report of a ten-member public inquiry on 18 October 2006 a total of 199 people (193 civilians and six policemen) were killed and 763 were injured (CNN, 18 October 2006). Meles laid the blame for the violence on a misguided attempt by the opposition to carry out a Ukrainian-style Orange Revolution and said that its leaders would be charged with treason (David Mageria, 10 November 2005).

While in 2001 Western ambassadors had supported Meles' purge of the EPRDF, during the 2005 election they not only condemned the government for its abuses of power but came close to aligning with an opposition which was not above using anti-Tigrayan racism. The election also made clear the growing influence of an expanding business class that favoured the development of a more liberal economy. However, the lack of unity within an opposition which called for both the return to an Ethiopian centrism and the devolution of more power to the regions, particularly Oromia, meant that the EPRDF was able to survive the turmoil, even though its legitimacy domestically and internationally took a beating.

With his extensive power Meles bore primary responsibility for the election chaos, but he again managed to avoid an evaluation of his authority and policies. Instead, he attributed the problem to the lack of jobs for a growing and educated urban youth and to party officials not carrying out their responsibilities. In response to such analyses and evidence of their increasing proclivity to engage in anti-regime activities, the government began rolling out programmes to deal with youth unemployment and good governance. The EPRDF focus, however, was almost entirely on urban youth (presumably because they were held to pose the biggest threat to stability) and it was some time before the problem of rural youth was even recognized, after which they figured prominently in the expanded membership of the EPRDF.

Bereket Simon, one of Meles' closest advisors, contrasted the violence and losses suffered by the EPRDF in the 2005 election with the relative calm of the 2010 election as due to the unclear transition the country had been undergoing, while in 2010 the positive results of the transition were apparent in terms of rapidly improving living conditions (Daniel Berhane, 4 February 2012). Given the lack of acceptance of the EPRDF in much of the country and what were held to be its TPLF bosses by large sections of the Ethiopian people, that view is not convincing. By Bereket's thinking, the 2015 election which produced no opposition representation in the federal parliament must have constituted a near total acceptance of the government, and that was clearly not the case. Indeed, as Clapham noted, Ethiopia had become 'a single-party state in all but name' (Christopher Clapham, 2018).

In defence of his one-man rule Meles no doubt reminded his Western interlocutors that the Asian Tigers – from which he claimed to draw his inspiration – also passed through a period of authoritarianism during their early industrialization, after which they became functioning democracies as understood by the West. But until the advent of Abiy Ahmed and the end of high growth rates Ethiopia was still a long way from achieving the level of industrialization or standard of living of the Asian Tigers that preceded their transition to democracy. Supporters of the EPRDF are thus not mistaken to ask why the lack of Western-style democracy in Ethiopia became the source of so much anger when South Korea, Taiwan, Hong Kong and Singapore, which also had authoritarian governments, were the focus of adulation.

Indeed, long-serving Singapore President Lee Kuan Yew, the admired leader of the Asian Tigers, pointedly rejected Western democracy believing it susceptible to short-sightedness and demagogy and preferred a meritocratic system to make enlightened long-term plans. According to Yew, 'Democratic procedures have no intrinsic value. What matters is good government' and that the government's primary duty is to create a 'stable and orderly society' where 'people are well cared for, their food, housing, employment, health' (Rakesh Krishnan Simha, 24 March 2015). Lastly, while the demand of South Korean and Taiwanese dissenters was for a democratic transition (albeit variously defined), in Ethiopia the opposition largely focused on overcoming ethno-national grievances, which in practice meant attacking the TPLF and sometimes Tigrayans generally.

## Countdown to the Abiy counter-revolution

The political activism of the youth was largely the product of major structural changes underway in Ethiopia and was used to advance the interests of increasingly powerful national-based elites. In the first instance youth discontent was due to the freeing up of rural labour in a context where agricultural production had increased enormously and there was no surplus land for the youth to take up, while at the same time there were insufficient employment opportunities in the urban areas (Bereket Simon, 10 November 2018). In addition to rapidly improving levels of education and health, increasing mobility and access to the internet and social media amplified discontent even while living conditions in the country improved. Social media and the spread of Western democratic values clearly played a role in the activism of the youth, but more important was ethnicity and economic interest.

Although addressing the concerns of the youth became a major objective of the Meles government, it failed to suppress the discontent, and this was primarily due to its focus on technical solutions and failure to appreciate that youth discontent was not only based on material conditions. Bereket attributed government failing to an 'obsession' with creating industrial parks and implied that its focus on ethno-nationalism served to divide Ethiopians and stress their differences while class would have served as a unifying factor because it cut across national divisions (Bereket Simon, 10 November 2018), a conclusion reached by the Bolsheviks more than a hundred years before. In 1990 Meles told the TPLF and EPRDF that they had to put politics before ideology, but that is precisely what he did not do. The approach of the Meles-led government never became a subject of ideological debate, in large part because Meles had purged those who would likely have taken up such a debate.

To the end of his life in 2012 Meles maintained an unchallenged stranglehold on power largely because the EPRDF held that Ethiopia's poverty represented an existential threat and under his leadership the country experienced some of the highest growth rates in the world. As he put it, 'what meaning did liberal civil and political rights have in a context of abject poverty or political chaos?' (Alex de Waal, 8 December 2012). Not holding office on the basis of free and fair elections, Meles and the EPRDF increasingly based their legitimacy on development. Indeed, it was announced that revolutionary democracy as a system of governance was to be replaced with 'developmental democracy', although the change was not readily apparent, was posited for the future and the Front's own cadres continued to use the term revolutionary democracy. Although badly damaged by Meles, the institutional structures of the Ethiopian government were maintained after his death, in part because EPRDF cadres (and many others) believed he had discovered the formula for continuing high levels of growth and his successor only had to follow his charted direction.

This explains how Hailemariam Desalegn, who had little charisma and few leadership attributes, could first be raised by Meles to the position of deputy prime minister and upon the death of Meles, selected as prime minister. There was, however, important symbolism in his appointment because only a few years before it would have been inconceivable that a member of a long-discriminated small community in southern Ethiopia, the Wolayta and an evangelical pastor in a country which has always been led by Orthodox Christians could become prime minister. But Hailemariam's lack-lustre leadership, technocratic approach and frequent resort to state violence to stem dissent led many Ethiopians to discount the significance of his social origins and instead consider him simply a stooge of the TPLF. This assessment was almost certainly overstated, and according to a former official in the Ministry of Foreign Affairs he faced most opposition in the EPRDF from the Amhara.

As with the crisis of 2001 the EPRDF leadership met at great length under Hailemariam to consider issues that the Ethiopian people were not a party to. The Front was able to get away with this approach in 2001 because it was still riding high after the military victory over Eritrea, it maintained a hegemonic position in the countryside, and its urban critics could be contained. But fifteen years later the EPRDF confronted a much larger and more politically aware people who were not prepared to have their fate decided upon by an unaccountable elite meeting in secret. Hailemariam's subsequent claim that he did not have the power to open up the system, unite the EPRDF, and lead a reform movement may be true, but the prevailing view was that he was simply incapable and as a result his term of office was widely viewed as a failure.

By 2014 the crisis in the EPRDF was openly acknowledged by the leadership, and as well as reverting to gim gima, the Front also introduced *metekakat* or leadership renewal and a commitment to *tiluq tihadeso* or deep reforms. But these measures did not involve engaging the Ethiopian public. EPRDF decision-making remained opaque, and in practice was largely limited to repeatedly changing ministers, discharging hundreds of civil servants, carrying out party purges and holding even more inconclusive closed-door meetings. In 2016 the EPRDF leadership, including future Prime Minister Abiy Ahmed, voted to institute a six-months state of emergency and began imprisoning thousands and according to Human Right Watch the government had banned nearly all speech that it disagreed with (nazret.com, 31 October 2016). Nor was this the last state of emergency declared. Hailemariam's subsequent claim that he prayed for a successor to lead the country and that Abiy, another evangelical pastor, was the answer to his prayers emphasized the limitations of his leadership and the ideological decline of the EPRDF, a process that began with Meles' 2001 purges.

Although facing multiple challenges, what brought the regime to the point of collapse was the threat posed by a highly mobilized and politicized youth. Apart from the structural causes there are three main reasons why youth discontent became so politicized in Ethiopia: first, the tight control of public debate and the heavy-handed approach of the security services which encouraged rather than dampened dissent; second, where political life is structured around ethnicity and pan-Ethiopian identities and class have been down-played ethnicity shapes discontent; and third, nationalism, particularly its extreme forms, developed in Ethiopia's predominately subsistence economy where peasants are weakly linked, parochial and, as Marx famously described them, 'like a sack of potatoes' (Karl Marx, 1852). Indeed, as Stalin pointed out, peasants are quick to support national movements when they think their access to land is threatened (Joseph Stalin, 1913), and that was the case during government land grabs over the expansion of Addis Ababa and Bole airport.

The Meles- and Hailemariam-led governments were slow to appreciate the extent of the opposition, failed to draw the link between government policies which fostered ethno-nationalism, and were blinded by the conviction that simply raising living standards would overcome dissent. Instead, the EPRDF focused on industrialization which could not begin to absorb all the unemployed from the countryside. Despite many achievements and the birth of a promising textile industry, manufacturing constituted less than 5 per cent of GDP and Ethiopia had one of the smallest industrial bases in the world (International Crisis Group, 21 February 2019). Hence a conundrum: an increasingly productive agricultural sector was producing a surplus of labour, but only a fraction of this labour could be absorbed by industry. The problem, however, would have been irrevocably worse if the EPRDF permitted a market in farmland because that would have swelled the reserve army of labour as well as undermining the bargaining position of Ethiopia's working class.

Also fuelling discontent was the widespread conviction of massive inequality in Ethiopia. However, a 2014 World Bank study reported Ethiopia to be one of the most equal societies in the world and government policies had dramatically decreased in percentage terms those living in poverty (World Bank, 2015). The study found that agricultural growth drove reductions in poverty, bolstered by pro-poor spending on basic services, while rural safety nets produced growth rates averaging almost 11 per cent a year. An IMF study in 2015 reinforced this conclusion and found that unlike other rapidly growing economies, Ethiopia had not experienced a significant increase in inequality, and that with a Gini coefficient of 30, 'Ethiopia remains among the most egalitarian countries in the world' (IMF, 2015).

Other figures show that between 2004 and 2019 Ethiopia's growth averaged over 9 per cent, while poverty declined from 46 per cent in 1995 to 24 per cent in 2016 and industry's share of output rose from 9.4 per cent in 2010 to 24.8 per cent in 2019 (Chowdhury and Sundaram, 30 August 2021). And despite Western and IMF pressures state-owned enterprises still dominated the banks, utilities, airlines, chemical, sugar and other strategic industries and although Ethiopia opened banks to domestic investors it kept foreign banks out. The EPRDF thus maintained a level of national sovereignty that was exceptional in a world governed by neoliberalism.

Ethiopia's Human Development Index increased 65.8 per cent between 2000 and 2018, while life expectancy at birth increased by 19.1 per cent between 1990 and 2018 (UN Development Program, Ethiopia Human Development Report, 2019).

However, few people in Ethiopia believed such statistics, and critics of the regime argued that the data used by the World Bank and IMF were drawn from government agricultural figures that were overblown and did not always take account of high levels of inflation. Indeed, high inflation together with government efforts to keep a low-valued *birr* made serious inroads into the incomes of many workers on the margins and resulted in an increasing number of strikes (Geiger and Moller, 2015). While not discounting such critiques which reinforce the contention that the EPRDF failed to serve as the leader of the working class, a range of social indices make clear that under the EPRDF there had been an enormous improvement in the living standards of ordinary people. Indeed, this was a phenomenal achievement even it was not widely appreciated outside the international development community. But it speaks to the level of alienation in Ethiopia during the final years of the EPRDF that studies by agencies whose statistics are accepted for other countries were denied by many Ethiopians. As a result, the achievements of the government were widely considered failures and provided the rationale for the dramatic changes in economic policy announced by Prime Minister Abiy Ahmed after 2018.

The disconnect between growing improvements in the living standards of ordinary Ethiopians and collective denial was partly due to the widely held belief that the benefits had gone exclusively to Tigrayans, either in the government and ruling party or their friends and relatives. However, evidence in support of the belief that Ethiopia suffered from high levels of corruption compared to other countries is hard to come by. What measurements are available suggests that Ethiopia under the EPRDF was slightly below the global average with respect to corruption and had been slowly improving over many years (WorldData.info, 2018) even though corruption is a typical feature of countries undergoing the high growth rates that Ethiopia experienced. Ethiopia under the EPRDF became a major recipient of international assistance because it was perceived as a source of stability in a conflict prone region, a strong partner in the American Global War on Terror, and a major contributor to UN peacekeeping operations. Crucially Ethiopia was viewed as 'a reasonably honest and efficient user of the aid that it received, and this technical "good governance" in large measure compensated for its shortcomings in political liberalism' (Christopher Clapham, 2018). Where the EPRDF clearly failed was in politically challenging the one-sided narrative of its faults in the social media.

However, there is at least anecdotal evidence that a minority benefitted disproportionately from Ethiopia's extended boom as reflected in the 108 per cent growth in the number of millionaires in Ethiopia between 2007 and 2013, the biggest increase of this group in Africa (New World of Wealth). Many of these millionaires were beneficiaries of the government's privatizations and the individual who gained the most was Mohammed Hussein al-Amoudi. An Ethio-Saudi dual citizen (of Amhara background), richest man in the country, and close to Meles, his companies gained control of 60 per cent of the privatizations (Wikileaks).[4]

More difficult to gauge is the performance of the four large EPRDF-affiliated endowments, which constituted a major part of the nominally private sector. These endowments fostered the emergence of a class closely linked to the EPRDF and the state which sometimes crossed the line from being party functionaries to in practice and lifestyle becoming part of an emerging state bourgeoisie. With the EPRDF committed to capitalism this did not pose a major ideological problem,

---

4. Al-Amoudi was one of many rich and powerful businessmen arrested by the Saudi Arabian government in November 2017 and in 2019 was placed under house arrest.

but it created conflicts of interest and a shift from the collectivist and peasant-focused concern of an earlier generation of cadres to one of personal interest and increasing identification with global capitalism.

Uneven development also became a problem, but the most serious case was and is Addis Ababa, which is not only the national capital, but also the capital of Oromia and is the only region that does not receive most of its financing from the central government (Assefa Fiseha, 2019b). But the premier position of Addis Ababa was rarely noted and instead it was widely held that Tigray received a disproportionate share of central government funding, and this was used by opposition parties to discredit the government since its rise to power in 1991. Forgotten is that Tigrayans came close to revolting in the early years after the EPRDF gained office because of the slow pace of development (John Young, 1997), and this at a time when many Ethiopians believed that there was so much industrial development underway in Tigray that you could not breathe the air in the region. Surprisingly neither the EPRDF nor the TPLF did much to challenge such beliefs and with the collapse of TPLF power at the centre it is accepted as a truism, although whether Tigray benefitted disproportionately from central government disbursements has never been convincingly established.

If there was more development in Tigray, it may have been because the region was able to benefit from a higher level of mobilization and organization than elsewhere in Ethiopia and Tigray's diaspora has been more willing to invest in the region than the Amhara or Oromo diasporas in their respective regions because they often opposed the government. Conversely, the Oromo administration was long recognized as the weakest in the EPRDF, and it also stood out for refusing to acknowledge the rights of national minorities within the region. That this was not contested speaks to EPRDF fears that to do so would upset Oromo sensitivities and advance the interests of the OLF, a conclusion that challenged the contention of TPLF domination of the OPDO. TPLF and Tigray bashing has gone on since before the EPRDF took power and while no region should be privileged some of those now held up as esteemed defenders of human rights have in the past – as witnessed by the author – called for Tigrayans to be driven into the sea (largely because they were held to be dupes of Eritrea, a notion put to rest with the Ethio-Eritrean War of 1998–2000 and further emphasized by the brutal conduct of the Eritrean army in Tigray during the November 2020 war). This racism also prepared the ground for targeting Tigrayans living outside Tigray, particularly in the Amhara region.

Even before the outbreak of the November 2020 war some Tigrayans attributed the negative view that many of their fellow Ethiopians had of them to Meles' policies. Also, not appreciated is that although Tigray experienced a high level of mobilization during the war which empowered the people and ensured a responsive TPLF administration, in recent years the quality of governance in the region declined (Assefa Fiseha, 2019b) and with it support for the ruling party. Ironically, it was the widely held perception of Tigrayans that Prime Minister Abiy and his government were opposed to both the TPLF and the people of Tigray that not only lost him support in the region, where he was initially viewed positively, but served to renew popular backing for the TPLF and regional president, Debretsion Gebremichael, as the best means to ensure their security in threatening times.

In February and March 2018 Queerroo, an Oromo group which identified as a 'national youth movement for freedom and democracy' and claimed to have links to the OLF became increasingly active (Queerroo, 16 September 2020). But appeared to be a disparate unorganized grouping of discontented youth with little clear politics. Nonetheless, Queerroo was used by the OLF and together with dissident Amhara youth groups they brought much of the road network from Addis Ababa to Tigray to a halt, and for a year and a half before the outbreak of war the only consistently open route to Tigray was through the Afar region.[5] The protests' base of rural, unemployed and underemployed youth was the product of the past twenty years of fast-paced but uneven development and rapid population growth. The unwillingness or inability of the central government to stop a state of siege against Tigray made clear its lack of concern for the well-being of Tigrayans. There were three further implications. First, Tigrayans who were increasingly disaffected by the failure of the central government to defend their nationals from attack elsewhere in the country now had additional evidence that they were targeted and needed to prepare for the worst. Second, once the last vestige of TPLF authority was removed at the centre divisions in the opportunist alliance came to the fore, particularly between Amhara who favoured a centralized Ethiopia and Oromos who wanted further devolution of powers to Oromia. With the authority of the centre demonstratively weakening, the states developed their militias which were to become a major problem. And lastly, the blockade precipitated the resignation of Prime Minister Hailemariam Desalegn and after virtually non-stop meetings of the EPRDF, Dr Abiy Ahmed was appointed prime minister.

Crucially Abiy identified as an Oromo, an evangelical pastor and a retired lieutenant-colonel in the intelligence services where he founded and led the Information Network Security Agency. This agency targeted diaspora-based dissidents with sophisticated intrusion and surveillance software which led to the arrest of many journalists, politicians and activists who were subsequently charged with treason and terrorism. Knowing little about his problematic background most Oromos thought Abiy's ascendency would end the increasingly violent rounds of demonstrations and protests in which hundreds had been killed and thousands arrested, and Abiy's initial actions suggested they were right.

Abiy announced an ambitious programme of reforms which included ending the state of emergency, terminating censorship, releasing political prisoners, reconciling with the armed opposition, privatizing major sections of the economy, ending the state of war with Eritrea, replacing leading TPLF officials in the security agencies and elsewhere in the state, upending Ethiopia's foreign relations, and appointing a gender balanced cabinet. With the elevation of Abiy and the

---

5. I tried to take a public bus from Addis Ababa to Mekelle at this time, waited four hours for a bus that never came, and was told that buses on that route had been fire-bombed, after which all the buses were removed from this route.

subsequent dissolution of the EPRDF (which was pushed through by Abiy in defiance of the EPRDF statutes) and founding of the Prosperity Party minus the TPLF in December 2019 a new narrative was pressed in Ethiopia. EPRDF rule was now held to be an unambiguous dark period in the history of Ethiopia in which the TPLF – who Abiy called 'daylight hyenas' – had imposed its authoritarian will on the country for the sole benefit of Tigrayans (Giulia Paravicini and Maggie Fick, 11 November 2020). He further held that national federalism would bring about the dissolution of the country, a claim Amhara elites had been making for almost three decades. Moreover, Abiy perpetuated the belief that the TPLF continued to rule the country until his elevation to power and the formation of the Prosperity Party, even though TPLF authority had been in decline since Meles' purges of 2001 and the TPLF had not held the position of prime minister since 2012. Although a long-term and senior EPRDF apparatchik, Abiy presented himself as an outsider and a liberator who would bring an end to this tyrannical past and usher in liberal democracy.

Apart from a handful of dissidents, mostly associated with the TPLF, Abiy's reforms were initially greeted with overwhelming support within the country, from the Ethiopian diaspora, international commentators (ICG, 21 February 2019), and were even welcomed in Tigray. Indeed, the good-looking and young Abiy quickly became an international celebrity topped off when he won the Nobel Peace prize in 2019 for making peace with Eritrea in July 2018. Abiy's international status was further propelled by being named African of the Year in 2018, one of Time's 100 Most Influential People, and one of Foreign Policy's 100 Global Thinkers in 2019. But the so-called Eritrean peace process obscured more than it revealed, and it would become clear that the real focus of the many meetings between Abiy and President Isaias Afwerki was not about building peace since even the border between Eritrea and Ethiopia remained closed but were primarily concerned with unleashing a multi-pronged war against Tigray.

As changes were carried out, exhilaration started to give way to doubt and then disenchantment, particularly among Oromos when Abiy began singing the praises of the nineteenth-century Amhara emperor, imperialist and great centralizer, Menelik II. Abiy called for a centralized administration and wanted Ethiopia to return to a mythical past when its disparate peoples lived in peace and unity. But there was little sign of Abiy's Ethiopian unity as supporters and opponents of the OLF clashed on the outskirts of Addis Ababa for three days in September 2018, leaving at least fifty-five dead and thousands homeless (Abdur Rahman Alfa Shaban, 14 September 2018). While the OLF announced plans to create an independent Oromia, Ginbot-7, an Amhara-Gurage armed group based in Eritrea, demanded the return to a centrist Ethiopia.

Ultra-nationalist groups in the Amhara region called for an independent Amhara state and urged people to take by force of arms territories in neighbouring Tigray and Benishangul-Gumuz, claimed to be part of the historical region. As would be the case during the November 2020 Tigray War, fighting involving Amhara militias aided by national government forces led to hundreds being killed in Benishangul in late 2020 and there have been periodic bouts of violence since then. On 22 June 2019 Brigadier-General Asaminew Tsige, head of Amhara security bureau, attempted a coup and this coincided with the yet to be fully explained killing of the chief of staff of the Ethiopian army (Reuters, 23 June 2019). Asaminew had been jailed for attempting a coup in 2009, was pardoned by Abiy, and was closely associated with Amhara nationalist groups and openly advised Amhara to arm themselves in a video circulated on Facebook. Meanwhile, the Internal Displacement Monitoring Center reported that with the largest number of displaced people in the world Ethiopia's displaced were being forced to return to the homes they had fled by the Abiy government under the threat of having their assistance stopped (Johan Schaar, 11 February 2019).

While claiming democratic bone fides Abiy used unconstitutional means to achieve his ends: arbitrarily replacing regional presidents with his own allies, establishing a commission to oversee the country's many internal territorial disputes that would report directly to him, instead of to the House of Federation which is constitutionally responsible for this task, and centralizing power in the prime minister's office. Although gaining applause for removing a claimed Tigrayan-dominated government, Abiy appointed Oromo supporters to key federal positions (Hone Mandefro, 4 July 2019, p. 2). During the first six months of his rule Abiy generally supported human rights, but as he consolidated power the state became an instrument for his self-aggrandizement and his rhetoric and concerns changed from creating a Western liberal democracy to resurrecting a mythical past Ethiopian greatness. Seeing this and the increasing Amhara hue of the government his support among Oromos plummeted. The Amhara elites were the one major group in the country that supported centralized administration, presumably so they could resume the leading role they had held before the EPRDF gained power.

Oromos got a further reality check when on 29 June 2020 Hachalu Hundessa, a pop star whose songs popularized the marginalization of his Oromo followers, was killed, after which dozens of people were killed and 9,000 arrested in the ensuing protests (Ermias Tasfaye, 1 June 2022). In the wake of the killings, leaders and thousands of cadres of Oromo's two leading parties – the OLF and the Oromo Federalist Congress – were jailed. The media, academics and ordinary people were also targeted by the Abiy government and there were mass arrests, police beatings and killings, shutdowns of the internet, and closing of media networks on a larger scale than had taken place under the EPRDF. Moreover, while former Prime Minister Meles Zenawi ran an austere regime, Abiy established his own multi-million-dollar Republican Guard, spent millions of dollars refurnishing his office, and on frequent state banquets costing many millions more (Hone Mandefro, 4 July 2019, p. 2).

In his zeal to overturn everything of his predecessors Abiy announced that Ethiopia would go to the international money markets to fund the Renaissance dam, thus upending the EPRDF policy of Ethiopian control of the dam and of its sovereignty. The authoritarianism that Abiy attributed to the EPRDF could not be overcome by forming the Prosperity Party when its membership, minus a small number of Tigrayans, had largely the same membership. Ironically, while the

EPRDF found that its Marxist agenda overtaken by the end of the Cold War, Abiy employed the rhetoric of liberal democracy and free markets at a time when both were in crisis in the West.

Piling all the blame on the TPLF for Ethiopia's ills more than eight years after the death of Meles was disingenuous, even though it was both successful and popular. The TPLF clearly dominated the EPRDF and the national government in the early years of its rule and it is hard to imagine how it could be otherwise given that TPLF fighters formed the large majority of EPRDF fighters that defeated the Derg. The TPLF was the most politically qualified, and after sixteen years of struggle had developed an experienced administration beyond compare to other EPRDF or anti-Derg forces. And in the early years of EPRDF rule it was found that some of the regional governments did not have the capacity to administer the demanding responsibilities imposed by the new regime of national federalism and TPLF cadres stepped into the breach. But even before Meles died few of these cadres remained, and their numbers were not significant in Oromia where the EPRDF was concerned with the popularity of the OLF. The problems in Oromia were largely due to the failings of the OPDO which the EPRDF insisted on supporting despite its lack of legitimacy among Oromos.

It also must be borne in mind that the TPLF was only one of four components of the EPRDF and with about 6 per cent of Ethiopia's population, Tigrayans only held a small number of seats in the House of Representatives, and a negligible number of cabinet positions. Moreover, key figures in the TPLF were being retired under a programme inaugurated by Meles in 2008 and few of the old guard held office by the time Abiy assumed power. Where TPLF influence continued was in the security services and again this can partly be explained by the greater numbers and experience of the TPLF. But here too, their numbers had been in decline for years. Abiy's subsequent dismissal of thousands of Tigrayan officers and soldiers from the Ethiopian National Defense Force was a popular move in Ethiopia, but the loss to the army was made clear when it was roundly and repeatedly bested by the Tigray Defense Force in the early stages of the November 2020 war before the sheer numbers of forces provided by the Ethiopian and Eritrean armies and Amhara militias overwhelmed the TPLF.

Where blame can be directed is with Meles who was so committed to dramatically growing and re-structuring the economy that ideological debate, much less opening up the political system, was considered a threat to both EPRDF achievements as well as the powers he held over the country from 2001 when he purged the Front and until his death in 2012. Indeed, Meles was neither accountable to Ethiopians, the government or to the Fronts he led and thus despite his contribution to the economic and social welfare of tens of millions of Ethiopians he must be recognized as a dictator and bears considerable responsibility for the dissolution of the EPRDF, and thus indirectly for the subsequent destruction and costs of the 4 November 2020 Tigray war. However, Abiy probably concluded that launching a campaign against the long dead former leader who was still viewed with respect in many parts of the country was not wise, and it was better to focus on the TPLF at a time when it was at a low ebb, but still held to be the biggest obstacle to his plans to upend the EPRDF programme. This conclusion would also have been strongly reinforced by the very strong anti-TPLF bias of his mentor Isaias. And given the character of the TPLF and its intimate links to most Tigrayans an attack on the TPLF was considered an attack on all Tigrayans, and the scorched earth policy of the Abiy-led war on Tigray confirmed the validity of that assessment.

There were further indications of the authoritarian tendencies of the incoming Abiy government when it was announced that because of the corona virus pandemic the national elections scheduled for September 2020 would be postponed. This decision caused particular upset in Tigray and the TPLF decided to go ahead with regional elections and won a resounding victory in October 2020. By then it was obvious that Abiy was on track to a war with the TPLF and the election had the result of both providing a rationale for Abiy's war and uniting and mobilizing Tigrayans behind the Front to face the growing crisis.

## *Conclusion*

The programme of the EPRDF was ideologically upended by the overwhelming victory of the United States and its Western allies in the Cold War on the eve of attaining power in Addis Ababa. Whatever the Front's vision of a socialist Ethiopia, Meles convinced his comrades that its time had passed, and they had to establish workable relations with the West. Meles was not alone in assuming that with the triumph of the West the issue of capitalism which had been at the centre of an ideological division for a century and a half was over, and it was the task of the EPRDF to salvage as much of its programme as was possible within those constraints. But it was crystal clear to the EPRDF leadership that their objectives could not be achieved by adopting Western democracy.

As a result, EPRDF priorities after coming to power included bringing security to a country that suffered long years of war, maintaining Ethiopia's unity, ending the oppression of Ethiopia's nations at the hands of an Amhara elite through national federalism, quickly growing the economy through state-led development to overcome endemic poverty, which was held to be an existential threat, and establishing a system of governance that ensured the rights of peasants were advanced. These objectives have a better claim to being democratic than the focus on the political rights of individuals and a market economy championed by Western liberal democracy and better met the needs of ordinary Ethiopians.

These achievements were not lost on the West which did not want a collapsed Ethiopian state and appreciated the stabilizing impact of the EPRDF in the turbulent HOA. But the West and the International Financial Institutions never accepted the developmental state, were uncomfortable with the EPRDF's close relations with China, opposed the Front's limited acceptance of a Western conception of human rights and remained sceptical about its commitment to capitalism when it repeatedly made clear its opposition to neoliberalism. Meanwhile, there was little support in the academic world for the EPRDF's system of national federalism, in part because few of the academics bothered to understand the theoretical basis of the system and were committed to the notion of the liberal nation-state. The Front's notable achievements outweigh its failings, but those failings, and particularly its unwillingness to construct viable systems of democratic governance, opened the door to Abiy, his reactionary programme and war.

In Tigray the TPLF commanded a high level of support, and this permitted generally cooperative relations with the peasants, but in the rest of the country that was often not the case. Part of this failure can be attributed to the difficulty of charting a political direction for a Marxist-oriented party that came to power at the end of the Cold War and the triumph of capitalism. But the problem runs deeper and raises the question of the revolutionary objectives of the TPLF. For example, during the armed struggle the TPLF was a strong advocate of women's rights, clearly a democratic pursuit, but when faced with the opposition of Tigrayan elders the Front stopped recruiting young women who at the time amounted to one-third of the fighters (John Young, 1998, pp. 178–81). Likewise in the face of opposition from the same quarter it ended a programme to train women to plough. Upon coming to power the TPLF tried to introduce gim gima, its system of popular accountability, into the federal civil service, but backed down in the face of resistance. A party committed to democratic transformation would have prioritized objectives like women's rights and making federal bureaucrats accountable to the people and overrode the dissent even if that opposition claimed majority support, but the TPLF repeatedly compromised in such situations.

In our 2003 paper Medhane Tadesse and I argued that the crisis in the EPRDF began with Meles' purge of the EPRDF in 2001 to the extent that the purge ended inner party democracy, open debate and made Meles a virtual dictator that is true. But elements of authoritarianism emerged before 2001 were intrinsic to key institutions of the Front and were shaped by the increasingly powerful Meles. The problem began with the narrow ideological perspective of the TPLF leadership and the dogmatism – albeit shared by other liberation movements of the era – that shaped its understanding of the problems facing Ethiopia, its political objectives and the means to achieve them. This led to the conviction that the Front's programme was superior to that of other groups and differences with these groups would ultimately be resolved through brute power and not by negotiations. Although it would not be known by studying post-imperial Ethiopian politics, socialism is a broad house with many rooms. But the politics of the liberation movements was restricted to a narrowly interpreted Marxism-Leninism and largely focused on gaining power and was further constrained by the parochial environment in which it was formulated and pursued. This was most graphic in the TPLF's dealing with the national question and the OLF with whom its vision of a decentralized federalism was closest. Instead of developing a strategic alliance with the OLF the TPLF established and supported the OPDO as an alternative and this proved to be an abysmal failure.

The EPRDF and its affiliates held that class formed the fundamental contradiction in society, but in a context where there were few capitalists, a tiny working class, and most peasants held their own plots of land the burning issue for the majority was Amhara domination and the constriction of their national rights. The EPRDF concluded – not mistakenly – that without championing the rights of the national communities and constructing a system that involved these communities in governing themselves that key components of Ethiopia, including Tigray and probably Oromia, would likely secede. Although not entirely successful and to some extent undermined by the commitment to the developmental state the EPRDF's national federalism went far to realizing the democratic aspirations of the marginalized nations of Ethiopia. Far from this system imploding as repeatedly claimed by the EPRDF's critics, national federalism ensured the survival of the fragile state of Ethiopia for thirty years and when it did spin into crisis it was caused by Abiy's attempt to centralize decision-making.

While the approach of the TPLF leadership on the national question largely derived from the work of the early Bolsheviks, the objective of the latter was to end national oppression to ensure that socialism was not derailed by bourgeois nationalists. But for the EPRDF eliminating national oppression became an end in itself and produced petty-bourgeois elites who used nationalism as the means to mobilize people – mostly youth – in opposition to the government and the TPLF. The legitimacy of these elites was based on ethnicity which became the surest route to power and the most effective means to challenge the powers of the ruling party. The otherwise close readers of *Marxism and the National Question* ignored Stalin's injunction that 'the complete democratization of the country is the *basis* and condition for the solution of the national question' (Joseph Stalin, 2013). The EPRDF, and specifically Meles, compounded the problem by undermining its own system of national federalism and the regional governments it created by empowering the centre through state-led development instead of constructing an acceptable balance of power.

Since both the developmental state and national federalism were designed to advance the welfare of Ethiopia's peasant majority, programmes to overcome class oppression in conjunction with advancing the rights of oppressed national groups could have served to both reduce the country's ethnic tensions and provide a basis to unite people – particularly poor and middle peasants – across national units. Although the EPRDF paid lip-service to class and class struggle its commitment to constructing a capitalist Ethiopia meant that class was not highlighted in its approach to policy and programming. While considerable emphasis was placed on mobilizing the peasantry, little was done to organize the growing working class into trade unions and as a result living conditions for many stagnated or deteriorated during the final years of the EPRDF.

This speaks to the incongruity of the Front whose leaders were inspired by leftist notions and relied on Leninist tools of administration and mobilization, but increasingly lost sight of the material conditions of the workers who were emerging as a class due to EPRDF policies. But alas this was a class that did not align with the EPRDF. Following the Asian Tigers model Ethiopian industrialization was largely based on cheap wage labour and migrant women workers which produced jobs and capital accumulation in the short-term, but this led to wildcat strikes and high labour turn-over and was not sustainable.

The EPRDF was ultimately caught up in its own contradictions. Foremost, the Front was a Leninist party that claimed an unconvincing commitment to parliamentary democracy. If the Front had established a truly Western parliamentary system, it would have brought classes to power that would have dismantled the developmental state, opened farmland to the market with the ensuing massive social dislocation, ended its virtual monopoly of power and almost certainly never achieved the high rates of economic growth of the Front. While the West would have considered this democratic, it would have been disastrous for most Ethiopians. Instead, the EPRDF ruled through revolutionary democracy, an opaque top-down system of party administration that only had internal mechanisms for accountability and under its long-time supreme leader, Meles Zenawi, those mechanisms were overruled. As a result, the EPRDF approach, which involved using Leninist tools of governance to achieve capitalism, meant that neither liberal democracy nor any version of socialist democracy was practised or aimed for.

Important to setting the EPRDF on the road to dissolution was the growth of a militant youth, part of a demographic bulge, the slowness of the EPRDF to appreciate the cause of their anger, failure to provide jobs and opportunities, respond to unequal development, and the consolidation of an enriched sub-stratum, some of whose wealth derived from links to the government, ruling party and EPRDF-affiliated companies. Moreover, in an environment in which the EPRDF encouraged sub-state nationalism, youth were drawn to ultra-nationalist movements which threatened the viability of the state. The experience of the EPRDF project makes clear that the pursuit of nationalism on its own cannot lead to higher forms of political development, much less resolve the social problem and that a party concerned with the interests of oppressed nations must also take up the class issue. Indeed, until the endorsement by social democratic parties of neoliberalism and rejection of class-based politics in the 1980s, for more than a century parties of all political stripes on the left made class struggle the centre-piece of their pursuit of democracy. The EPRDF refusal to lead a class struggle became a refusal to lead a popular struggle for democracy.

Meles opposed neoliberalism, was the author and chief implementer of state-led development and an accomplished economist. But he lacked democratic sensibilities and favoured technical solutions which precluded considering the broader social and ideological context of his policies. By dismissing the president of Ethiopia, three of the four regional heads of the Front, jailing his defence minister, placing the chief of defence staff under house arrest and running roughshod over Front rules, Meles carried out an internal coup in 2001. This ended collegial decision-making and open debate and by extension undermined revolutionary democracy, democratic centralism and the vanguard party. Equally important by making regional heads effectively agents of Meles, he seriously undermined national federalism and the legitimacy of the government, and irrevocably impaired the EPRDF.

Rosa Luxemburg expressed fears that Lenin's democratic centralism would lead to the centralization of power under one person and the alienation of the workers and that is what happened under Meles Zenawi. Marxism-Leninism in Meles' deft hands became a theory to be manipulated to achieve his ends. He was equally effective internationally where according to a senior TPLF member, 'he told the Chinese he was a Communist and the Americans he was a Jeffersonian democrat'.

Increasingly Meles' colleagues became his students who meekly took their instructions from the master. The adoration he received from some in the international community increased his haughtiness and further distanced him from the domestic constituency to whom his efforts were directed and to whom his power ultimately derived – the peasantry. Moreover, it was precisely his failure to overcome the problem of a growing rural surplus labour that could not be absorbed by industry and fuelled discontent that took an increasingly nationalist focus and set the stage for the unravelling of the EPRDF. However, believing that the ideological problems had been settled, the government directed its energy to resolving technical issues and policy implementation and as a result there was little time or place for consultation with either the EPRDF or the people. Ultimately the failure of the EPRDF was the failure of Meles.

With his death in 2012 the country was ripe for change, but Hailemariam and the EPRDF he led still suffered from the 2001 purges, did not have a clear vision, was beset by internal conflicts, and the Front could only resort to state repression and technical fixes to deal with the far-reaching problems afflicting the country. Meanwhile, Abiy Ahmed's much-vaunted efforts to implant Western democracy are being sunk by his domination of the political process in a manner far worse than that of Meles.

## Chapter 4

## SUDAN, THE UNITED STATES AND THE PROPAGATION OF DEMOCRACY

The US involvement in Sudan from independence in 1956 to the present makes clear that although turned off and on to meet its foreign policy needs, democracy propagation was just one of a number of tools employed to achieve its ends. During almost seven decades Washington often had closer relations with Sudan's dictators than it did with the short-lived democratic regimes and even initially welcomed the Islamist coup in 1989. Not only were the dictatorships often more compliant (because they did not have to respond to democratic constituencies) but they – including the Islamist regime – found common ground in a commitment to capitalism and neoliberalism.

As befitting its support for Islamist movements internationally because of their typically anti-leftist views, the United States tacitly supported the overthrow of the democratically elected Sadig al-Mahdi government through a coup in 1989 by the National Islamic Front, a Muslim Brothers' off-shoot. It was only when the NIF was held to pose a threat to the regional interests of the United States that it raised the banner of democracy and began assisting the Sudan People's Liberation Army, a movement that had been supported by the Soviet Bloc and the Ethiopian Derg and had an appalling human rights record. Although the SPLA under its leader, Dr John Garang, was dedicated to a united New Sudan, with his death the party switched to support for the secession of southern Sudan which it eventually achieved through an internationally conducted referendum in 2011.

As a result, the United States was left to deal with a rump Sudan still controlled by Islamists. But since the Islamists had been tamed and increasingly adapted their foreign policy to American dictates, US democracy rhetoric was dropped even though the regime's authoritarianism remained unchanged. And things might have continued except that first, the Sudanese youth launched a popular uprising against the regime in 2018 that gained widespread support, and second, powerful actors in the Gulf and Egypt had long wanted to see the last of a regime rooted in the Muslim Brothers and viewed any democratic transformation in Sudan as a threat and the uprising provided an opportunity to be rid of the al-Bashir Islamists, but keep the military in power.

The United States likewise did not want its regional client states destabilized by developments in Sudan and largely went along with an approach designed to marginalize the protesting youths on the street in favour of a power-sharing arrangement between civilian technocrats and al-Bashir-appointed generals and the Rapid Support Forces. This arrangement, however, proved highly unstable and left the United States in the contradictory position of trying to balance the demand of the street for a democratic transformation with client states irrevocably opposed to democracy.

## US relations with Sudan in historical context

An examination of US relations with Sudan makes clear that national interests led by security concerns have always dwarfed efforts to promote democracy and human rights, even if the rhetoric suggests otherwise. In international relations terms, realism consistently eclipsed idealism. General Ibrahim Abboud took power due to a coup in 1958 that was precipitated by widespread opposition to a neo-colonial aid package as part of the Cold War 'Eisenhower doctrine' (New York Times, 29 May 1957). Abboud went on to dissolve the political parties and popular movements of workers and peasants and pursued a programme of Arabization and Islamization in southern Sudan as part of an increasingly brutal counter-insurgency operation.

But because Abboud opposed Communism, he had good relations with the United States, was invited to Washington and publicly praised by President John F. Kennedy (YouTube, 4 October 1961). Abboud's regime ended as a result of what in Sudan is called the 'October Revolution' of 1964 and led to a short-lived civilian administration and democratic freedoms. Although the incoming government improved the condition of workers and at least urban women, it was unable to end the conflict in southern Sudan, did nothing to restructure centre-periphery exploitation and broke relations with the United States because of Washington's support for Tel Aviv in the June 1967 Israeli war.

The failures of that government provided the background for Jaffir Nimeiri to launch a coup in May 1969 with the support of leftists, after which he proclaimed socialism and outlined a policy of granting autonomy to southern Sudan, thus laying the grounds for the subsequent peace agreement (John Markakis, 1987, p. 203). Nimeiri was initially shunned by the United States because his regime had close ties to the Sudan Communist Party and that led to cordial relations with the Soviet Union, which also angered the Americans. Under the influence of the Communists the Nimeiri regime carried out a wave of nationalizations, particularly of Sudan's banking sector, and endeavoured to undermine the power of the traditional Islamist parties.

But after a faction of the SCP launched a failed coup in 1971 Nimeiri declared the party illegal and finding himself politically isolated reached agreements with Ethiopia and Uganda to stop support for one another's armed groups and reach a peace agreement with southern Sudanese rebels to consolidate regional and domestic support. He also turned dramatically to the right, reconciled with the traditional parties and brought NIF leader Hassan al-Turabi into his government as justice minister. The Islamists expanded Sharia law, introduced Islamic banking and supported IMF policies on lifting subsidies, liberalization and privatization. The United States still did not support the Nimeiri government because its ambassador to Sudan was murdered in 1973 by the terrorist group, Black September (US State Department, June 1973), but Nimeiri had created the conditions for a full-blown alliance.

The alliance was based on Sudan ending its non-aligned foreign policy and supporting American policies in the region, including standing virtually alone in the Arab League with President Anwar Sadat after the US-brokered Camp David peace agreement with Israel led to Egypt's isolation. Nimeiri also played a key role in transporting *Falasha* Jews from Ethiopia to Israel, which angered the Islamic world and in 1976 he helped arrange the release of ten Americans held hostage by an Eritrean rebel group. In a further effort to gain American favour, he supported President Reagan's opposition to Libyan President Muammar Gaddafi, allowed the transit of US weapons to the Chadian army of Hissen Habre and permitted the CIA to establish a base in El Fashir (Veronica Nmoma, 2006).

Nimeiri's regional significance to the United States further increased with the rise to power of the Ethiopian Derg which was supported by the Eastern Bloc and as a result Nimeiri's regime served as the frontline in the HOA during the Cold War. Sudan became the largest recipient of US economic and military aid in sub-Saharan Africa – $160 million of which $100 million was for military assistance (Donald Petterson, 1999, p. 9). In 1983 Nimeiri introduced *Sharia* law, announced himself to be an *Imam*, and after peacefully ending the southern civil war in 1972 broke the agreement at the behest of the traditional parties and plunged the country back into war (The New Humanitarian, 23 November 2010). Although relations with the United States were deteriorating because of growing internal opposition to his regime, human rights abuses and massive corruption, the United States stood by Nimeiri to the bitter end which came as a result of a popular insurgency on 5 April 1985 against IMF austerity policies while he was in Washington begging for additional military support.

Strains quickly emerged between the US and the post-Nimeiri governments. A Transitional Military Council (TMC) held power for one year, after which a Sadig al-Mahdi-led coalition took power as a result of elections. Although the 1986 national elections could not be held in parts of southern Sudan because of insecurity, in the rest of the country they were free, fair, involved a multitude of parties and there were few complaints about the voting or the outcome according to the US government (US Department of State, 1986, p. 314). During the three years of the Sadig government human rights were generally respected, there was freedom of assembly, speech, and as I can testify as a journalist who worked in the country during that period there was a lively and unhindered media that ranged from Islamist on the right to the Sudanese Communist Party and a host of small southern parties, some strongly opposed to the government's policies in southern Sudan.

None of this, however, impressed the United States which undermined the government because it did not abide by its foreign policy objectives. Foremost, the Sadig coalition government did not support the US policy of overthrowing the neighbouring government of Muammar Gaddafi because it wanted Libyan weapons to fight the growing insurgency in southern Sudan and for Libya to stop supporting the SPLA (New York Times, 10 May 1986). In return Khartoum would end assistance to US-supported groups opposed to Muammar Gaddafi. Relations were also hindered by residual anger in Sudan with American support for the Nimeiri dictatorship and this led Prime Minister Sadig al-Mahdi to muse that the United States preferred dealing with dictators than with democracies because they did not have to respond to democratic constituencies.

The United States in turn was upset that Sadig permitted Muammar Gaddafi to use territory in Darfur to assist rebels opposed to the American-supported Chadian regime of Hissen Habre. Nor did the United States accept Sadig's efforts to formulate a non-aligned foreign policy, his government's failure to end the southern war and opposition to IMF proposals on the imposition of another round of austerity measures. Showing how far it would go, the United States suspended concessionary food sales to Sudan, thus endangering the lives of many. As de Waal noted, 'The US was "playing politics with food" and would have been pilloried in the media if Sudan had been under closer scrutiny' (Alex de Waal, 1997). Going still further the United States began speculating according to a number of American diplomats that a military coup might be preferable to the Sadig-led government (Campbell and Scroggins, 1989). The timing of the Islamist coup on the eve of the National Assembly accepting a framework agreement between the government and the John Garang-led SPLA made clear the Islamist and military opposition to the prospects of peace.

Three conclusions can be drawn from the Sadig al-Mahdi coalition government. First, despite its democratic bone fides in Western terms, the government was a failure because it did not end the civil war, overcome Sudan's economic crisis and its preoccupation with replacing Nimeiri's Islamic laws demonstrated its lack of concern for the welfare of Sudanese. Indeed, so bad was the government's performance that many Sudanese were not unhappy – at least initially – to see its overthrow by an NIF coup. Second, while the United States supported the dictatorships of Abboud and Nimeiri, its relationship with the Sadig government was largely conflictual, thus casting into doubt its commitment to democracy in Sudan. And lastly, the US understanding of democracy involves states in the Global South subjecting their policies to the demands of Washington.

## US relations with the Sudanese Islamists

The United States miscalculated in initially supporting 'constructive engagement' with the Omar al-Bashir coup government, an Islamist party with policies that challenged its regional hegemony. Moreover, the United States was slow to understand that the NIF represented a break from Sudan's past political civility, the Front had no qualms about the application of violence and viewed Sudan's culture with contempt. The biggest break from the past was al-Turabi's construction between June 1989 and December 1989 of a 'totalitarian' regime (Abdúllahi A. Gallab, Spring 2001). The Islamists understood the capacity of civil society and particularly the trade union movement under leftist leadership to upend governments and it worked effectively to neutralize them. While unsuccessful in introducing its civilizational project, through control of schools and post-secondary institutions the NIF and NCP indoctrinated a generation in its Islamist values and undermined the capacity of academics to lead popular uprisings as they had done in 1964 and 1989. The Islamists also vastly increased the intelligence services to the extent that it was widely believed both in and outside government that they had eliminated the possibility of being overthrown.

However, NIF support for Iraq in the 1990–1 Gulf War, close relations with Iran, shipments of arms to Gaza from ports on the Red Sea, hosting Carlos the Jackal, Osama bin Laden, Abu Nidal and others whom the United States viewed as terrorists, and ramping up the war in southern Sudan ended American illusions. Also upsetting the United States was the leading role of Hassan al-Turabi, the Front's leading ideologue, in holding the Popular Arab and Islamic Conference which brought together militants from around the world (J. Millard Burr and Robert O. Collins, 2003, p. 58). Claiming that Sudan supported international terrorism, destabilized neighbouring states (which were US clients) and abused human rights, President Clinton introduced sanctions and declared the NIF government a 'state sponsor of terrorism' on 12 August 1993.[1]

Supporting the SPLA, which had an even longer record of human rights abuses than the NIF, was widely opposed in the United States but Clinton's liberal interventionist allies endeavoured to re-package the SPLA leader, John Garang, as a freedom-loving democrat (John Young, 2019, pp. 47–50). Moreover, de Waal held that this policy served to endorse Garang's authoritarianism and undermine the efforts of those struggling for reform in the movement (Alex de Waal, 6 June 2016). In addition, the United States granted $20 million in military aid to the so-called 'front line states' of Eritrea, Ethiopia and Uganda to defend themselves against Sudanese excursions. Most of this money went to Ethiopia whose armed forces used it to buy Hercules transport planes, while together with Eritrea and Uganda it sent armies deep into Sudan and turned over the captured territories to

---

1. In 1994 Anthony Lake, Clinton's national security advisor, called North Korea, Cuba, Iraq, Iran and Libya 'outlaw states' for their pursuit of weapons of mass destruction, support for terrorism, abuse of their own citizens and strident criticism of the United States, and Sudan was sometimes added to this list (US State Department, 2003). In an effort to punish and isolate such states the US imposed economic sanctions against Iran, Libya, Cuba, Afghanistan and Sudan (American Foreign Relations). This concept was replaced by the Bush administration with the 'Axis of Evil', which included Iraq, Iran, North Korea, and according to some Sudan. This group overlapped with the 'State Sponsors of Terrorism' list which included Sudan, Cuba, Iran and North Korea.

the SPLA, which often lost them in short order (Lt-General Tsadkan, 1 November 2018). Nonetheless, this coalition together with the National Democratic Alliance (NDA, an Asmara-based group of northern Sudanese parties and the SPLM) proved remarkably successful and appeared to be on the verge of overthrowing the NIF were it not that the Ethio-Eritrean war broke out in May 1998, after which both Addis Ababa and Asmara were anxious to gain the support or at least neutrality of Khartoum (John Young, 2012).

Disinformation also figured in the US attempt to collapse the regime and the Americans accused Sudan of supporting a 'slave trade' in southern Sudan, although it turned out that it was conducted by military commanders of the SPLA and the Swiss-based Christian Solidarity International, which raised money from naïve supporters, sometimes American children, to free the 'slaves' (The Irish Times, 23 February 2002). The United States then demanded that Sudan deport Osama bin Laden who had established a large construction company in the country, and in May 1996 he and 100 of his operatives were expelled and subsequently took up residence in Afghanistan. In February 1997, al-Bashir sent President Clinton a personal letter offering to allow US intelligence, law-enforcement and counterterrorism personnel to enter Sudan and go anywhere and see anything, to help stamp out terrorism (Tim Weiner and James Risen, 21 September 1998). The United States never replied to that letter which Susan Rice described as meaningless and part of a Sudanese 'charm offensive'.

According to numerous sources Sudan offered to turn bin Ladin over to the United States, provide information about his al-Qaeda network and deliver material on the group involved in the bombing of the US embassies in East Africa in 1998 (Stephen Mbogo, 7 July 2008). In addition, the NIF promised information on Hezbollah, Hamas and the World Trade Center bombers in an effort to end the economic embargo. But these efforts came to naught (Tim Carney, 30 June 2002 and Mansoor Ijaz, 5 December 2001). So committed to regime change were hard-liners in the Clinton government led by Rice that they were not prepared to cooperate with the Sudan government even when US national security interests were at stake.

In August 1998 the United States launched cruise missiles against the al-Shifa pharmaceutical plant in Khartoum North based on the claim that Sudan was involved in the bombings of US embassies in Nairobi and Dar Salam and that the plant was producing chemical weapons, which former Ambassador David Shinn denied (David Shinn, 30 September 2011) and the *New York Times* found 'inconsistent' (Tim Weiner and James Risen, 21 September 1998). According to the *New York Times*, National Security Adviser Sandy Berger and Secretary of State Madeleine Albright believed that Osama bin Ladin was using the al-Shifa plant to experiment with poison gas. The plant was under contract to supply the UN with medicines and Washington's mistake became a propaganda victory for Khartoum which invited international journalists to the Sudan capital to visit the bombed al-Shifa site and present itself as a victim of US aggression. The NIF quickly had demonstrators on the streets carrying placards linking the bombing to Clinton's need for a diversion while facing a scandal over his affair with Monica Lewinski.[2]

In retrospect the bombing can be seen as a precursor to the US invasion of Iraq in 2003 when Washington fabricated evidence to 'prove' a link between Saddam Hussein and weapons of mass destruction. As in the case of Sudan, those efforts backfired. Nonetheless, Sudan was placed on a list of seven countries that the Bush administration planned to overthrow within five years according to US General Wesley Clark (Joe Conason, 12 October 2007). Neoconservative eminence Paul Wolfowitz, the former deputy secretary of defence under Donald Rumsfeld, explained this hit list: 'With the end of the Cold War, we can now use our military with impunity. The Soviets won't come in to block us' (Joe Conason, 12 October 2007).

According to present and former NIF leaders the United States grossly exaggerated the power of the government in the region, which Washington attributed to Sudan's proximity to the Middle East, an area of primary security interest to the United States and the NIF's relations with radical elements in the region. On at least one occasion according to an US Ambassador Donald Petterson, he presented al-Bashir with a non-paper in which the United States threatened to obliterate the Sudanese economy for supporting international terror. Petterson subsequently wrote that although he regularly passed allegations of Sudan's support for terrorism to the government, the State Department never provided him with any evidence to back up those charges (Donald Petterson, 1999, p. 69). The Sudan government knew it could not defend itself against the United States but reasoned that the thousands of *jihadis* trained for combat in southern Sudan and the even larger Popular Defense Force provided deterrence against a ground attack.

Contravening previous laws which forbade the funding of belligerents in combat, on 29 November 1999 President Clinton signed a bill authorizing the United States to directly supply the SPLA with food and shortly thereafter it was reported that US supplies were reaching the SPLA (Veronica Nmoma, 2006). By the end of the Clinton presidency the Sudan Islamists had been so demonized that they were thought to be capable of almost any crime, to the extent that Secretary of State Madeleine Albright described Sudan as a 'viper's nest of terrorists' (Tim Weiner and James Risen, 21 September 1998).

In the view of a senior NIF official, American policy was shaped by 'malice and naivety' and that a broken-down country in the Global South would challenge the United States. President Clinton hoped that sanctions and isolation would turn the Sudan government and when that failed, he committed to regime change with

---

2. Talking to people on the streets of Khartoum in the wake of the bombing, it was clear that ordinary citizens including those opposed to the government were dumbfounded at the Americans' actions. One respondent said that he would have welcomed a US missile attack on the Presidential Palace but was upset at the United States chose to attack of a pharmaceutical plan producing malarial drugs.

the SPLA, internal allies and US supporters in the region serving as proxies. But that approach too was unsuccessful and with the end of the Clinton presidency the problem of Sudan was passed to the incoming Bush government. The secular liberal interventionist activists who did much to shape the narrative on Sudan were augmented by evangelical Christians who were part of Bush's political base and for them the Sudan civil war represented a 'biblical conflict' between Arab Muslims in the North and African Christians in the South (Asteris Huliaras. 2006). They wanted Bush to take up this cause and he delivered, but to the surprise of many he chose to back peace efforts.

Although President Bush announced that spreading democracy was to be the centre-piece of his government's foreign policy, his engagement in Sudan was a response in the first instance to the demands of his evangelical Christian constituency who wanted him to end what they considered a northern Moslem jihad against southern Christians and, second, to security concerns, which grew exponentially after 9/11. Unlike Clinton who employed military means to deal with Sudan, Bush supported liberal peacemaking which it was hoped would end the north-south conflict, remove or lead to the democratic transformation of the NIF, and win him prestige as a peacemaker, particularly in the Islamic world where many saw him as a Christian crusader. But the more engaged the United States became in the peace process, the more it needed the NIF's cooperation, and this continued to be the case as the United States required Sudanese assistance in the Global War on Terrorism, the southern Sudan civil war and other issues. As a result, demands for democratic change and efforts to overthrow the regime ended, making clear that democracy was only propagated when it corresponded to US interests.

The sanctions introduced by Clinton, expanded by the US Congress, extended by Bush in response to the NIF's counter-insurgency operation in Darfur, and the US declaration that genocide had taken place in Darfur became the central focus of Sudan-US relations and played a major role in shaping developments in Sudan until the formation of the 2019 transitional government. After breaking with the NIF's chief ideologue, Hassan al-Turabi, however, the Islamists under Omar al-Bashir lost their radical zeal and became increasingly ideologically pragmatic, and bent to the will of the Americans, including bringing the government's foreign policy in line with US dictates.

The NIF took power in Sudan as the world's first Sunni Islamist government with seemingly radical domestic and foreign policies. But in the face of growing US opposition and military defeats in the region the NIF revised its offending policies, thus demonstrating both the party's ideological weakness and the leadership's willingness to dispense with their convictions to survive. NIF cooperation with the Americans did not, however, end the sanctions and instead they deepened an economic crisis which threatened to bring about the collapse of the regime that ironically the United States became interested in preserving to ensure regional stability. But so much virulent rhetoric had been expended on Sudan that even though in 2004 the United States removed Sudan from a list of countries considered non-cooperative in the GWOT (Small Wars Journal, 9 April 2011), and indeed was playing a positive role in the GWOT, Washington found it politically difficult to remove the sanctions.

## US pursuit of democracy and peace in Sudan

While arguably the United States has been committed to spreading democracy since the presidency of Woodrow Wilson, and Jimmy Carter made human rights the hallmark of his foreign policy, it was only with George W. Bush that a president made democratization the signature element of his foreign policy as he announced at his 2005 Inauguration (Steven R. Weisman and David E. Sanger, 22 January 2005). And in the wake of the 9/11 attacks Bush insisted that as well as a moral calling the quest for freedom was a strategic imperative and 'the urgent requirement of our nation's security, and the calling of our time'. In his second inaugural address to Congress on 20 January 2005, Bush said, 'It is the policy of the United States to seek and support the growth of democratic movements and institutions in every nation and culture, with the ultimate goal of ending tyranny in our world' (George W. Bush, 20 January 2005). Bush also said that freedom is 'God's gift to humanity', and that it is America's responsibility to spread it.

However, US interests changed, and Washington increasingly viewed Africa's underdevelopment and 'failed states' as a threat to its security and the continent became a major theatre for the GWOT and this involved engagement in a series of peace processes. Sometimes these peace processes were led by the United States and its allies, but to give the illusion of 'African solutions to African problems' and not appear over-bearing the preference is for African organizations to lead them or – in Obama's words – for the 'US to lead from behind'. Thus, the Inter-Governmental Authority on Drought and Development (IGADD), a largely technical body made up of countries in the HOA and East Africa, was expanded in 1996 at Western instigation to become the Inter-Governmental Authority on Development (IGAD) and assume responsibility for peacemaking, including that in Sudan.

As well as its leverage over IGAD, US influence was further buttressed by the decision of the International Criminal Court to charge President al-Bashir with leading a campaign of murder, rape and mass deportation in Darfur since 2003 (Peter Walker, James Sturcke, 14 July 2008). The ICC could not arrest al-Bashir in Sudan, but there were numerous attempts to capture him when he travelled abroad, he was restricted where he could travel, and diplomats of the US, Europe and other countries in Khartoum refused to meet him because of the charges. Being the first sitting president of a country to face such charges was humiliating for al-Bashir and discredited Sudan internationally. The NCP accused the EU and the United States of being behind the charges and having them dropped became a foreign policy priority.

But the ICC charges did not have the domestic impact the West hoped, many in Sudan and elsewhere in Africa saw them as politically motivated, and South Africa, Burundi and Gambia announced they were pulling out of a court that unfairly focuses on their continent (Joan Leishman, 16 November 2016). Meanwhile, the NCP attempted to cast al-Bashir in the role of victim. While the United States was a leader in the campaign to have al-Bashir appear before the ICC, it did not recognize the authority of the ICC to judge American citizens, particularly its military which has been widely accused of abuses. Although

Islamist radicalism had been in decline for years, anger at al-Bashir's indictment rallied opposition to the West and demonstrated the capacity of the NCP to turn off and on its Islamist ideology to meet the needs of the hour (al-Maboob Abdelsalem, 28 November 2018).

While Bush led a global campaign in support of democratization, al-Bashir was equally anxious to ensure that it did not succeed because of fears that the American crusade was designed to replace him with someone favoured by the United States. But as Bush acknowledged, after 9/11 security shaped the US commitment to spreading democracy and this led to American demands that the NCP cooperate on a range of security issues. And to the surprise of observers who did not appreciate the pragmatism of the party after the marginalization of al-Turabi, it had few problems accommodating the United States, even when it impinged on Sudan's sovereignty. Indeed, the NCP believed it had information on groups that was of great value to the United States and could be traded for improved relations. Thus, Salah Gosh, al-Bashir's head of the National Intelligence and Security Services (NISS), was specifically tasked with expanding and coordinating anti-terrorist intelligence with the CIA. So desperate were the Americans for intelligence in the wake of 9/11 that they did not see the irony in fighting terrorism by cooperating with a government that the United States considered to be terrorist (Ken Silverstein, 29 April 2005).

The Bush administration was constrained in its efforts to improve relations with Khartoum, however, by Americans, including the president's evangelical followers, who found the regime abhorrent, even if the information gained was considered vital to American security. The problem for Bush worsened when Salah Gosh publicly bragged about his relationship with the Americans and claimed it protected Sudan from being bombed by the United States (Ken Silverstein, 29 April 2005). Indeed, Gosh, who was linked to atrocities in Darfur, was flown to the United States on a CIA plane to thank him for his support in the GWOT and this caused outrage and forced the US government to subsequently keep him at a distance. This did not end the relationship with Gosh, but he was then handled more circumspectly. Meanwhile, the US State Department admitted in 2005 that no al-Qaeda elements had been present in Sudan with the knowledge and consent of the Sudanese government since 2000, and its 2007 country report on Sudan stated that Khartoum had become a 'strong partner' in the Global War on Terrorism (Stratfor, 9 November 2010). All of which begged the question of why the sanctions were still in place.

The answer has to do with politics in the United States, not Sudan, and with bipartisan secular and religious constituencies that competed in demonizing the al-Bashir Islamists and that made it very difficult for any US administration to change course. What became an extensive US engagement in the peace process also proceeded from its role as the global hegemon in the post-Cold War period, its efforts to pacify an area in Africa that could destabilize key client states in the Middle East, an attempt to deepen Africa's integration into the US world order, and to fulfil its self-designated role as the bearer of democracy.

## 4. Propagation of Democracy

The leading US role in the peace process led to an overwhelming referendum vote in favour of the secession of southern Sudan in 2011 (see below), but that did not change the US need for Sudan's cooperation in the GWOT, and thus the commitment to democratization and abuse of human rights continued to be ignored. The willingness of the Sudan government to accept American demands was based on the promise it thought it had from the United States that in return for assisting in the peace process through to the independence of South Sudan that relations would rapidly improve, and the sanctions would end. Although some in the Western media had elevated al-Bashir to the status of a statesman and peacemaker for agreeing to the 2005 Comprehensive Peace Agreement with the SPLM, his image and that of his regime remained negative in the view of most American law makers and the United States maintained both the sanctions and the state sponsor of terrorism designation.

Barack Obama replaced Bush and began his presidency by attempting to extradite the United States from its many failing military engagements, but soon his administration was indistinguishable from that of his predecessor as he ramped up the war in Afghanistan and began new wars in Libya and Syria. Sudan could not be forgotten because as John Kerry, secretary of State under Obama, explained, the US helped 'midwife the birth of the new nation' of South Sudan (Ty McCormick, 26 February 2015). Although the rhetoric about democracy receded, confrontation could not be avoided because Susan Rice who had played a leading and unhelpful role in formulating policy on Sudan during the second Clinton presidency was again made responsible for Sudan policy under Obama. While the newly appointed presidential envoy, General Scott Gration, attempted to build on efforts by the Bush administration to work with the Government of Sudan, he lost the internal battles with Rice who wanted a more confrontational approach, and was dismissed.[3]

With the outbreak of civil war in South Sudan in December 2013 the United States found that it again required Sudan's cooperation. Washington wanted to first ensure that Sudan did not militarily support the rebel forces of the Riek Machar-led SPLM-IO (SPLM-In Opposition) or give sanctuary to Riek because the United States backed the South Sudanese government of Salva Kiir (John Young, 2019). Not known at the time was that Khartoum and Washington were carrying out secret negotiations over the removal of presidential sanctions against Sudan (Washington Post, 13 January 2017). While there was unhappiness among some in the NCP at US interference in Sudan's internal affairs during the negotiations, President al-Bashir was not prepared to change course. Despite misgivings about the role of the United States in the South Sudan peace process and its efforts to

---

3. Although a registered Republican, General Gration gained his Sudan appointment because he was a major backer of the presidential campaign of Obama who author Lemann considered 'The most mystical believer in Obamaism whom I met' (Nicholas Lemann, 6 October 2008). After his dismissal as special envoy, he was appointed ambassador to Kenya where he was hated by his staff and dismissed from that position as well.

dictate Sudan's foreign policy, in order not to upset the Americans the Government of Sudan restricted its involvement to established organizations supported by the United States, like IGAD (John Young, 2019, pp. 173–4).

However, once the Obama administration was replaced by the Trump administration, which did not share the attraction of the three previous administrations for the SPLM and democracy propagation, there was no major objection to Sudan assuming a more active role in the peace process. As a result, Sudan led the US-initiated South Sudan peace process and it quickly produced an agreement between the belligerents, even if its sustainability remained in doubt. Most important to Sudan was the economic appeal of ramping up South Sudan's oil industry and the money gained from its transit through Sudan. The need for financing became ever more pressing as Sudan's economic crisis deepened, the United States failed to end its terrorism designation, and Saudi Arabia and the UAE did not provide the finances Khartoum expected.

Not only did the Trump administration end two decades of support for the SPLM and drop rhetorical calls for democratic transformations in Sudan and South Sudan, but its policy of putting America first meant using the continent to pursue a Cold War against China and Russia. This was made clear in the government's 2018 Africa strategy when National Security Advisor John Bolton said, 'The predatory practices pursued by China and Russia stunt economic growth in Africa; threaten the financial independence of African nations, inhibit opportunities for U.S. investment, interfere with U.S. military operations and pose a significant threat to U.S. national security interests' (National Security Council, 13 December 2018). Bolton also said that US aid would only go to countries that advanced US interests, although significantly he made no mention of democracy propagation. On 8 August the Biden Administration announced its 'Africa Strategy' and continued the emphasis of the Trump era on the values-based struggle with China and Russia and that the 'War on Terror' would continue unabated (The White House, August 2022). What the Trump and Biden administrations made clear is that Sudan and the rest of Africa were not to be permitted to have foreign relations of their own choosing.

## *Decline of Islamist radicalism*

The NIF emerged as a radical movement under the charismatic and intellectual leadership of Hassan al-Turabi who was dedicated to Sudan becoming a leader internationally in the struggle against the Christian West. But the dependence of the NIF on al-Turabi and his aggressive foreign policy agenda brought the government into confrontation with the West, and this ultimately led to his marginalization and retraction of his Islamist agenda. As well as domestic influences, the NIF's ideas were moulded by the international environment, and both served to lay the basis for conflict with US governments.

Al-Turabi was ambitious, global in his thinking, and capable of innovative and progressive interpretations of Islam. He was also a pragmatist who organized a coup against the Sadig al-Mahdi government in 1989 when it became clear that the NIF could not gain power through elections, and the Front stood to lose if its political opponents could reach a peace agreement with Garang's SPLA. The coup represented for one NIF intellectual 'a loss of innocence' because Front plans for sharing power in a broader based alliance never materialized. Instead, the NIF monopolized power, frequently resorted to extreme brutality and became 'a bureaucratic organization concerned with holding power which had no objectives' according to one leading Islamist while its leaders developed into a 'class separate from the people' according to another official.

Ghazi Salahdien, who held numerous leading positions in the government, wrote in similar language about his colleagues forming 'a conservative elite who would cling to power as a way of protecting their position and possessions' (Ghazi Salahdien, 17 June 2018). In this light, the NCP 'joined the mainstream' as another put it since he claimed that all the major Sudanese parties operated at a strictly tactical level, their leaders could jump from one position to another and no party had any real concern for the people. That the NIF abandoned its ideological convictions so quickly after assuming power speaks strongly to the fact that although it was led by intellectuals, the Front leadership was ideologically weak, ill-prepared for government and largely dependent on al-Turabi for both leadership and inspiration (al-Mahboob Abdelsalem, 2018).

The NIF came to power in 1989 at the end of the Cold War, and while socialism as a system had been discredited, notions like anti-imperialism still had wide popularity and were reflected in various movements, including the early NIF. Thus, the NIF supported the arch secularist, Saddam Hussein, in his war with Kuwait whose leaders claimed legitimacy from Islam, and as a result much of Sudan's economic assistance from the Gulf dried up. Also noteworthy of this trend was the hosting by al-Turabi of three Popular Arab and Islamic Conferences between 1991 and 1995 which brought together 500 Islamic militants and nationalists from forty-five countries, as well as a handful of Christian revolutionaries such as George Habash to consider the way forward in the wake of the Soviet withdrawal from Afghanistan and the Iraqi defeat in the Gulf War (Gilles Kepel, 2002, p. 184). The conferences aspired to unite and support Islamic groups from Tajikistan to the Philippines and Bosnia through the former Soviet republics in Central Asia.

These conferences cum movement were also meant to serve as an alternative to the conservative Saudi-led Organization of the Islamic Conference and made clear that Sudanese Islamism was to be distinguished from Saudi Wahabism. While it soon became apparent that the Islamic Conference participants were too ideologically divided to operate under one umbrella, the meetings expressed the global aspirations of al-Turabi, the importance of anti-imperialism to the early NIF agenda, and for some gave meaning to the Huntington thesis of the clash of Christian and Islamic civilizations. The conferences were not, however, supported by most of the NIF leadership and when the West expressed its anger with them, moves were made to isolate al-Turabi, according to al-Mahboob Abdelsalem, a leading Front ideologue (al-Mahboob Abdelsalem, 2018).

Further ammunition to target al-Turabi was provided by the attempted assassination of Egyptian President Hosni Mubarak during a visit to Addis Ababa for a summit of the Organization of African Unity on 25 June 1995. Although most of those involved in the assassination attempt were Egyptian, Mubarak quickly concluded that it was masterminded by al-Turabi (AFP, 29 June 1995). Current thinking is that former Intelligence Chief, Dr Nafi Ali Nafi, and not al-Turabi, was the key person behind the conspiracy,[4] but it added to the backlash Sudan was experiencing because of al-Turabi's adventurist foreign policies. The failed assassination attempt led one leading NIF official to conclude 'Sudan stabbed Meles [Zenawi, the Ethiopian prime minister] in the back' at a time when his government had been on good terms with the NIF.

al-Turabi was convinced that Muslims constituted a majority in Ethiopia and had a burning desire to be free from Christian domination and in response Sudan provided hard and soft support to assist them. al-Turabi belatedly discovered that instead of mobilizing dissident Ethiopian Muslims he had mobilized Sudan's former ally, the EPRDF, which threw its considerable weight behind the SPLA to fight Sudan and was joined by Eritrea and Uganda in whose affairs the NIF was also meddling.

Trying to export al-Turabi's vision and objectives were increasingly at odds with his erstwhile followers in the NIF, most of whom wanted to enjoy the benefits of state power. The Sudanese joked, 'We followed the Islamists to the mosque, and they went to the souk.' Comfortably ensconced in the state NIF leaders did not want their good life threatened by pursuing Islamist dreams that angered powerful countries in the West and the Middle East and had no support in Sudan. In 1999 the Islamists split into two factions, the NCP led by al-Bashir and the smaller Popular Congress Party (PCP) led by al-Turabi, and in 2001 al-Turabi was jailed for the first of what would be many times by his former colleagues.

After the dismissal of his mentor, al-Turabi, al-Bashir worked to centralize power in his person and that meant sidelining his own party and removing key leaders like former Vice President Ali Osman Taha and Dr Nafi Ali Nafi. Although in contravention of the Interim National Constitution of the CPA which stipulated that the tenure of office of the President of the Republic was five years and could only be renewed once (Constitutionnet, 17 August 2018), on 9 August 2018 the NCP passed a resolution at the Annual Meeting of its Consultative Council authorizing President Omar al-Bashir to run for a third term. Abolishing limits on presidential terms permitted al-Bashir to become a president-for-life, provided protection against being arrested by the International Criminal Court and avoided a destabilizing struggle within the ruling party over a successor to run in the 2020 presidential elections.

The contravention of the national constitution highlighted a long process by which the Government of Sudan (and its counterpart SPLM government in South Sudan) overruled their CPA and constitutional commitments to democratic

---

4. Dr Nafi was jailed by the Transitional Military Council in April 2019.

transformation. But despite some grumbling by the United States, what was most significant was Washington's apparent lack of concern at the increasing power of al-Bashir in the party and his undermining of the CPA, a document which only a few years earlier the United States considered a major US foreign policy success, and which would set the regimes in Khartoum and Juba on the road to democracy. However, because of the widespread opposition to the regime and al-Bashir personally as was made clear by the country-wide demonstrations that broke out in Sudan in late 2018, it became increasingly doubtful that he would serve as the NCP 2020 presidential candidate.

In an effort to end the charges against al-Bashir and terminate the sanctions, the NCP supported Western efforts to overthrow Muammar Gaddafi, who in any case was long opposed to political Islam and was historically close to the Umma Party (even though the UN resolution gave it no such right), ended relations with Iran in 2015 after Saudi Arabia deposited $1 billion in Sudan's central bank (AFP, 13 August 2015), and signed and ratified regional and international treaties to fight terrorism. Indicative of the changes the NIF/NCP had undergone, it shifted from being an exponent of anti-imperialism to joining the Western-backed Saudi-Emirates War against the Yemeni Houthis. While the United States and UK supported the war from a distance and made money selling weapons to the Gulf states, al-Bashir sent the biggest foreign ground force to Yemen, many of its fighters drawn from the government supported RSF, made up of former *jangaweed* fighters with a notorious reputation for human rights abuses in Darfur where its members ravaged Africans, and in 2003 it is believed that Hemedti joined the organization. Sudan's involvement in the war was due to two factors: first, a desperate need for foreign reserves and investment from the Gulf states, and second, to have Saudi Arabia and the UAE appeal to the United States to end its sanctions. But as a former senior NCP official bitterly noted, the UAE and Saudi Arabia provided scant financial support and appealing to the subordinate in the Saudi-US relationship was a non-starter.

al-Bashir established militias like the RSF because he did not fully trust an army which in 1964 and 1985 had turned against their erstwhile leaders and sided with demonstrators. In addition, Hemedti, as leader of the RSF, was tasked with defeating insurgencies. The empowerment of Hemedti involved giving him and his family the right to mine gold in Darfur and beyond and then circumvent capital controls, sell it to the Sudanese central bank at preferential rates (Khalid Abdelaziz, Michael Georgy, Maha El Dahan, 26 November 2019) and export it to Dubai, where he developed powerful links. Not only did this give Hemedti enormous financial resources that could be used to further empower his RSF, it also deepened his links with influential people in the UAE.

Although never appearing in formal statements, the NIF/NCP opposition to Israel was a major point of contention with the United States, according to former NCP officials. The NIF had cooperated with Iran and Qatar in smuggling weapons to Hamas in Gaza through its Red Sea ports and this led to Israeli bombings of suspected weapons in Port Sudan in 2009 and a weapons factory in Khartoum in 2011 (Radio Free Europe, 24 October 2012). While Sudan was sometimes paid for its support of these operations, they served to buttress the NCP's legitimacy as an Islamist movement. However, the Israeli bombings proved effective, and the al-Bashir government ended its involvement in the transit of weapons to Hamas.

In addition, Sudan had to contend with the bedrock support of all US governments since 1967 for the security of Israel. Indeed, in response to the Palestinian-led Boycott, Disinvestment, and Sanctions (BDS) campaign against Israel's policies in the occupied territories and failure to abide by the conditions of the Oslo Agreement, Israel and the United States launched a counter global campaign (Dovid Efune,10 September 2020). This campaign ignores the rationale behind BDS, denies any distinction between opposition to Israeli policies and anti-Semitism and calls for, and has introduced, laws where even the advocacy of BDS can lead to fines, imprisonment and loss of employment. However, long before the anti-BDS campaign began the US government and lobby groups worked to gain the widest possible diplomatic recognition of Israel. The issue was also regularly raised in Congressional confirmation hearings of US ambassadors to Sudan, and NCP officials report that Sudan's recognition of Israel was frequently brought up in meetings with their American counterparts according to NCP officials. As a party official noted, 'American policy is Israeli policy.'

The NCP was also mindful that due to recent developments Saudi Arabia, the United Arab Emirates and Egypt, all of whom the Sudanese Islamists looked to for political support, finance and to positively intercede on their behalf with the United States had become strategic allies of Israel and the latter two formally recognized Israel. Meanwhile, US hostility to Iran is largely because of Tehran's leadership of an alliance which includes Syria, Hezbollah and Hamas in opposition to Israel. In its efforts to win American favour Sudan flipped its loyalties from the latter group to the former, launched an anti-Shia propaganda campaign and went to war against the Houthi Yemenis on the spurious grounds that they are Shia and supported by Iran.

Behind the scenes NISS chief, Salah Gosh, held secret talks with the head of Mossad, Yossi Cohen, on the sidelines of the Munich Security Conference in a meeting arranged by Egyptian intermediaries with the backing of Saudi Arabia 15–17 February 2019 (Hearst, Hooper, and Mustafa, 1 March 2019). Israel wanted al-Bashir's removal because he opposed normalizing relations with Israel. It was alleged that Gosh, who had close ties with the CIA during the GWOT, was selected by Israel's Gulf allies to become president when Omar al-Bashir was toppled from power. Although al-Bashir was overthrown only two months later Gosh was a victim of the fallout of that event (Middle East Eye, 1 March 2019).

Whether under Gosh or al-Bashir it had been widely anticipated that Sudan would diplomatically recognize Israel. Possibly as a means to prepare the Sudanese public for yet another ideological flip-flop, in late 2018 the state media openly debated the merits of recognizing Israel. As one former non-Islamist minister in the government noted, 'al-Bashir is ready to do anything to win the favour of the US and end the ICC charges against him.' When the NIF first came to power recognition of Israel would have been inconceivable because the only Islamist government in Sudan's history could not recognize Israel when all other Sudanese governments had refused; moreover, recognition of Israel challenged many core NIF convictions and would cast it into repute among Islamists internationally. But in an environment of economic decline, political demoralization, anger on the street and against a long history of compromising principles, recognition of Israel became likely were it not that the regime was overthrown.

Although the United States was successful in getting Sudan to rebalance its foreign relations and cooperate in the GWOT, the country remained outside the American orbit. And thus former Special Envoy for Sudan and South Sudan, Donald Booth, announced a 'Five-Track Engagement Plan' in 2016. This plan called for Sudan to cease military offensives in Darfur, Southern Kordofan and Blue Nile, improve humanitarian access to the conflict zones, refrain from interfering in South Sudan's civil war, increase cooperation on regional and counterterrorism issues, and cooperate on the threat posed by Uganda's Lord's Resistance Army (US State Department, 13 January 2017). In return Washington would lift its trade embargo and economic sanctions and begin cooperating in bilateral areas and this is what occurred after the revoking of sanctions in late 2017. Unfortunately for the NCP this did not produce the economic turnaround that was expected.

The Sudanese Islamists hoped that cooperation with the United States would serve to improve relations, but it produced meagre results. President Bush announced a $100 million counterterrorism initiative for East Africa and the HOA in 2003 as part of the GWOT for the region and in 2007 the Pentagon declared it would establish AFRICOM to bring together its varied programmes on the continent (Karl Wycoff, 1 April 2004). Within Africa the HOA was the object of the most militarized US response to confronting terrorism in Africa. Sudan, however, was not invited to participate in the US-led Operation Enduring Freedom – HOA, a counterterror operation, which included Ethiopia, Kenya and Djibouti. Nor did Sudan participate in the related Trans-Saharan Counterterrorism Initiative, which included forces from Chad, Niger, Mauritania and Mali.

But on 16 March 2017, the United States and Sudan announced the resumption of military relations after exchanging military attachés and a month later it was revealed that the CIA would open its largest office in the Middle East in Khartoum (Sudan Tribune, 1 February 2017). In April 2017 Sudan's Chief of Defence Staff, Emadeldin Adawi, attended meetings for the first time at AFRICOM headquarters in Stuttgart and the army was quick to announce the consultation as 'evidence of the breakthrough in the relationship with the United States and a move towards lifting Sudan's name from the US list of countries sponsoring terrorism and fully lifting the American economic sanctions' (Dabanga, 18 April 2017). But that was wishful thinking and nor did the meeting between Kamal Abd al-Marouf, the incoming chief of staff of the Sudan Armed Forces (SAF) and senior US military officials produce the long-anticipated break-through in relations.

Instead, and to the shock of the Government of Sudan, incoming President Donald Trump placed Sudan on a list of six Muslim countries subject to a US travel ban. Sudan was removed from the travel ban of Muslim-majority countries in September 2017, probably because of UAE lobbying on its behalf (Grim and Emmons, 25 September 2017). And on 6 October 2017 Trump lifted the 1997 sanctions after Sudan cut all ties with North Korea, a last-minute addition to meet the changing needs of US foreign policy, even though there was no evidence of a North Korean trade in weapons with Sudan (Small Arms Survey, May 2019).[5] But this did not produce any improvement in the Sudanese economy, and to the fury of al-Bashir the United States continued to keep Sudan on the list of state sponsors of terrorism, which made it impossible for Sudan to benefit from the World Bank debt-relief programme and receive financial support for its development plans.

Instead, the United States announced that there would be a second phase upon which the removal of Sudan from the state sponsors of terrorism list would depend and for the first time human rights together with religious rights were mentioned (Human Rights Watch, 'US Considers Lifting Sudan's 'Terror State' Designation.' 7 November 2018.) But as Human Rights caustically notes, 'No wonder the US and Sudan prefer to celebrate their deal in private.' Lost on supporters of the US global agenda, Sudan and other countries on the list of state sponsors of terrorism had never attacked or threatened to attack the United States while Saudi Arabia was a financial supporter of al-Qaeda which attacked the United States, but nonetheless remained a close ally.

Significantly the second phase did not include any reference to democracy, and this is not surprising since a senior NCP official involved in many negotiations with the United States said, 'In all my meetings with US diplomats they never once raised the demand that Sudan democratize.' The new list included demands for counterterrorism cooperation, improving humanitarian access, ceasing hostilities in Darfur, Southern Kordofan, and Blue Nile to create a conducive environment for negotiations, while demands that Sudan cooperate on the South Sudan peace process and end support for Uganda's Lord's Resistance Army were removed as being accomplished. The focus on 'religious freedoms' appeared to be concerned with church leaders from the war-afflicted Nuba Mountains because of their perceived support for the SPLM-North (Mohamed Osman and Magdi el Gizouli, 25 November 2018). There was evidence of discrimination by Sudan's NCP of Christians, but there was far more evidence of such discrimination in a number of countries in the Gulf and that did not prove to be an obstacle to the United States having close relations with them.

## United States and Islamists find common ground in commitment to capitalism

While al-Bashir was successful in resisting US pressures for regime change, he had no objection to establishing a market-based economy, albeit one that maintained

---

5. Although there was no documentation of North Korean weapons or ammunitions in Sudan's war zones, there was documentation that neighbour states and US allies, such as Kenya, Ethiopia and Somalia, had military relations with North Korea, all of which escaped US censure.

Islamic banking, ensured his government was free to dispense the patronage upon which its survival depended, and made only token and largely public relations efforts to tackle endemic corruption. In any case, systemic corruption and patronage was a common feature in the economies of many of Washington's allies and clients and was far from absent in the United States, so it was disingenuous to lay this charge solely against Sudan. The one potential obstacle to bringing Sudan into the international (i.e. Western dominated) financial system was Islamic banking. In 1970 under the influence of the SCP, the government began nationalizing the country's banks. But after the attempted SCP coup two years later and his sharp turn to the political right, Nimeiri brought the NIF of al-Turabi and the Umma Party of Sadig al-Mahdi into the government and they agreed to privatize banks and establish an Islamic banking system.

The fundamental difference between the Islamic- and Western-dominated banking system is that the former does not accept interest and is based on a partnership that shares risks and rewards. Under Nimeiri it was announced that all financial institutions operating in Sudan must fully comply with Islamic laws and prohibit *riba*, an increase in wealth not related to productive activity. Between 1989 and 2005 a fully developed and integrated Islamic banking system developed in Sudan (Mohamed Khair, 6–7 November 2013). Most of these 'reforms' were overseen by Abderrahim Hamdi, the NIF finance minister who has been called the 'godfather of economic liberalization policy', a policy which impoverished many Sudanese (Altaghyeer Archives, 19 April 2021).[6]

Some in the NCP claimed that Islamic banking, which involves investors in the ownership of concerns and supports programmes for the poor, represented a fundamentally different and superior form of banking to that of the West and Islamists noted the system's financial stability in the wake of the international economic crisis of 2008. But the former NCP officials interviewed during the course of this research did not see Islamic banking as being opposed to Western banking and pointed to the presence until recently of the US-based Citibank in Khartoum which had an Islamic banking window, the growing popularity on Wall Street of Islamic banking and the listing of Islamic banks on Western stock exchanges. Indeed, there has long been a close relationship between right-wing economists associated with the Chicago school and Islamist bankers and politicians and once in office Islamist regimes pursued neoliberal policies. This is consistent with support for neoliberalism by other Muslim Brothers groups since 2000 (Wael Gamal, 31 January 2019) and their rejection of class struggle. Despite Islamic concerns with social justice and helping the poor, the regime's endorsement of an unfettered market economy left the poor to their own devices and was, in the words of one former official, 'callous', but entirely understandable for a doctrine that in its modern manifestations endorsed capitalism. Moreover, a

---

6. Hamdi is most remembered for the 'Hamdi Triangle' which encompassed the northern riverine core of Sudan in which he proposed that the government concentrate development because this is the area in which the NIF had the most support.

study of Sudan's Islamic banking found the poor were deprived of banking access as a result of inequality and discrimination (Sudan Democracy First Group, 29 May 2019).

Sudanese Islamists capitalized on Islamic banking and developed corporate ties in ways that enabled them to amass wealth and tighten their political grip (Abdullaihi, 2018). Nor are Islamic banks free of corruption as made clear by the arrest of directors of the Faisal Islamic Bank, Khartoum Bank and the Islamic Insurance Company and there were links between those arrested and senior figures in the NCP government (Suliman Baldo, November 2018). A major obstacle to the Sudanese banking system, however, was US sanctions which limited links to international banks and led to the US fining banks trading with Sudan. The most graphic example was that of the Omdurman National Bank which was held to have imported raw materials that could be used for the manufacture of weapons through the French bank, PNP-Paribas, thus running afoul of US sanctions against Sudan. As a result, BNP-Paribas was fined $8.9 billion (Sudan Democracy First Group, 2018).

Islamists frequently voiced their disapproval of 'socialism' and in meetings with the author al-Turabi repeatedly spoke of his desire to 'get the government off the backs of the people' and support for the market in similar language as that of US Republicans or UK Conservatives. Moreover, he claimed that ending 'socialism' was one of the major accomplishments of the government. As one former NCP intellectual noted, 'There was no philosophical difference between us and the IMF.' Upon coming to power, the NIF announced its *Al Tamkeen* policy (literally 'consolidation of power'), which in the economic sphere was the same policy it pursued under Nimeiri: selling state assets and companies, often at knock-down prices to supporters, ending subsidies, welcoming foreign capital and encouraging a free market economy.

Indeed, following the Bretton Woods agencies a key element of the Islamist government's economic programme was the privatization of the Gezira Scheme, Sudan Railways and Sudatel which produced massive job losses in the country's largest industries. One study of the NCP privatization programme concluded that 'even if privatization contributed to improved efficiency in some sectors (such as telecommunications), it had a negative effect on the distribution of wealth, income, and political power' (Osman Suliman, 2007). The privatization of the Gezira Scheme and Sudan Railways which had been the centre-piece of the national economy since the colonial era also served to undermine the unions that represented the workers in those industries and in turn the Sudan Communist Party which based much of its authority on its control of those unions.

Instead of Africa's links to the Western-dominated global economy being considered a cause of underdevelopment and chronic instability as a generation of radical intellectuals contended, the NCP endorsed the view of the IMF and the West that Africa's relative exclusion from globalization was the central problem. Trade liberalization and market deregulation were held to be ladders by which poor countries could harness the dynamism of capitalism, traditional economies were deliberately undermined and social welfare programmes reduced or eliminated. Structural Adjustment Programs were imposed to inject dynamism into the economies of peripheral states, introduce more effective forms of governance and demonstrate acceptance of the West's conception of democracy. SAPs involved the same kind of restructuring imposed in the West: privatization of state assets, reduction of social, health and education programmes, ending subsidies, emphasizing export-led development, eliminating trade barriers, floating currencies, removing obstacles to the repatriation of profits, and other measures, which are sometimes considered the 'Washington Consensus', misnamed because there was never a consensus.

As was the case in the West, neoliberal policies in underdeveloped countries have lowered living standards for the majority, increased inequality, fostered social tensions, weakened national autonomy and left national economies in Africa and Sudan dangerously exposed to international and particularly Asian competition. Aping the position of modernization theory, the Bretton Woods agencies insist that the only road to development is that pursued by the West, and this involves acceptance of free markets and liberal democracy which are held to be universal values.

While the NIF developed a system of Islamic banking, it failed to produce an economy in any other way distinctive from the capitalism that was at the core of the Western society that its leaders abhorred and aspired to surpass. The political revolution and religious revival of the NIF did not challenge the fundamental structures of the economy and this despite Islamist influence over the economy by its commercial affiliates was held to be a first step towards establishing a modern Islamic state as an alternative to capitalism and globalization. Likewise, its vision of a 'civilization project' was never realized. The NIF tried to harness political ideology to a kind of totalizing state control over culture and society that was unprecedented in its scope (Abdullaihi Gallab, 2018), but as one analyst noted, 'Sudan's al-Turabi donned the mantle of Islamic revolution, but Sudanese society is not undergoing revolutionary transformation' (Zachary Karabell, 1996). When the regime faced international isolation its leaders raised slogans about self-reliance, but they fell flat. Indeed, it is capitalism and globalization that changed the Islamists, and not vice versa. As a result, 'the Islamic model had failed' according to an NCP official, and this produced cynicism and increasing devotion to personal gain by party cadres.

However much the NIF wanted to make Sudan a free-market paradise along the lines of that proscribed by the IMF and the United States, its leaders were stymied by the economic sanctions against the country, adherence to demands for austerity, costs associated with the independence of South Sudan, endemic corruption, dependence on patronage politics and the opposition of an aroused population. While sanctions undermined the technological and social development of the country, the austerity measures served to exponentially increase debt, cause social disruption, and produce horrific inflation and instability (John Young, June 2020, p. 57). The independence of South Sudan in 2011 and the impending loss of oil revenues which provided almost half of the government's income were known six years before when the CPA was signed, but little was done to plan for the transition. However, promises had been made by the government of South Sudan to ease the transition through cash and oil payments to Khartoum that did not happen because of the country's civil war. Further pain was caused by the oil installations being damaged during the civil war and the collapse of oil prices.

One of the most pernicious elements of the IMF programme was encouraging foreign investment in Sudan by selling at minimal cost large tracts of land with little or no judicial oversight or concern for those whose livelihood depended on the land to foreign commercial agricultural corporations. According to the reasoning of the IMF, which was accepted by the government, the land sales and anticipated commercialization of agriculture would go far to making up for the loss of oil revenues with the secession of South Sudan. The IMF's recommendations to make Sudan suitable for foreign investments usually mean facilitating land grabs away from Sudanese farmers into the hands of foreign oligarchs by 'lifting judiciary's oversight over land sales, reforming land relations, and in allowing foreign investors to grab as much land as possible', according to El Gizouli (Raven Rakia, 25 March 2015). Successive Sudanese governments turned over land from rural communities to large-scale agricultural national and multi-national corporations but hopes this would produce positive change have never been realized. Neither the IMF, the US government nor the NCP expressed any concern at the abuse of human rights these measures caused nor the resulting mass protests and sometimes loss of lives. US democracy and its circumscribed conception of human rights failed to address the concerns of ordinary Sudanese.

The NIF/NCP government's acceptance of IMF dictates was largely because it wanted to end the country's enormous debt burden or at least obtain debt relief. Most of Sudan's debt of approximately $56 billion was the result of it being compounded from loans taken out by the Nimeiri regime in the 1970s and 1980s to finance large-scale (and frequently failed) development projects (Jubilee Debt Campaign). Although Sudan had the second highest debt load in Africa (after South Africa), it was not able to benefit from debt relief under the Heavily Indebted Poor Country (HIPC) Initiative because of the US state sponsor of terrorism designation, a shortage of funds and opposition in the US Congress to the provision of funds (Nehanda Radio, 17 April 2019). Acceptance under this initiative would have allowed Sudan to normalize relations with its creditors, including the World Bank and the African Development Bank, pave the way for new financing and eliminate Sudan's arrears to the International Financial Institutions and bilateral creditors.

Removing subsidies on basic commodities was the most politically explosive feature of the IMF 'reforms', and the government repeatedly backtracked because of fears of a backlash that could bring about the collapse of the NCP government, a realistic assessment as it turned out. Over many years Sudan developed a system of subsidies that included bread, fuel, sugar and electricity that set it apart from neighbouring countries with the exception of Egypt, which faced similar IMF demands, but not the same threat because Cairo was a close ally of Washington. However, under the NIF/NCP, and consistent with IMF demands, user-fees were introduced into the educational and health systems to the detriment of the poor and working people. The IMF contends that subsidies are an inefficient means to keep prices down, supply up and they lead to smuggling. But the country's farmers, workers, poor and shrinking middle class view such subsidies as a right, necessary to their survival, and have repeatedly resisted government and IMF attempts to entirely remove them. Nonetheless, as a result of the pernicious influence of neoliberalism, health care was privatized and as a result costs increased dramatically, while education declined in quality and likewise increased in costs.

Another impact in recent years has been an increase in crime, particularly in Darfur, made worse by the virtual state-like powers of the RSF, a militia established by al-Bashir because of his fears of the national army. A further element in the crisis was reached in late 2017 when the government following IMF recommendations removed long-standing subsidies and raised the customs exchange rate. This produced an immediate and enormous increase in the price of fuel and bread and runs on the currency by those anxious to protect the value of stocks and real estate and was manifest in a growing black-market exchange and long queues at ATM machines in late 2018. Under the US rendering of democracy, the interests of the market and those who control the market rank higher than the welfare-seeking people.

The same al-Turabi who wanted to challenge the United States through instruments like the Popular Arab and Islamic Conference turned out to be a believer in the redeeming value of the market, but opening up the market did nothing to improve the general well-being of Sudanese. What the regime could point to is that despite suffering civil war, sanctions and not being showered with foreign aid like neighbouring Ethiopia, it significantly increased the number of educational institutions, hospitals, roads, heavy industry, military industry and established an oil industry. Probably the biggest initial achievement of the NIF was to improve governance from its virtual collapse during the Sadig al-Mahdi years, despite its political purge of the civil service. Although this achievement did not last, the Sadig government was so dysfunctional that democracy had become a bad word for many Sudanese. The unfettered economy favoured by both the IMF and the Islamist government – and which was held to be a critical component of democracy – produced growing inequities that were highly visible in 2018 and early 2019 when demonstrators across the country protested at a marginal increase in the price of bread at the same time that the streets of Khartoum and other urban centres were bursting with late model cars and upmarket restaurants filled to capacity.

The NCP ended the southern war, but only after it carried out a coup in 1989 to abort a peace process and the eventual peace agreement led to the secession of South Sudan, the loss of oil revenues on which the country had grown dependent, but despite American promises, the sanctions were not ended. In line with international experience, most Sudanese suffered because of the sanctions, while leading government officials, their relatives, political allies and those with access to foreign currency were largely untouched. As a result, US policy had the effect of punishing the innocent majority of Sudanese, while leaving the elites who bore responsibility for Sudan's supposed unacceptable policies and practices largely untouched.

With the United States acknowledging that Sudan largely met the requirements demanded by the imposition of sanctions, outgoing President Barack Obama decreed in January 2017 they would only be lifted after a further six months of continuing cooperation by Khartoum and pending the final assessment of his successor (Charles Capito, 24 January 2017). Unusually there was agreement between Obama and incoming Donald Trump to end the sanctions against Sudan. However, Obama's decision to make this ruling in the final days of his presidency and Trump's delay in first making a decision and then adding more requirements before the designation of Sudan as a supporter of terrorism would be removed made clear the controversial nature of the decision. Both presidents were sensitive to the sentiments of Congress and American public opinion which had been shaped by the widespread belief that the sanctions were designed to ensure a democratic transformation in Sudan which had clearly not occurred. Also crucial to the decision was the lobbying carried out by Saudi Arabia and the UAE of the Obama administration to normalize relations with Sudan after Khartoum cut diplomatic ties with Iran (Grim and Emmons, 2017).

Gone were fears of the NCP's adventurist foreign policies or its radical Islamist ideology since both had been emasculated. Instead, and in contrast to the Clinton years, the United States feared the weakness of the government, fragility of the state (Carson and Vertin, March 2018), and in the absence of an opposition deemed capable of ruling the country the collapse of the government would create a power vacuum into which extremist groups could operate and threaten US interests in the region. As a result, the United States wavered between either supporting the regime or trying to facilitate its soft-landing. Meanwhile, European governments feared instability in Sudan could produce new waves of migrants across the Mediterranean and viewed al-Bashir as a key partner due to Sudan's role as migration hub for the entire HOA, a development according to Traugott that involved outsourcing European border security 'at the whim of foreign dictators' (Leopold Traugott, 21 September 2016).

But the inconsistencies of US policy did not stop there. While endeavouring to preserve the regime, the US designation of Sudan as a state sponsor of terrorism increased the country's economic pain and the prospects that the government and country would collapse. Although liberal peacemaking is premised on the conviction that development and economic integration are crucial to sustainable peace, the United States pursued policies in Sudan that deepened the country's isolation and undermined prospects for global integration. Further, while considered a terrorist state, Sudan was acknowledged to be a valued supporter of the US GWOT (Johnathan Schanzer, 5 July 2012).

But perhaps the biggest knot the United States tied itself in is that sanctions reduced US influence in Sudan, which in any case was waning because of declining US investment and engagement in Africa. US influence also suffered from the reduction of the State Department budget and the failure of Trump to appoint an assistant secretary of state for African affairs, ambassadors to several African countries, or to even visit the continent during his term of office and as a result US influence in Africa markedly declined according to *Foreign Policy* journal (Reuben Brigety, 28 August 2018). This was in contrast to Chinese President Xi Jinping who visited Africa four times between 2014 and 2019 and in 2018 promised $60 billion in investment and aid over the following five years (China Daily, 27 November 2021). Against this background, China, Russia, the Gulf states, Turkiye and others were increasingly filling the vacuum, and this caused growing alarm in Washington (Jeffery Herbst, March 2018).

## *The post-al-Bashir era*

While the regime was never popular, Sudanese attitudes towards it changed over the years. Thus, the coup which overthrew the Sadig al-Mahdi government was not completely unwelcome given conditions in the country at the time. But very soon the brutality of the NIF shocked the Sudanese who – following their famous author, Tayeb Salih – asked, 'Where did these people come from?' (Teller Report, 22 April 2019). NIF ruthlessness declined somewhat after power was consolidated, but the regime remained very unpopular until 1998 when oil production came on stream and in 2000 Sudan began exporting oil and this led to a reduction in inflation, improvement in the exchange rate, a building boom and employment prospects picked up (Haitham Abdualaziz and Fung Deng, January 2014, p. 29).

But with the secession of southern Sudan and the loss of oil revenues, the economic crisis returned and bowing to IMF pressures the government reduced wheat and fuel subsidies in September 2013. The youth responded by going to the streets, and in clashes with the security forces, mostly from the RSF, Amnesty International reported that 200 were killed (Sudan Tribune, 4 October 2013). This brutal response led to the formation of the first resistance committees to mobilize the people and lay the basis for more concerted struggles in 2018–2019. In December 2014 the opposition parties met in Addis Ababa and launched the 'Sudan Appeal' and agreed to 'dismantle the system of one-party rule for the sake of a nation based on equal citizenship' and for this to be achieved 'through daily efforts by the people that should develop into a popular uprising' (Dabanga, 3 December 2014).

Unlike the past where dissent was largely centred on university campuses, the resistance committees were rooted in neighbourhoods and thus directly linked to the people. In late 2018 opposition reached new peaks with demonstrations organized by the committees to oppose increases in bread prices and shortages of fuel as the government attempted to implement IMF demands to end subsidies. Unlike 2013 the resistance committees were informed by WhatsApp and varied from the upper-class Khartoum neighbourhood of Riyadh to the working class and poor neighbourhood of Kalakla. According to Magdi El Gizouli, 'While Kalaklaka is hungry for work, Riyadh's agitators are motivated by the depreciation of their middle-class purchasing power' (Magdi El Gizouli, January 2020).

Four months of country-wide demonstrations and sit-ins across from the military headquarters in fourteen Sudanese towns ensued, especially in Khartoum which Magdi described as a 'a Woodstock of sorts on the Nile' (Magdi El Gizouli, 2023). al-Bashir was jailed on 11 April 2019 by the security forces subsequently headed by Lt-General Abdel-Fatah al-Burhan which then demanded that the leaderships of the army, national security, police and the Rapid Support Forces lead a two-year transitional government until national elections were held. They followed the footsteps of the army generals in 1985 by constituting a Transitional Military Council without consultations with the leaders of the popular uprising (Lam Akol, 3 September 2021). The security forces' coup was not carried out to usher in democracy; quite the contrary, it was carried out to prevent the displacement of the entire Islamist-infused state apparatus, and thus it represented continuity more than genuine change; indeed, it was intended to pre-empt change. Hemedti was briefly very popular among many ordinary people in Khartoum because of his supposed refusal to obey al-Bashir and fire on the demonstrators and in the arrest of the dictator.

al-Burhan has a checkered history and while serving in Darfur he was the head of the Border Guard Forces militia, which later became the Rapid Support Forces commanded by his deputy Hemedti who seconded him during the war on Darfur groups and was largely directed to ensuring 'Arab' dominance in the region. El Shafee Abdallah, one of the leaders of the camps for displaced people in Central Darfur, said, al-Burhan is the architect of the genocide that took place in Darfur, where, as the first official in charge of popular security in the region, he armed the militias known as the border guards. He distributed the weapons to the militias that were used in the massacres since 2009' (Dabanga, 15 April 2019). In other words, far from representing a clear break from the former Islamist regime, the supposed 'coup' led by al-Burhan represented links to the crimes of the past.

A group of opposition parties organized under the label Forces for Freedom and Change (FFC) supported the demonstrators and rejected the demand that the military rule on its own. Meanwhile, Saudi Arabia and the UAE rushed to back up the Transitional Military Council with pledges of USD 3 billion which led one commentator to conclude that Egypt, Saudi Arabia and the UAE are 'keen to snuff out democratic revolutions in the Arab world and have the resources to do so' (Michael Woldemariam, 2019). Indeed, this was the same game plan that the UAE and Saudi Arabia employed to support the el-Sisi dictatorship and fend off demands for a democratic transformation in Egypt. But the resolve of the demonstrators continued, and together with the AU decision to automatically sanction and freeze the membership of any country in which the military takes power by force, this opened the way for negotiations between the civilians and the military on how to share power in the transitional period (Lam Akol, 3 September 2021). Although some in the opposition were adamant that the military be excluded from any role in the transitional government, and that was the view of the demonstrators, apart from the leftist parties the mainstream parties were prepared to share power and were backed up by the West, Egypt, the UAE and Saudi Arabia (John Young, 2020a).

Meanwhile, Hemedti met with Saudi crown prince Mohammed bin Salman while al-Burhan met with Egyptian President el-Sisi and UAE crown prince

Mohammed bin Zayed, after which the generals stated that the sit-in constituted a 'threat to national security' (Reuters, 2019b). And early morning on 3 June 2019 a force led by the RSF attacked the sit-in in Khartoum and other urban centres. More than 100 unarmed demonstrators were killed, many women were raped and the encampments were burned down. The day after the RSF attack – 4 June – al-Burhan went on national television and said that the TMC no longer recognized the FFC or the agreement the military had reached with it and that it would rule on its own until elections were held in nine months.

However, the demonstrators were not cowed and returned to the streets on 30 June. This set the stage for an all-out war which might have ensued, were it not that the United States, the international community, including Abiy Ahmed who participated in discussions in Khartoum, and even the TMC's allies in the Middle East appreciated that the massacre of the civilian demonstrators had lost the generals legitimacy and they must agree to share power with civilians. On 17 July a power-sharing agreement was signed that established an eleven-person Sovereign Council that would govern for thirty-nine months, after which elections were to be held (Al Arabiya English, 17 July 2019). In the first twenty-one months of the transition the Sovereign Council was to be headed by a general (al-Burhan) and would be followed by a civilian for the remaining eighteen months of its tenure. The Sovereign Council would be Sudan's highest authority and would be composed of five military personnel chosen by the TMC and five civilians selected by the FFC, with the eleventh member being a civilian selected by consensus. The government was officially formed on 21 August, when the head of the TMC, Lt-General Abdel-Fattah al-Burhan, was sworn in as head of the Sovereign Council with Hemedti serving as his deputy, although there were always tensions between the professional commander of the Sudanese armed forces and his unprofessional deputy who made no secret of his ambition to become leader of Sudan and his opposition to the RSF being integrated into the Sudanese armed forces.

The FFC selected Abdalla Hamdok as prime minister who as an international economist (even though once a member of the SCP) provided a useful link between the regime and the Western powerbrokers that the regime wanted to impress. Hamdok's first Finance Minister, Ibrahim Elbadawi, was a former World Bank economist, and the cabinet was led by technocrats, many from international financial institutions (John Young, 2020a). Hamdok in turn chose one of three FFC-proposed candidates to head each of fourteen ministries, excluding the interior and defence ministers, which would be appointed by the military. Four national councils were also to be established and members assigned by the prime minister. Lastly, a 300-member Legislative Council composed of two-thirds FFC members and one-third others who had supported al-Bashir's overthrow was agreed to, but its formation was postponed until the other governance institutions started functioning. In the event, the transitional government extended its term of office until 2024, repeatedly delayed the appointment of the Legislative Council, and with the subsequent military negotiated agreements with some of the armed groups, the Sovereign Council membership was expanded with individuals broadly sympathetic to the generals.

Crucially the agreement kept the existing socio-economic system intact and did not hold the military responsible for their killing of civilian protestors or contest their vast private sector holdings. For many demonstrators and the SCP this agreement constituted a hijacking of the revolution. The old order was challenged, but the continuing major role of the al-Bashir era generals and RSF made clear that the transformation called for by the protestors was not on the cards and there would be considerable continuity. Also clear was the failure of the Trump administration to champion the cause of the protestors who used a democratic discourse that drew much from the United States. Instead, the United States under Trump was happy to have its autocratic clients in the Middle East play the leading role in the transition. Those Middle Eastern leaders were keen to see the last of al-Bashir, but anxious to keep his military in a dominant position and contain the democratic demands from the street (Declan Walsh, 26 April 2019). Meanwhile, Egypt was the most alarmed by Sudan's democracy movement and Cairo became the refuge of choice for former spy chief Salah Gosh and other members of the displaced regime (Mohamed Amin, 31 January 2022).

Although highly educated, most of the Hamdok cabinet had lived much of their professional lives outside Sudan, had supped deeply on neoliberalism, held that the country's failure was due to its lack of integration with the Western led international community, and set about correcting that. Not only did this mean submission to the West and undermining Sudan's sovereignty, it also represented a continuation of policies that the al-Bashir regime attempted to carry out to win the favour of the United States. With the formation of the Hamdok government legions of United States, EU and other international officials descended on Khartoum to give advice. The cooperation agreement between the civilians and the military, together with the wholesale adoption of the programme of the World Bank and the IMF, led the Communist Party to abandon the FFC, declare its opposition to the transitional government, and in September 2021 call for it to be toppled (Guardian, 13 September 2021).

Having surrendered its economic policy Sudan followed the well-trodden path of all supplicants of the global financial masters including the endorsement of austerity as a pre-condition to debt relief and issuing new loans. After accumulating some of the highest debt levels relative to the size of its economy in the world, the transitional government imposed a structural adjustment programme to meet the conditions of the IMF's Heavily Indebted Poor Country Initiative. Access to HIPC was also the hope of the al-Bashir regime (see above) and it remains equally misplaced because the programme is not designed to cancel debts but ensure they are paid, and it is not concerned with enhancing human development, reducing poverty or even increasing growth (Focus on the Global South, 4 October 2000). It is primarily concerned with regularizing the country's debt arrangements with its foreign donors and permitting the infusion of more loans. However, in the face of a collapsing economy Hamdok trumpeted the HIPC and other debt relief measures as evidence of the confidence that the international community (read the West) had in his government and that a new age of prosperity was just around the corner.

Such programmes are dedicated to the integration of subject countries into the Western-dominated global economic system, which further limits the prospects of Sudan developing autonomous economic and foreign policies. National governments are severely constrained in carrying out economic reforms unless they fall within the IMF-prescribed neoliberal framework (Boas and Gans-Morse, 2 June 2009). This framework limits the role of the state in tackling economic injustices, emphasizes the market and fosters the economic inequality and unequal development the transitional government had to overcome if it was to improve the lives of Sudanese, end the wars in the country's peripheries and stay in power. The transitional government had the choice of representing the interests of the majority of Sudanese or the demands of the West and without hesitation it followed the West. Just as debt placed severe constraints on the al-Bashir regime, the transitional government faced similar obstacles, and just as the former regime felt compelled to introduce austerity measures, there was no chance the transitional government could avoid them.

Indeed, within days of coming to power Hamdok announced his commitment to rolling back subsidies, and this predictably led to growing bread shortages and increased fuel costs, all of which severely affected the poor and working class while the rich could ride out the economic chaos, as they did during the al-Bashir regime. These measures together with devaluing the Sudanese pound against the US dollar by almost 700 per cent resulted in skyrocketing prices for everyday goods including bread (Jahn and Kurtz, 9 April 2021).

It was not until six months after these austerity measures were introduced that the government met with representatives of the outraged civil society, thus making clear that the government viewed itself as primarily accountable to the Western IFIs and not the Sudanese citizenry which placed it in power. That meeting was meant to reassure the people of the good intentions of the government and distinguish it from the former regime, but the government did not bend to the concerns of the demonstrators, some of whom continued to go to the streets to express their dissatisfaction. The willingness of the civilian government to stare down the welfare concerns of the demonstrators together with the leading role of the military in the envisaged three-year transitional period provided further assurance to the United States that its liberal international order would be adhered to.

While the space for individual freedom expanded under the transitional government, the Strategic Initiative for Women in the HOA (SIHA) reported that crimes of gender-based violence against women by Sudanese security and military forces continued to be the norm in the public and private spheres across the country and that Sudan's notorious Sudan Public Order Law was still being implemented (Dabanga, 3 September 2021). Indeed, although women played a major role in the uprising, neither they nor people from the non-riverine core had a significant presence in the transitional government. Even key Western criteria for achieving democratic status such as a free press remained in doubt, appointment of the Legislative Council was extended to 2024, and the military remained powerful in both the political and economic spheres where it owns many industries.

The government committed itself to reaching peace agreements within six months of assuming office, but two years later it had only signed agreements with largely paper rebel organizations and failed to reach agreements with the two most powerful armed groups – the SPLM of Abdelaziz al-Hilu in the Nuba Mountains and South Blue Nile and the Sudan Liberation Movement of Abdel Wahid al-Nur in Darfur. The civilian component of the transitional government was excluded from the negotiations, which were held in Juba and led by Tut Gatluak, the security advisor to President Salva Kiir, who had been brought up in the home of al-Bashir (hence his nick name 'son of Bashir') and has long had close contacts with the al-Bashir security agencies. The agreements and subsequent appointments to the government and Sovereign Council increased the power of the generals in the transitional government.

Despite expectations of a positive response to the dismissal of the al-Bashir regime, the Trump administration made clear that the end to US sanctions was not dependent upon the coming to power of a post-al-Bashir transitional government committed to democracy or even its embrace of neoliberalism, but the incoming government must also recognize Israel. In the event, that was not a major problem and the new Foreign Minister, Asmaa Abdallah (trumpeted as the first woman foreign minister in Sudan's history and thus a mark of women's advancement in the country), was quick to signal the impending normalization of relations with Israel (Al-Jazeera, 9 September 2019). This was despite the fact that the prime minister had said that normalization could only be made by the transitional assembly which had not been appointed and by revoking the Israeli Boycott Act of 1958 which could only be done by an elected parliament. This was not accepted by the Americans and the Hamdok government again bent to the will of the United States and on 23 October 2020 announced that Sudan officially recognized Israel after a meeting between al-Burhan and Prime Minister Netanyahu in Uganda (Times of Israel, 4 February 2020).

Blackmailing Sudan into recognizing Israel is comparable to the US inducing Morocco to recognize Israel in return for Washington recognizing the country's illegal annexation of the former Spanish territory in the western Sahara, the Sahrawi Arab Democratic Republic (Marina Ottaway, 17 December 2020). In both cases these initiatives (called the Abraham Accords) were held by Washington to represent milestones on the road to Middle East peace, but in fact they demonstrated both the brute power of the United States and its willingness to overrule the sentiments of the people in both countries which remained staunchly anti-Israel. As Whitbeck explains, 'The only principle consistently adhered to by the U.S. government in such matters is the fundamental principle of contemporary international relations: It is not the nature of the act that matters but, rather, who is doing it to whom' (John Whitbeck, 24 February 2022).

The United States went on to press the financially starved Sudan transitional government reach agreements with the families of those killed in the 1998 US embassy bombings in Kenya and Tanzania, the 2000 bombing of the USS Cole because of 'alleged' material support for these attacks provided by the al-Bashir government and the killing of a USAID employee in Khartoum, although the perpetuators were jailed. That all of these alleged crimes were committed by the al-Bashir regime and that the Hamdok government and its supporters had overthrown that government and bore no responsibility for them were of no interest to the Americans. In late March 2021 US Secretary of State Antony Blinken announced that United States had received $335 million from Sudan as compensation for the victims of attacks that Washington linked to Khartoum (Middle East Eye, 31 March 2021). Hamdok apparently thought that this would lead to rapid financial assistance from the United States and IFIs to pay for his economic reforms, but the Americans were prepared to have his government collapse and wanted to see results before contributing.

The United States surprised the professionals and the youth by first tolerating the al-Bashir regime after it had been defanged, and second, by largely sub-contracting its policy to its autocratic Middle Eastern client states during the uprising and their primary concern was to ensure there was no democratic transition. 'By supporting the UAE-Saudi axis of counterrevolution, the US opposed democrats and supported tyrants while maintaining some form of distance and deniability' (Sam Hamad, 15 December 2021). Also shocking was the extent to which the United States would press a poverty-stricken – but pro-American – government to do its bidding.

After the uprising Sudan's transitional government ended its positive relations with Addis Ababa and began developing a strategic partnership with Egypt. Sudan's switch in alliances had little to do with its national interests and instead was a product of the role Egypt played in assisting the Sudanese military. As a result after supporting the construction of the Renaissance Dam under al-Bashir, Sudan condemned Ethiopia's position on the dam and demanded guarantees that Ethiopia reduce any adverse effects it might suffer (Ayah Aman, 3 November 2021). Egypt believes it needed to continue maintaining strong relations with the Sudanese military as part of its strategy to geo-politically encircle Ethiopia and pressure Addis Ababa to sign a binding agreement on the dam to secure water rights to the Nile (Andrew Edward, Yaw Tchie, and Jihad Mashamoun, 7 January 2022).

Like Hamdok the FFC did not want to harness the revolutionary forces unleashed by the uprising, but instead to contain them. Most of those who led the FFC had cooperated with Sudanese military regimes in the past or had been part of military regimes and were not in principle opposed to a transitional government composed of both civilians and generals. Indeed, Hamdok lauded the civilian-military transitional government, viewing it as a model, and went on to 'pay tribute to the role of all the regular forces in protecting democracy' (Sudan Tribune, 25 December 2019). But what was praiseworthy for Hamdok and the FFC was unacceptable to the youthful protestors. The FFC looked to the West, US client states in the region and the International Financial Institutions to ensure a peaceful transition. However, as one analyst has noted, 'The Sudanese political elite should carefully study the unfolding Afghan crisis and understand that prioritising international support over domestic needs and becoming overdependent on the international community can lay the path for the resurgence of fundamentalists triumphantly eulogising the failure of liberal democracy' (Kholood Khair, 3 September 2021).

Despite efforts to buttress his government with foreign support the transitional government was very fragile as Prime Minister Hamdok acknowledged. Speaking in Paris on 17 May 2021 he expressed fears that the country could experience another civil war between multiple armed groups and different factions of the military and said, 'The big question today is will Sudan exist or not exist?' (Yasir Zaidan, 13 July 2021). Hamdok was mistaken, however, in thinking that his government and the country were only threatened by armed groups and instead his government was also threatened by its inability to overcome Sudan's economic problems through a neoliberal restructuring of the economy which produced widespread discontent. In addition, a weak, divided civilian politics with a narrow focus on political advantage has since Sudan's independence fostered disenchantment and virtually encouraged the military to intervene.

The failures of the Hamdok government gave all sections of the opposition, particularly the only recently ousted Islamists, renewed confidence. In the wake of large anti-government demonstrations in July 2021, a senior official of the former regime emailed me on 4 July 2021 saying, 'Sudan is now warming up for a new regime change. A revolution is simmering and possibly already in the making. This time it is spearheaded by the Islamists.' My informant was not entirely mistaken and on 25 October 2021 al-Burhan's military carried out a coup. Acting on the belief that because the Sudanese were increasingly disenchanted due to declining living standards, increasing crime and power-hungry politicians, they would either support a military take-over or prove passive as they did in 1989 after the overthrow of the failed Sadig al-Mahdi government.

The military also could count on its regional backers – Egypt, Saudi Arabia, the UAE and Israel – because the generals were the guiding force behind Sudan normalizing relations with Tel Aviv in exchange for removal from the US list of state sponsors of terrorism (Joseph Krauss, 22 November 2021). Indeed, the UAE probably played the key role in both formulating the transitional arrangements and in reconciling the Sudanese military with Israel. al-Burhan may also have noted that the West did not condemn the coups of General-Abdel Fattah el-Sisi in Egypt in 2013 against Mohamed Mursi or that of the Zimbabwean military which overthrew President Robert Mugabe in 2017 (Christopher Rhodes, 3 December 2021).

However, in the face of massive street level resistance, the military reached out to Russia for support in similar fashion to that of al-Bashir four years earlier. On the day that the Russian Federation launched an invasion of Ukraine and the West announced new sanctions against Russia, General Hemedti announced his support of the invasion after a meeting in Moscow with Foreign Minister Sergey Lavrov who affirmed his country's interest in strengthening cooperation with Sudan in the areas of energy, agriculture and mining (Sudan Tribune, 25 February 2022). Analysts contended that Hemedti's visit was not only intended to improve Sudan's desperate economic situation, but also provided a means for him to gain a foreign supporter in his competition with al-Burhan (Mat Nashed, 16 March 2022).

With a supportive international network, continuing opposition from the street, and the failures of the Hamdok government, al-Burhan carried out a coup against his civilian partners in the transitional government on 25 October 2021. As well as placing most of the cabinet in prison and Hamdok under house arrest, al-Burhan released from prison leading figures associated with al-Bashir's NCP (Sudan Tribune, 31 October 2021). Additionally, al-Burhan placed generals, Islamists, and politically reliable people in state and federal institutions, the state-owned media and companies, the Central Bank, and restored the intelligence services' powers to arrest and detain.

The Sudanese were shocked at the measured response of the United States and UK to the coup and were further surprised when they welcomed an agreement on 21 November 2021 between al-Burhan and Prime Minister Hamdok to reformulate a military-civilian transitional government and appoint a 'technocratic' cabinet (Arab Press Updates, 17 December 2021). This was what al-Burhan had been demanding to ensure the security of the military, that they and their RSF allies would not be held accountable for their crimes and could continue to reap the benefits of their enormous financial holdings. What the Sudanese liberal democrats failed to understand in spite of ample evidence was, 'the US, under the logic of foreign policy realism, views democracy in the Middle East and North African region as a threat to stability and its interests' (Sam Hamad, 15 December 2021).

Hamdok contended, just as he had after his first agreement with the military, that it was necessary to protect lives (Murat Sofuoglu, 25 November 2022). Even though most of Hamdok's cabinet resigned in disgust, the FFC could not accept the agreement, and dozens of protestors were killed by the security forces, the United States and the West together with their client states in the Middle East sought to put a positive gloss on these developments. Indeed, it is likely that Hamdok's decision to surrender to al-Burhan was because he did not think he had the support of the United States and EU. The United States, EU and UN were relieved at Hamdok's agreement with al-Burhan since they had invested so much in the transitional government which allowed the military to foster the illusion that Sudan was still a civilian-led transition. Hamdok was also going up against US client states in the region, notably Egypt which worked tirelessly to provide political and diplomatic support to al-Burhan and to oppose mounting international pressure on him to end the coup and reinstate Hamdok (Khalil al-Anani, 22 December 2021). Meanwhile, the FFC and the resistance committees pressed for the end of military rule and for all militias, including the RSF, to be integrated into the Sudanese armed forces, which Hemedti opposed.

What Hamdok never understood was that his power depended on the street and not the West and the Arabs to whom he had sold Sudan's sovereignty, and when the street turned against him for selling out to the military, his days as prime minister were over and he resigned on 3 January 2022. Referring to the post-coup Hamdok agreement with al-Burhan, a demonstrator said, 'It has revealed that the conflict is not actually between the civilians and the military – as claimed by the FFC – but it is actually a conflict within a certain political class, unconcerned with the aspirations of the Sudanese people for a civilian rule' (Toward Freedom, 17 January 2022).

During the first stage of the uprising most of the demonstrators displayed considerable naivete in thinking that the realization of their demand for removing al-Bashir would usher in democracy and solve the country's ills. Due to their political immaturity, most believed that the West was a partner in their democratic struggle against the military and that made them amenable to manipulation. They were likewise mistaken in thinking that a civilian transitional government which linked Sudan's fate to an alliance of Saudi Arabia, the UAE, Egypt and the United States, and an economic policy determined by the IFIs, was a viable formula for a democratic transition.

A major difference between the coups that overthrew the governments of Sadig and Hamdok is that in 1989 the coup was a largely internal affair, while in the case of the coups of 2019 and 2021 regional states played a major role. According to the *Wall Street Journal* there were close consultations between Cairo and the Sudanese junta and al-Burhan followed a script laid down by el-Sisi (Benoit Faucon, Summer Said, and Joe Parkinson, 20 December 2021). As one analyst concluded, Cairo 'will not accept civilian authority, whatever the price, even if direct intervention is needed to abort it' (Khalil al-Anani, 21 December 2021).

During the wave of demonstrations that spread across the country in the wake of the 25 October 2021 coup, the youthful demonstrators showed they were not going to back down on their demand for a civilian government. Their 'Three Nos' – no negotiations, no partnership and no legitimacy for the military – made that clear (Muzan Alneel, 24 November 2021). But for many and maybe most of the demonstrators, achieving a civilian government was still their primary political objective, and only a minority stressed the need that the government be controlled by the people in the interest of the people and not in the interest of foreign powers and domestic powerbrokers.

Indeed, there were complementary interests of the United States, EU, Saudi Arabia, UAE and Egypt in not destabilizing the region by endorsing a genuine democratic transformation in Sudan. Moreover, on 28 October, the UN Security Council issued a statement (SC/14678) that did not refer to the army action of 25 October as a 'coup' and called on the military to 'restore the civilian-led transitional government on the basis of the Constitutional Document and other foundational documents of the transition' (Aljazeera, 28 October 2021). Similar sentiments were expressed in a statement released on 16 December 2021 by the United States, UK, Saudi Arabia and the UAE which formally approved the 21 November agreement between al-Burhan and Hamdok and their 'civilian-military partnership' (US Department of State, 16 December 2021). Although the UN established a peacemaking mechanism in the wake of the 25 October coup, it was quickly marginalized by the African Union which one analyst has called 'a club of dictators' whose task was to legitimize the junta (Khalid Mukhtar Salim, 30 July 2022). All of which made clear just how out of touch these organizations were with the sentiments of the people, particularly as represented by the resistance committees which across the board rejected any political initiative involving the military.

Against the failures of now three post-uprising civilian governments, it is not realistic to have any faith in the major Sudanese political parties, although the protestors were clear and correct in holding that the military should have no role in the governance of Sudan. Indeed, the resistance committees turned against the FFC as part of their deepening distrust of politicians and because they were staunchly opposed to any negotiations with the military. As a result, they opposed any peace initiative that involves power-sharing with the military. It remains to be seen, however, if the committees can move beyond their rejectionist politics to providing a map for Sudan's democratic transformation.

## *Conclusion*

According to Yoshiko Kurita, 'the Sudanese ruling classes, when faced with the upsurge of popular protest movements and unable to cope with them by ordinary means, were ready to take recourse even to military coup d'ètats, abandoning in that process the facade of democracy such as parliament, political parties, and respect for civil and political freedoms' (Yoshiko Kurita, 2019). The United States was equally disingenuous. Rhetoric about democracy and concerns with the human rights abuses of the NIF/NCP peaked during the second Clinton administration, both because of the adventurist foreign policy of al-Turabi and pressure from American liberal interventionists. But with the failure of both sanctions and proxies to displace the regime, President Bush addressed the issue through a peace process conducted by the region but dominated by the United States and its Western allies.

However, by the end of the Bush era, the elections of a Muslim Brotherhood president in Egypt, Hamas in Palestine and Hezbollah in Lebanon dampened support for democracy promotion. It was becoming increasingly clear to leading sections of the foreign policy establishment that democracy promotion conflicted with US national security interests. In any case, US support of the Abboud and Nimeiri dictatorships, opposition to the democratic government of Sadig al-Mahdi, leadership of a Sudan peace process which entrenched military regimes in Khartoum and Juba, and Washington's acceptance of NCP rule made clear that human rights and democracy in Sudan were at best secondary concerns for the US and at worst completely fraudulent.

The US-dictated Sudan's economic and foreign policies humiliated the post-al-Bashir civilian transitional government before the Sudanese people. That the demands were so crass speaks not only to Washington's arrogance, but an appreciation that Hamdok's government had nowhere else to go and if the prime minister objected to the demands, he could be readily replaced by the generals waiting in the wings. Although these actions were taken by a haughty Trump administration, they are consistent with US policy in Sudan over the past sixty-five years which does not accept developing countries having non-aligned foreign policies. Ultimately the political character of Sudanese governments and whether committed to democracy or not was of little concern to Washington so long as they met the interests of the United States and its regional client states.

At the core of the opposition in Sudan to authoritarian rule is a civil society which has proved strong enough to overthrow governments, but not strong enough to carry forward a transformative project. Since independence Sudanese civil society has had well-developed political parties, unions, academic associations, a critical media and a culture of openly debating political issues. However, civil society has always been centred in the riverine north and urban areas where education levels are high and government/military repression generally constrained. In the periphery it has been weak and barely existed in southern Sudan which has mostly been under martial law. Moreover, in recent years Sudanese civil society has been increasingly shaped by Western donors whose liberal values are superseding the collective, socialist and anti-imperialist values that underpinned the 1964 and 1985 uprisings.

The weakness of Sudanese youth movements has been its inability to move beyond Western values, emphasize national sovereignty and chart alternative conceptions on how society could be organized to meet Sudanese needs. Its strength during 2018–2019 and 2021–2022 was in neighbourhood resistance committees that operated with considerable independence, had a limited hierarchy, were largely leaderless and not controlled by the professional politicians. This made the resistance committees difficult to co-opt, but the inexperience of its members meant that its initial demands did not go beyond ending the al-Bashir regime. As a result, following the pattern of 1964 and 1985 the youthful protestors forced the military to jail al-Bashir, but had no influence on the resulting transitional government and the participation of the military in that government.

## Chapter 5

## SOUTH SUDAN: ANOTHER FAILED US DEMOCRACY PROJECT

The United States faced multi-decade opposition in Afghanistan and Iraq to its nation-building and democracy promotion policies, but over an even longer period from the second Clinton administration to the election of President Trump in 2016 the United States pursued not dissimilar policies in Sudan, southern Sudan and South Sudan. There were two main differences between US policies in Iraq and Afghanistan and those in South Sudan. First, in South Sudan these policies were not pursued by tanks and helicopter gunships and instead by an army of diplomats, international NGOs and peacemakers. And second, South Sudanese overwhelmingly supported these efforts and attempted to graft Western models of governance onto their very different country. Like Iraq and Afghanistan, however, US and Western efforts at nation-building and democracy promotion have failed and South Sudan has been left with an entrenched dictatorship, continuing war, economic collapse and has not had an election since 2010.

South Sudan encompasses large numbers of Nilotic, Bantu and other peoples. It has virtually no modern economy apart from a petroleum industry geared to exports, and its agricultural sector is largely made up of subsistence farming and traditional pastoralism. It is one of the poorest, most underdeveloped and isolated states on the planet. Most South Sudanese live in preindustrial rural isolation and often have conflictual relations with their neighbours or even within their own communities. Some like the Zande, Shilluk and Anywaa have a history of kingship and hierarchy, but the majority Dinka and Nuer have never established systems of permanent administration. South Sudan does not conform to any model of a nation-state and attempts by sections of the Dinka to impose a nation-state have led to endemic violence. While extended armed struggles have sometimes served to bring nationally heterogeneous societies together in Africa, under the leadership of the Dinka-based SPLM, the armed struggle fostered tensions which have made the country virtually ungovernable. It is thus hard to imagine a more unlikely candidate for the establishment of a Western-modelled democratic state, but this is what three US presidents and a host of American and Western diplomats and NGOs have attempted over three decades.

## Historical context

Sudan was made up of a polyglot of peoples brought together by the Ottoman, Egyptian and British empires, but the post-colonial state has been dominated by people from the same three groups – Shagiya, Jalien and Dangala – called the *Awlad al bahr* or 'children of the river' because they are from the country's riverine core. The departing British handed over state power to elites from these communities and they used state power as a tool of extraction of wealth from the periphery to the centre. Fearing the influence of Egypt, wanting to gain control of the Nile, and produce cotton for Lancashire cotton mills, the British colonial power oversaw a relatively high level of economic development and institutions of governance in the northern Sudanese riverine core.

The counterpart to a relatively developed riverine core rooted in Arabism and Islam was a destitute periphery that repeatedly responded with revolts, notably of the southern Sudanese in the 1950s and 1960s, the SPLM revolt of 1983, and rebellions in the Nuba Mountains, southern Blue Nile, eastern Sudan and Darfur. In part because it involved not only economic and political marginalization, but also issues of race (in the Sudanese sense where northern 'Arabs' were contrasted with Africans) and religion (the north being made up almost completely of Muslims and the African south of followers of traditional faiths, Christians and Muslims), the north-south conflict assumed central stage until the secession of South Sudan in 2011. In Sudan's march to independence in 1956 the few southern leaders permitted by the British a voice expressed fear of northern domination and demanded either federalism or independence. They received neither, were marginalized in the post-colonial governments and a low-level rebellion began even before Sudan's independence, and under the South Sudan Liberation Army (SSLA) or Anya-Nya an insurgency was launched in the 1960s to achieve southern Sudanese independence (John Markakis, 1987, pp. 207–10).

Independence was not achieved, but the Addis Ababa Agreement of 1972 granted southern Sudan autonomy and a multi-party elected parliamentary regional government. However, there were two problems with the agreement that made it unsustainable. First, northern Sudanese did not have comparable powers and as a result the agreement was opposed by the traditional northern elites. Second, Equatorians of southern Sudan contended they were dominated by the region's largest people, the Dinka, and demanded control of their own separate territory. Not only did these developments lead to the collapse of the Addis Ababa Agreement and set Sudan again on the road to war in 1983, but it caused distrust between the Equatorians and the Dinka that persists to the present.

Sudan's second civil war was led by the SPLM but breaking from the past the SPLM did not identify as a southern Sudanese party even though almost all its members came from southern Sudan and the Nuba Mountains, and under its leader, Dr John Garang, it struggled for a united New Sudan. From the outset, the SPLM bore the imprint of its biggest foreign supporter, the Ethiopia Derg, and that meant pursuit of a united Sudan and adoption of a Marxist ideology of the type favoured by the Ethiopians, that is, statist, centralized and beholden to Addis Ababa and its Eastern Bloc supporters (John Young, 2005a). With this backing the SPLM achieved some military successes, but most were due to the direct engagement of supporting armies from Eritrea, Ethiopia and Uganda. Garang's dedication to unity was also held to be necessary to gain support in northern Sudan and ease concerns that the SPLM intended on breaking from the Arab world, but in the wake of the earlier failure of federalism he was repeatedly challenged by southern Sudanese who wanted the SPLM to commit to southern Sudanese national self-determination.

Garang's commitment to a united Sudan together with his authoritarian rule set the stage for the biggest schism in the SPLM when in August 1991 Drs Riek Machar and Lam Akol and General Gordon Kong broke from the movement (John Young, 2012, pp. 54–7). Although probably most southern Sudanese shared what was called the Nasir group's pro-secessionist sensitivities, Garang held the brunt of the movement together and the Nasir group was forced into an alliance with the Khartoum Islamists. The split made clear not only the ideological divisions within the southern movement but the fragility of the national alliance on which the SPLM was constructed because it unleashed a war between Dinka, particularly Garang's Bor Dinka, and the Nuer of Riek and Gordon. In time, however, the mainstream SPLM was forced to endorse national self-determination of southern Sudan, although Garang – but few of his colleagues – continued to reject secession.

Self-determination was not the only divisive issue and allegations of Dinka domination were a constant during the 1983–2005 civil war. This led to a host of local-based militias being established in greater Equatoria and other parts of the country opposed to the SPLM, and most significantly the founding of the South Sudan Defense Forces (SSDF) (John Young, 2005b). Although made up mostly of Nuer, it brought together groups from virtually every corner of southern Sudan under the loose leadership of General Paulino Matieb. While opposition to Dinka domination was its primary focus, the SSDF was a strong proponent of an independent southern Sudan, even while it was supported by Khartoum. The national government, actually the Military Intelligence, never permitted the SSDF to develop a political wing, but its leaders often doubled as administrators in their territories and although dubbed as 'warlords' often had considerable local support. In time the SSDF had a comparable number of fighters as the SPLM, and by the final years of the war, it was the SSDF and not the Sudanese army that largely confronted the SPLM.[1]

## US enters the fray

It is not obvious why the United States would devote so much political and financial capital and the direct engagement of three presidents to a territory with less than 12 million people in central Africa with little strategic or economic

---

1. I worked as a monitor with the US-supported Civilian Protection Monitoring Team between 2004 and 2006 and I estimate that 70 per cent of the conflicts we investigated during that period were between the SSDF and SPLM.

significance. Although claims have been made that the oil of southern/South Sudan or its position on the upper reaches of the Nile explain US engagement in the country, by international standards South Sudan's oil is not significant and US legal prohibitions against investment in Sudan meant that the oil concessions had long since been taken by others – largely China, India and Malaysia. Meanwhile, the battle over the Nile is largely a contest between Egypt and Ethiopia (the first as the primary consumer of the Nile waters and the latter as the overwhelming producer), and the role of South Sudan is at best secondary.

Instead, the disproportionate US interest in the country must be explained by security concerns and fears that Sudan's civil war was producing a failed state that threatened to destabilize neighbouring client states. But also influential were notions of the United States as the bearer of a torch of world freedom and that its unmatched global power bestowed on the United States the responsibility to come to the aid of the victimized southern Sudanese. Reinforcing that perspective, secularists largely linked to the Democratic Party, and evangelicals with ties to George Bush's Republican Party pressed their own agendas and both served to give ideological cover for US imperialism.

It was a secular lobby group – the Friends of South Sudan – with close links to the Democratic Party, particularly Susan Rice, that proved crucial in highlighting the plight of southern Sudanese during the second term of the Clinton presidency (John Young, 2019, pp. 47–51). The Friends of South Sudan were in the first instance inspired by the charismatic SPLM Chairman, Dr John Garang, and believed that the United States had a key role to play in resolving the southern conflict. But they had a major problem in promoting Garang in the United States because he identified as a Marxist-Leninist and was allied to the ruthless Ethiopian Derg which was backed by the Soviet Bloc. Moreover, the SPLA had a long record of human rights abuses. By the 1990s many human rights organizations had published studies of SPLA abuse of civilians, ethnic cleansing, mass rape, large scale theft, killing of aid workers, diversion and sale of humanitarian aid, and the killing of prisoners of war (John Young, 2019, p. 45). With the collapse of the Eastern Bloc and the Derg in 1991, Garang was desperate to expand his foreign support network and the liberal interventionists who would form the Friends of South Sudan were a ready partner.

It speaks to their public relations skills, political connections and the naivete of many Americans, including the US Congress, that the Friends overcame these obstacles and transformed Garang into a democrat and an African hero. Equally contrived was the contention that the SPLA was conducting a united struggle of the southern Sudanese for national self-determination. Garang was authoritarian, southern Sudan was deeply divided, and until after his death the SPLM was committed to a united New Sudan, not a secessionist South Sudan. South Sudan was divided along both ethnic and political lines, and the notion that the SPLM was a unifying force could only be maintained by refusing to acknowledge that much of the fighting in southern Sudan was between southern Sudanese and many of these fighting forces, including the SSDF, were aligned with the northern army (Young, 2012). Moreover, northern Sudanese 'Arabs' also struggled against the Khartoum regime, but their struggles did not fit the prevailing north-south Arab-African narrative. As a result, they were largely discounted in the West even though the SPLM was a member of the northern-dominated opposition National Democratic Alliance (NDA) and Garang was the head of its military wing.

The Friends of South Sudan had a direct route to the presidency through Susan Rice and John Prendergast who was appointed by Rice to the National Security Council. The Friends exerted influence in the Congress through Ted Dagne who served as the very influential head of the US Congressional Research Service. The Friends' perspectives and support for the SPLM were highlighted in the Department of Agriculture and USAID by senior officials Brian D'Silva and Roger Winters. And the message of the Friends was widely and effectively disseminated through the writing skills of English Professor Eric Reeves who had only spent two weeks in southern Sudan but was considered an authority on the civil war and regularly appeared before the US Congress as an expert. The Friends also briefly had a direct engagement with the Government of South Sudan when, with the support of Susan Rice, Ted Dagne served as a presidential advisor to Salva Kiir (Sudan Tribune, 12 August 2012). Dagne's career, however, ended abruptly, and he was forced to flee the country after he sent a letter in Salva's name to hundreds of present and former SPLM leaders asking that they return an estimated $4 billion President Salva Kiir said had been stolen from the South Sudan government to a Kenyan bank account (Sudan Tribune, 20 August 2012).

Despite their long and considerable involvement in Sudanese affairs the Friends' misunderstanding of the SPLA was graphically expressed by Roger Winters who in Congressional testimony in 2009 said, 'The people of the SPLM are democrats. They respect the kind of approach to governance that is taken in the United States of America' (Roger Winters, 29 July 2009). Prendergast went on to form the Enough Project and the Satellite Sentinel Project, quickly dubbed 'NGOs for the stars' because of the high-profile membership of George Clooney and Angelina Jolie who like Reeves became instant 'experts' on South Sudan and appeared before Congressional hearings. For his role in spreading disinformation and causing great confusion over US policy on Sudan and South Sudan, Prendergast was awarded seven honorary doctorates (Enough Project).

## Mythologizing South Sudan's conflicts

Support for the SPLA and highlighting the issue of southern Sudan in the United States served as a means for liberal Americans to confront issues of racism in their own society just as Zionist support for persecuted Darfuri Muslims through the Save Darfur Coalition cast in a positive light their defence of Israel, widely viewed as a racist state (Mahmood Mamdani, 2010). While the future Black Lives Matter (BLM) and their white liberal supporters found in America's civil war a moral basis from which to launch their movement, an earlier generation of liberals found in southern Sudan a conflict that mirrored problems of racial injustice in the United

States. Moreover, by standing up for Black Africans they affirmed their liberalism and belief in the benefice of the United States and of US exceptionalism. That these activists had little understanding of southern Sudan and its conflicts would soon become clear, but not before the Clinton administration had been replaced by that of George W. Bush and his evangelical constituency which held that the conflict in southern Sudan was rooted in Muslim oppression of Christians.

The American Christian link with southern Sudan began with the support of American churches in the World Council of Churches peace mediation that ended the first war between northern and southern Sudan in 1972 at Addis Ababa. More significant was the involvement in Sudan of the US international NGO Samaritans Purse operated by Franklin Graham, son of Billy Graham, an intimate over his long life with thirteen presidents, particularly President George W. Bush, and was known as the 'pastor to presidents' (BGEA, 21 February 2018). With the end of the Cold War, evangelicals who constitute 25 per cent of the US population shifted their ire from Communism to Islam and the al-Bashir Islamists were an easy target given the widespread human rights abuses of the regime (Ivar Iverson, 1 January 2007). Advocacy by the evangelicals and other Christians led to the passing of the International Religious Freedom Act in 1998 which required the US government to prepare annual lists of 'countries of concern' and that increased the focus on Sudan. Nina Shea from Freedom House and later from the Hudson Institute declared Sudan to be 'the world's most violent abuser of the right to freedom of religion and belief' (quoted in Melani McAlister, 2008). Racist portrayals of Islam were common, and the Grahams publicly expressed the view that Islam was 'evil and wicked' (Franklin Graham, 3 October 2010).

Always ideologically flexible, the SPLA under John Garang which had previously presented itself as Marxists to gain support from the Ethiopian Derg, and then as heroic African democrats to win the favour of the Democratic Party and its liberal lobby groups, rapidly switched gears upon the coming to power of Bush and his evangelical followers. As a result, the SPLA used 'Christianity and the bad Muslim/good Christian narrative to generate support for their cause in the US' (MERP, 2012). Critical to the mobilization of American evangelicals was the campaign to free supposed southern Sudanese slaves as widely reported in the Western media. John Eibner, the US director of Christian Solidarity International (CSI), claimed to have redeemed 80,000 slaves and defended CSI's actions in terms of Christian charity and the R2P declaration (Allen Hertzke, 2004). Elements of slavery and forced wife-taking have existed in parts of Sudan for generations, but often these actions are resolved later through reconciliation conferences. However, much of the slave-taking highlighted by CSI was subsequently revealed to be organized by pale skinned SPLA commanders who took payments from CSI to free the 'slaves', but not before many in the West, including American school children, contributed to CSI (The Irish Times, 23 February 2002).

These actions and beliefs also reinforced the 'clash of civilization' thesis of Huntington which held that the countries in the Islamic and Christian world were in a global conflict, and in the case of Sudan the conflict was characterized as a

Muslim north persecuting a Christian south.[2] This portrayal found favour across the US political divide even though Christians only formed a minority in southern Sudan and the flexible (one might say open-minded) southern Sudanese typically did not draw the hard, fast and bitter lines between religions that were the norm in the United States and the West. As elsewhere in Africa, evangelical churches, often supported by Americans, are growing quickly in South Sudan and Franklin Graham is a powerful figure, having met President Omar al-Bashir many times to advocate for the country's Christians and he has also prayed with President Salva Kiir and First Vice President Riek Machar (Antony Loewenstein, 18 March 2015).

## US-sponsored South Sudan peace process

Appreciating that lining up with the Christians in the United States and southern Sudan would not only alienate northern Sudanese Muslims, many of whom were sympathetic to the United States and looked upon it as a means to dislodge the hated Islamist regime, but also cast him in a poor light in the Middle East, President Bush opted to support a peace process to resolve the conflict. The instrument he chose was the regional-based Inter-Governmental Authority on Development (IGAD), an organization which had been proposed by the West, funded by the West, directed by the West, and during the Sudan peace process the United States, UK and Norway participated directly in the negotiations as a Troika (John Young, 2012, pp. 354–5). Moreover, the mediation was led by Kenyan General Lazarus Sumbeiywo, who had spent much of his career defending the aging dictator and US client, President Daniel arap Moi, and had a history of working closely with the CIA (John Young, 2019, p. 91). The United States could thus be confident that IGAD would protect its interests and at the same time leave the impression that African states were leading the peace process along the lines of the much favoured 'African solutions for African problems'.

Crucially this exercise in liberal peacemaking was not only limited to ending the Sudan conflict, but included issues of governance, creating political institutions, defining their authority, and establishing links between political units and the international community. The role of Kenya, Djibouti, Uganda and sometimes Ethiopia in hosting US military bases, to intelligence cooperation between Khartoum and Washington, to the close security relationship between Addis Ababa and Washington and later Nairobi and Kampala in Somalia, made clear that peacemaking, much less democracy, were only elements in the pursuit of a broad set of American interests in the region.

---

2. The author was in Khartoum at the time of the US bombing of the al-Shifa pharmaceutical plant and met with US diplomats and later their counterparts in Nairobi after the evacuation of the US Sudan embassy and they frequently made references to Huntington's clash of civilization thesis in explaining these developments.

Democratization was ostensibly at the core of the peace agreement between the NCP and the SPLM which the United States, its Western allies and IGAD oversaw and made clear in the Machakos Protocol, the statement of principles on which the CPA was based. The Protocol is replete with references to 'democratic governance, accountability, equality, respect and justice for all citizens of Sudan' (CPA, Section 1.1, 2005) and that Sudan 'establish a democratic system of governance' (CPA, Section 1.6, 2005).

But this commitment to democracy was immediately contradicted by the reality of a peace process which was elite driven, not only denied popular engagement, but, apart from the NCP and SPLM, denied even the participation of other political parties and armed groups, and was run by a Kenyan general obsessed with secrecy. Moreover, there could be nothing democratic about handing over power to the SPLM, an organization which took the form of a largely Dinka military cabal which the United States and its allies mistakenly concluded represented the will of the disparate peoples of southern Sudan. The SPLA only controlled a portion of the territory it was given to rule by the international community's peace agreement and was feared and hated by a large section of the non-Dinka population.

Crucially the mediators did not permit the SSDF a place at the negotiating table, contending that although of similar size to the SPLA it was northern dominated, forgetting that not only was the SPLA a member of the northern-dominated NDA, but by isolating the Nuer-led SSDF the mediators virtually ensured a post-agreement conflict between the Dinka and Nuer.[3] The monopoly position of the SPLA in the negotiations also angered people in Equatoria where tensions had reached new heights during the war after Dinka pastoralists followed the SPLA soldiers into Equatoria in search of grazing lands and water and clashed with local farmers.

When questioned about the emphasis on democratization in the Machakos Protocol one senior NCP official said that it had already figured prominently in Sudan's 1998 constitution and did not constitute a concession by the government (even though it was clearly not practised), while a government negotiator said it was inserted at the request of a South African mediator (Nicholas Haysom, who subsequently became head of the UN Mission in South Sudan) but had little relevance for either the belligerents or the Americans. An NCP negotiator told me at the time, 'there was no real democratic conviction on either side', surely an accurate assessment and one that the United States and its Western partners ignored. But such was the level of cynicism that the Machakos Protocol and the subsequent peace agreement were sold as the basis for a democratic transformation in Sudan and should it vote to secede, an independent South Sudan. But instead

---

3. The size of ethnic groups in South Sudan is highly contentious and made more problematic by weak statistics, considerable intermarriage, the capacity of South Sudanese to change their ethnicity, and the often marked divisions within ethnic communities. However, most would accept that the Dinka are the largest ethnic group, followed by the Nuer and Azande.

of viewing the Protocol and the CPA as a formula for democracy, they served to galvanize opposition across the south and north by those who feared that the entire national pie was being divided between two unaccountable parties, the NCP and the SPLA.

One of the most serious problems of the model of democracy bequeathed South Sudan is that its neoliberal focus did not address the overwhelming poverty of the country and unequal development which has long been a factor in fuelling both north-south and south-south conflicts. As befitting neoliberalism, the prevailing assumption was that to the extent that endemic poverty and economic inequality in the country were of concern, they would be resolved by the market. And the South Sudanese elite anxious to demonstrate its ideological soundness and understanding the need to keep their American benefactors on board repeatedly voiced their commitment to market-driven development. The problem was that apart from a handful of farmers in Equatoria, most rural South Sudanese were largely self-sufficient peasants, herders whose animals were raised to meet traditional needs, supported by the international aid agencies, by their relatives living abroad or lived in UN refugee and IDP camps. Not only could such an underdeveloped market not begin to overcome South Sudan's economic problems, but the model of governance bequeathed by the CPA (as befitting neoliberalism) did not envisage an activist state, which alone could have made a difference.

Bush had hoped that US leadership of the peace process would prove politically beneficial at a time when the United States was widely criticized for its failed policies in the Muslim world. In the event, by the time the CPA was signed in January 2005 US television screens were filled with images of a humanitarian crisis in Darfur and celebrating peace in southern Sudan would appear cavalier and not provide the desired political pay-off. Instead of basking in the glory of a peacemaker Bush imposed new economic sanctions on Sudan in May 2007 which blocked assets of Sudanese citizens implicated in the Darfur violence and sanctioned companies owned or controlled by the Government of Sudan (CNN, 29 May 2007). Although Garang had been proclaimed an African hero by the Americans, Bush maintained close relations with his successor, Salva Kiir, who he described as a 'friend' and a 'strong leader' (The White House, 5 January 2009). The Bush administration oversaw the peace process and prepared the ground for the 2011 referendum on the secession of southern Sudan, but it was under the watch of President Obama that it was carried out and it was his team that basked in the fulfilment of the peace process.

But before the 2011 referendum under the CPA the signatories were pressured to hold a national election which both opposed. The election caused the SPLM leadership a problem since from its inception the party had been firmly committed to a united reformed Sudan and with the large recent intake of new members from northern Sudan as a result of the peace agreement there was little doubt that was also the view of the majority of the members. But after Garang died, that was not the view of the southern based SPLM leadership under Salva Kiir which was almost universally in favour of secession, and it was their view that carried. Salva therefore did not run against al-Bashir for the presidency in the 2010 national elections and instead ran for the southern Sudan presidency, while an SPLM loyalist from the north, Yasir Arman, served as the party's candidate (Sudan Tribune, 14 January 2010). However, that caused another problem since Yasir performed surprisingly well in the campaign and if he had won on behalf of the SPLM, it would have been difficult to then call for southern Sudan's secession. As a result, he was pressured by both the NCP and the SPLM leadership to drop out of the campaign to ensure an al-Bashir victory, but officially because of claimed NCP rigging in Darfur (BBC, 31 March 2010).

Key to gaining international legitimacy for elections in developing countries (but not in the developed West) is that they be approved by international election observer missions. And during the 2010 national elections I served as the political advisor to The Carter Center, one of the international groups observing the election. That experience confirmed the emphasis of Schumpeter and Huntington on the technical focus of the exercise and commitment to the orderly circulation of elites approved by the West. As a result, a 'good' election from the perspective of international monitoring organizations is not necessarily one that represents the democratic will of the people, and instead is determined by whether the campaigning parties meet a series of technical requirements. This sometimes has the effect of training indigenous operatives on how best to game the system to gain the approval of the international community.

In that respect the NCP was far more proficient than the SPLM. The most effective cheating is carried out during the voter registration because election observation missions do not have the resources to follow this exercise, particularly in a large country with limited transport and communications like Sudan. The NCP concentrated on fixing the voter registration and for the most part got away with it, while the SPLM resorted to stealing and stuffing ballot boxes.

Ruling on the 2010 Sudan national elections placed the international observers in a quandary – if they ruled that the election was unfair, and there was considerable evidence to indicate that was the case – the peace process might collapse and the parties return to war. But if the monitors endorsed the election, the international community would be making clear that its concern with security and keeping the peace process on track trumped its commitment to the conduct of a fair election as an important step in realizing democracy. While the internationals forced the unwilling NCP and SPLM to hold an election, the parties turned the tables and left the internationals with seemingly little option but to endorse what was clearly a flawed process.[4]

---

4. The Carter Center engaged in an internal debate over whether to endorse the elections and finally it concluded that the elections were fair except in Darfur. This was the conclusion that was reached in its report the day after the election, but after a lot of number crunching in the final report, which unfortunately few pay any attention to, it was concluded that the 2010 'election process was highly chaotic, non-transparent, and vulnerable to electoral manipulation and as a result the Center was concerned about the accuracy of the preliminary results announced by the National Elections Commission' (Carter Center, 10 May 2010).

Instead of considering democratic transformation as a necessary condition for sustainable peace as held by the proponents of liberal peacemaking, the international sponsors of the Sudan peace process, the ruling parties and the election observation missions passed over the election rigging. As well as endorsing and bestowing legitimacy on the resulting dictatorships in Khartoum and Juba, the election set the stage for the referendum and its inevitable outcome of a 99 per cent vote for the secession of southern Sudan (Josh Kron and Jeffrey Gettleman, 21 January 2011).

The vote in favour of South Sudan's secession was portrayed internationally as ushering in not only a new state, but a budding democracy and evidence of the collective endorsement of the South Sudanese of the new state under the leadership of the SPLM. It was also hailed as a great political and moral victory of the democratic West and particularly Washington which had led the peace process (Rebecca Hamilton, 9 July 2011). With the referendum completed the SPLM government of the soon-to-be fully independent South Sudan could begin to overcome the legacy of war and division and with the continuing support of the West rise to the challenge. But the illusions did not last long.

Contrary to this perspective, the referendum vote was an affirmation of the people's African character in a Sudanese state that downgraded their African identity and gave primacy to Arabism and Islam. The vote did not represent any overcoming of ethnic identities and even less did it represent an endorsement of the SPLM. The West had only permitted the SPLM to serve as the vehicle to gain national self-determination and thus the South Sudanese had little option but to accept its key role in that process. Moreover, despite the mistaken efforts of the United States and its Western allies the peace process deepened the distrust that many held for the SPLM. Indeed, in terms of the objectives of liberal peacemaking and the links drawn between liberal peacemaking and democratization, the election must be viewed as a failure. And after a brief flurry while American politicians, groups like the Friends of South Sudan and other international NGOs took a collective bow for their great achievements in ushering in the democratic state of South Sudan, they endeavoured to dissociate themselves from this engagement and hoped that it would soon be forgotten. Moreover, the completion of the election and referendum unleashed a rush for the spoils of the state by the incoming southern Sudanese elites.

The CPA was underpinned by three assumptions that quickly proved false. First, the various peoples that made up southern Sudan constituted a nation for purposes of national self-determination and statehood. Second, the central contradiction afflicting Sudan, and thus the cause of the war, was conflict between an 'Arab' Muslim north and an African and religiously heterogeneous south. And third, the assumption that the SPLA – to whom the international mediators handed over complete power in the fledgling state – was capable of administering the territory and carrying out a democratic transformation.

In spite of enormous international goodwill led by the United States and vast oil resources which made South Sudan in macro-economic terms probably the richest country in East Africa, SPLM governance was so bad that a crisis was already well advanced before the end of the CPA-stipulated six-year transitional period. This was not unexpected for any discerning observer since the SPLM failed to develop functioning and popular governance bodies in its liberated territories during its long war with the north. Unlike liberation movements that took power in neighbouring Eritrea, Ethiopia and Uganda and utilized their experience in public administration acquired during the war years when they assumed state authority, the SPLM gained little experience from which to administer a state government and instead was and remained highly dependent on the international community.

Learning from the Islamist north, the SPLM set about constructing a state that privileged a Dinka elite who looted the country's resources and used its party-army and ruthless intelligence services to contain the increasing revolts and lawlessness in the peripheries (John Young, 2019). The human rights abuses of the SPLM/SPLA were well known to the United States as made clear in the 2011 State Department Country Study of South Sudan which identified politically motivated abductions, government restrictions on the press, speech, assembly and association, harsh prison conditions, a corrupt judiciary, restrictions and harassment of NGOs, widespread violence against women and girls, discrimination and violence against ethnic minorities and homosexuals, government incitement of tribal violence, and child and forced labour (State Department, 2011). Reinforcing this, the UN Human Rights Office of the High Commissioner reported that members of South Sudan's government committed human rights violations 'amounting to war crimes' in the country's southwest, including abuses against children (UN Human Rights Office of the High Commissioner, 18 March 2022).

While the operations of the government were stymied by rampant kleptocracy, ethnic divisions, political battles, and limited communications between even President Salva Kiir and his First Vice-President, Riek Machar, the SPLM was ever sensitive to meeting the politically correct demands of its US sponsors. Thus, the National Assembly passed measures to ensure that 25 per cent of its members were female, established a gender ministry, and laws provided for the protection of women and girls against discrimination, forced marriage and gender-based violence, but the UNDP concluded that these legal provisions were 'often misinterpreted or ignored' (UNDP, August 2017). Other popular Western imports included a human rights commission that did nothing while the government arrested people at random, shut down newspapers, and arrested and killed journalists. The Western benefactors of the regime were particularly keen on introducing the latest approaches to overcoming corruption and as a result an anticorruption commission was established and staffed with highly educated young people who were provided with the latest technology, but alas the commission reported that it was stymied by the government and in 2008 nobody had been prosecuted in the previous three years (Skye Wheeler, 13 March 2008).

In the early years of independence when oil prices topped $100 a barrel Salva's kleptocratic government thrived even while the people of South Sudan gained little. But oil prices soon crashed and Salva was reduced to begging his present and former colleagues to return some of the $4 billion they had stolen from state coffers (see above). And without money to buy off critics, especially those who might go to the countryside and launch insurgencies, the government faced a deepening crisis. The crisis affected all the people of South Sudan, but it was the powerful Nuer people led by Riek Machar that provided the biggest threat to the regime.

## Civil war in South Sudan

It had long been apparent that the SPLM was not living up to US expectations and had completely ignored its commitment to democratization, but even the outbreak of the December 2013 civil war did not end American support. Indeed, while serving as Obama's Secretary of State, Hillary Clinton repeatedly overrode the Child Soldiers Prevention Act that banned military assistance to nations that use child soldiers even though US government agencies regularly documented that the SPLA before and after South Sudan's independence, and even after civil war broke out, employed child soldiers (Intercept, 9 June 2016). This was surprising because Clinton had publicly spoken in 2011 against child soldiers in South Sudan. Each waiver to ensure the flow of aid was justified on the grounds it was in 'the national interest of the United States' (Intercept, 9 June 2016) and was needed to help South Sudan transition to a civilian and democratic state and carry out necessary security sector reforms. As a result, the United States provided $620 million in assistance to South Sudan in 2012 and $556 million in 2013, of which $40 to $60 million was military assistance (Congressional Research Service, 22 September 2016). With the advent of the Trump presidency interest in South Sudan markedly declined.

This support, according to the State Department's 2013 Congressional Budget Justification, was designed to promote 'a military that is professionally trained and led, ethnically balanced, aware of moral imperatives, and able to contribute positively to national and South-South reconciliation' (Nick Turse, 18 May 2015). That rationale collapsed when a unit trained by the US military, the Presidential Guard, killed 'thousands' of unarmed Nuer civilians in Juba in mid-December 2013 according to the UN.[5] According to President Salva Kiir and backed up by the Friends of South Sudan this killing spree was the result of an attempted coup by his First Vice President Riek Machar. But the most exhaustive study carried out of the conflict by the African Union Commission found no evidence of an attempted coup and instead attributed the killings to a concerted plan by the government (AU Commission of Inquiry, 2014).

Nonetheless, the United States was there for the regime when Nuer quickly prepared for a revenge attack on the Dinka of Juba led by the 'white army', an irregular youth army drawn from the east bank of the Nile that was not controlled

---

5. In responding to the number killed, Hilde Johnson, special representative of the UN secretary-general in South Sudan and a strong supporter of the SPLM, said, 'We say thousands, but we do not know. We are deliberately not flagging numbers in any of our reports' (African Union, 2014).

by Riek or any other politician and instead by elected youth at the local level (John Young, 2016). The United States responded by bringing pressure on a range of actors to contain the white army, particularly Peter Gadet, a senior Nuer officer in the SPLA who had close links to the youth, while President Yoweri Museveni of Uganda sent his army to Juba to protect Salva Kiir's regime. Together they ensured that Juba was not attacked and the Salva kleptocracy survived. Thus began a two-year-long war between the remnants of the SPLA (many Nuer soldiers in the SPLA quickly defected to the opposition) and the white army and the remaining forces of the SPLA and militias under the control of Salva. Hundreds of thousands died before the United States and IGAD managed to press the parties to sign an agreement – the Agreement for the Resolution of Conflict in South Sudan or ARCSS on 26 August 2015 in Juba (ACCORD, 19 October 2016). Under ARCSS Salva was designated president and Riek the first of four vice-presidents, and power at the national- and state-level governments was divided between the government, SPLM-IO and some smaller parties.

But forcing the parties to the table did not overcome the distrust between Salva and his enemies and Salva obstructed the implementation of the agreement. As a result Riek had good reason to believe that his security and that of the SPLM-IO would be threatened if he returned to Juba. Those dangers, however, were ignored by Secretary of State John Kerry who pressed Riek to return to Juba, an action which in retrospect can be viewed as criminal. These pressures continued even though Human Rights Watch reported that in breach of the agreement between ten and twelve thousand SPLA forces were hiding in Juba dressed as civilians (Human Rights Watch, 15 August 2016).

Riek relented to overwhelming pressure from Washington as well as European and African capitals and returned to Juba. But Salva's opposition to the agreement and unwillingness to share government with his first vice president led to the widely predicted breakdown of ARCSS and another round of SPLA killing of Nuer civilians in Juba on 8 July 2016 (Human Rights Watch, 15 August 2016). In response Riek and his forces fled on a long march to the Congo under continuous attack by the SPLA. Never condemning the role of Salva and the SPLA in the breakdown of the agreement, Kerry went on to support Salva's appointment of Taban Deng, Riek's disloyal first lieutenant, to the position of first vice president, in another US-sanctioned breach of ARCSS (Daily Nation, 26 August 2016).

At this stage the United States gave up on the peace process and opted to let Salva and Taban give war a chance and eliminate Riek and the SPLM-IO, but in the event, they were not entirely successful. The SPLM-IO was weakened, but few in Riek's alliance defected to Taban and since the IO could not be defeated there was a need for another peace agreement. The authors of the agreement called it the Revitalized ARCSS and it was signed on 30 August 2018 by Riek and Salva (ACCORD, 11 February 2019). But minor insurgencies, insecurity and a growing humanitarian crisis did not end. US support for the Salva regime continued until the advent of Trump who felt no loyalty to the SPLM and was probably baffled at the enormous amount of money spent on supporting the regime and how instead of producing a democratic transformation it led to kleptocracy and war.

It is not the concern of this study to analyse the specific reasons for the failure of the R-ARCSS except to note that the entire approach to the construction of a Western-modelled state and peacebuilding in South Sudan has been beset by fundamental contradictions that have been studiously ignored by IGAD, the Western promoters of these efforts and local actors whose interests have rarely been beyond their narrow power and rent seeking. The implementation of R-ARCSS was to be completed before February 2023, after which national elections were to be held.

The failure to implement the agreement must foremost be the responsibility of Salva Kiir who was granted 60 per cent of state power and complete control over the state security apparatus. That said, Salva's repeated resort to violence to achieve his ends and stay in power speak to the weakness of state institutions, the absence of any attempt at formulating a ruling ideology, the fractured state of South Sudanese society which regularly throw up dissidents, and his ethnically divided army.

The implications of yet another failed Western instigated round of peacebuilding are clear: by late 2022 more than 400,000 South Sudanese had lost their lives in a continuing civil war, one-third of the country's 12 million people were displaced, and according to the UN in April 2022 more than the 7.7 million people – some 63 per cent of the population – faced a food crisis (Al-Jazeera, 9 April 2022). There was a mere 300 kilometres of paved road in a country of similar size to France (African Center for Strategic Studies, 13 September 2021). That road is between Juba and Nimule and was constructed by USAID, and its chief function is to provide an all-weather road link to Uganda to meet the commodity needs of the SPLM elite and a small urban population.

The regime has been linked to the murder of journalists and repeatedly told potential anti-government demonstrators they would be shot if they went to the streets. It has done nothing to advance the peace process or end an insurgency in Equatoria and its rule has been described by the International Crisis Group as 'slush-fund governance' (ICG, 6 October 2021). Meanwhile, Transparency International's 2021 Corruption Perceptions Index, which measures the perception of public sector corruption according to experts and businesspeople, found South Sudan was at the bottom of the list of 180 countries, making it the most corrupt country in the world (Rachael Bunyan, 25 January 2022). And despite a wealth of natural resources, South Sudan was deemed the second poorest country in the world in 2022 (Luca Ventura, 5 August 2022).

As well as the security forces, the critical tool employed by Salva and his dictatorial counterparts elsewhere was his power over appointments to the national bank and finance ministry. With this power he controlled the rate at which the local currency is traded and the access to foreign exchange which allowed him to confer benefits on friends, deny them to enemies and build a loyal band of followers even while his policies cripple the economy, a well-tested model for African kleptocrats (Robert Bates, 2010). Following a well-beaten path of dictators, Salva had 'converted markets into political machines', but in so doing has fostered the opposition that may eventually drive him from power.

Even the liberal lobby groups that played an outsize role in championing the struggles of the SPLA and sided with Salva Kiir in the civil war have been forced to change track and find other worthy causes which the United States could be prevailed upon to solve, without however acknowledging their years of misrepresentation and the harm they had caused. Although President Biden was vice-president for eight years while the Obama Administration supported the SPLA, South Sudan has not figured in his foreign policy concerns.

## South Sudan's future

The United States has been anxious to forget its harmful role in peacemaking, state-building, democracy promotion and overseeing the secession of South Sudan. As a result, the country has largely been left to its own devices, second-string diplomats, UNMISS (United Nations Mission in South Sudan) and a host of international NGOs. UNMISS and the international NGOs provide a kind of second-order government, delivering the services the Juba government either cannot or will not provide, as well as ensuring a modicum of security in a largely lawless South Sudan. The international community's optimism of yesteryear is long gone, replaced by cynicism, despair and a hope that the country does not descend into another major civil war.

All these failed peace processes have not led the countries of the US-led international order to question their approach or the philosophy on which it is based. But there was a passing note of wisdom from an unlikely source: the UN Panel of Experts on South Sudan. It concluded that 'rather than breaking the violent cycle of elite political bargaining in South Sudan, the 2018 Revitalized Agreement on the Resolution of the Conflict in South Sudan (the peace agreement) has become part of it,' and moreover 'almost every component of the peace agreement is now hostage to the political calculations of the country's military and security elites, who use a combination of violence, misappropriated public resources, and patronage to pursue their own narrow interests' (UN Security Council, 28 April 2022). Unfortunately, the statement fails to identify the authors and instigators of liberal peacemaking in South Sudan.

In the past Juba was blessed with oil riches that could be used to buy off rebel leaders, but that is no longer the case as the country is deeply in debt and the only thing of value it can offer is political power and that can only be distributed by taking from Salva's own kleptocratic partners. It is thus difficult to predict where all of this is going and under what conditions there could be a sustainable peace agreement. It is also not clear that a peace agreement would significantly improve the plight of ordinary South Sudanese since the Western-bequeathed model of peacebuilding is largely based on sharing power among elites and support for the status quo, both of which have been discredited. Indeed, experience in Sudan and South Sudan makes clear that Western-led peacemaking is not leading to a democratic transformation and instead has solidified the power of the dictatorial Salva regime.

Like the armed opposition, the civilian opposition is too weak to be taken seriously by a government only concerned with armed threats to its power. During the armed struggle the churches played an important role in highlighting human rights abuses, including those by the SPLA. But in the 2010 national elections key church leaders ran for office under the SPLM banner, after which the churches lost much of their independence (John Young, 2019, p. 124). This was most evident in December 2013 when Salva Kiir's army massacred Nuer civilians on the streets of Juba and the churches neither protected the victims nor subsequently advocated for them. Dominated by the Dinka, the churches descended into the same ethnic divisions that afflict the rest of the country.

Traditional leaders also represent a countervailing force to the SPLM government, but during the armed struggle they were viewed as reactionary feudals, agents of Khartoum and often forcibly displaced. But the SPLM was not able to eliminate the traditional rulers and while they have a negligible role in the national or state governments, they retain considerable authority at the local level. They could also play a role in formulating culturally rooted systems of governance if it is appreciated by the modern elites that Western models of governance have failed South Sudan. Unfortunately, many educated South Sudanese remain infatuated with the West and notions of modernity and to acknowledge the continuing significance of traditional leaders is seen as backward.

As leader of the National Democratic Movement, Dr Lam Akol has pointed out unlike Sudan, in South Sudan there are no professional unions for doctors, engineers or accountants, unions are weak, and some of the civil society organizations are heavily infiltrated by elements of the regime (Lam Akol, 3 September 2021). However, South Sudanese civil society is becoming more politically active, particularly through its growing diaspora in the United States, Canada, Australia, UK and countries in East Africa. These groups are trying to challenge the kleptocracy of Salva and his clique and the government-established National Dialogue called for both Salva and his chief competitor, Dr Riek Machar, to leave political life (Jale Richard, 17 December 2020).

Civil Society can appear formidable in social media, but they are up against a government that regularly threatens to kill protesting citizens and President Kiir who said, 'If anybody among [journalists] does not know that this country has killed people, we will demonstrate it one day, one time. … Freedom of the press does not mean you work against the country' (Refworld, 17 August 2015). Such threats have the objective of both intimidating people from going to the streets in a popular uprising and even supporting elections because of the violence that might accompany them. Indeed, a poll that found that 50 per cent of South Sudanese opposed the planned February 2023 elections, 10 per cent said that elections should be called off entirely, and two-thirds of respondents viewed the risk of violence as high should an election be held (David Deng, Sophia Dawkins, Christopher Oringa and Jan Pospisil, 2022). But Lam Akol argues, it is precisely the resort to such threats and the repeated postponement of elections[6] that makes clear the weakness of the government (Lam Akol, 3 September 2021). And while the security services are ruthless, they are also unreliable and their loyalty to the government in the event of a popular uprising cannot be safely predicted.

## *Conclusion*

Although of little strategic interest and its resources largely appropriated by others, three presidents, the Western media and key sections of American civil society took up the cause of southern and then South Sudan and endeavoured to recreate a US-styled democracy in this most unlikely territory. While US policy on Sudan was based on geo-political concerns, and these concerns were not absent in its approach to South Sudan, their policy sprang primarily from the mythology Americans had about their own country and the comparison they drew with the struggles of the southern Sudanese. The ignorance on which US engagement was based made clear that the Americans involved – white liberals, evangelical Christians, black politicians and human rights activists – used southern and South Sudan as a forum to fight domestic battles and pursue identity politics. Their engagement served to reinforce all the old American chestnuts – the United States as a democratic beacon for the world, the United States as the indispensable nation needed to end conflicts, the universality of American liberal values and an affirmation of the US world order. But US engagement did not end the conflicts in South Sudan, democracy did not take root and US involvement served to reinforce destructive domestic power relations.

It was only eleven years after independence that a report to Congress concluded that 'South Sudan remains a deeply fragile nation beset by weak governance, pervasive insecurity, fiscal mismanagement, and widespread corruption' (Report to Congress on United States Policy Toward South Sudan, 2022). This signalled the US announcement in July 2022 that it was cutting its funding for peace implementation, withdrawing funding from World Food Program projects, and ending funding for various organizations supported by USAID (Sudan Tribune, 31 July 2022).

But it was never a case of the United States simply forcing its notions of democracy on reluctant southern Sudanese. Having been subject to northern slave traders, British colonialism and the internal colonialism of successive Sudanese regimes, Western democracy offered the prospect of leap-frogging centuries of racial and cultural denigration and asserting a South Sudanese African identity. By joining the club of American democrats, South Sudanese would not only attain Western levels of development, but equally satisfying be

---

6. Salva Kiir and opposition leader Riek Machar overruled their agreement and delayed elections scheduled for February 2023 until December 2024 (Radio Tamazuj, 28 July 2022).

able to look down on their former overlords in Khartoum. For many South Sudanese intellectuals and politicians, it was as if the post-colonial era of neocolonialism, the Cold War and the demands of the US international order never existed. And moreover, that the radically different values, cultures, histories and economies that gave rise to American democracy could be replicated in a pre-industrial South Sudan wracked by ethnic-based conflicts and led by the dictatorial SPLM.

Just like in Iraq, Afghanistan and a host of other countries, US engagement exacerbated existing conflicts and when the extent of the failure could not be ignored, the activists and politicians simply moved on to other worthy causes, learning nothing from their failures. After the destruction caused by the United States and its allies, their departure should be welcomed and may provide a small window of opportunity for the South Sudanese to dispense with failed Western models and develop forms of governance that correspond to their unique conditions.

The Americans left behind a broken and war-ravaged country that could never conform to the models they and other in the West had of it. The US failure in South Sudan was in some ways worse than similar failures in Afghanistan and Iraq because the engagement was longer, and it was largely supported by the people who genuinely admired the United States. Or at least *did* admire the United States.

The problem for the United States is not simply that the enormous human and financial resources devoted over many years failed to produce a functional democratic state in South Sudan. The problem is that the United States cannot learn the lessons of that failure because to do so would involve questioning fundamental assumptions about the political character of the United States, assumptions that figure prominently in its people's national identity and are manifest in Washington's ideological confrontation with its 'authoritarian' undemocratic enemies.

# CONCLUSION

During the Cold War the United States underwrote authoritarian regimes as long as they opposed the Eastern Bloc and socialism. The United States also supported and fostered the emergence of Islamist movements in the Middle East to counter leftist and nationalist movements and governments that were held to threaten its interests or those of its allies. Democracy, human rights and support for the rule of law figured in US rhetoric, but its international engagements and alliances made clear that these values were trumped by concerns with security and efforts to ensure its dominance in the Cold War and the post-Cold War eras.

With the embrace by Western governments of neoliberalism all pretence of state neutrality ended as well as the right of states to control their own destiny, and a new era of neo-colonialism began in the Global South. As well as producing levels of inequality not known in a century, the adoption of neoliberal values and institutions have spawned political and economic polarization, restricted human rights and led to the proliferation of anti-system and neo-fascist movements. Further, this has produced alienation, disaffection and in the United States growing polarization and the loss of legitimacy of elections, long held to be the centre-piece of American democracy.

States in the Global South have been subject to the ideological twists and turns of the Western metropoles in their approach to democracy and governance, and because of the imbalance in power with few exceptions have bent to the demands of Washington. These elites have accepted Western forms of democracy and governance, including constitutions with the requisite commitments to the rule of law, human rights, regular elections, free markets, and the latest proclamations on gender and sexual orientation. However, these measures have rarely been fully implemented, have not led to fundamental change in power relations, are frequently at odds with the values and norms of the local people and have not gained popular endorsement. The adoption of foreign and imposed measures has distorted development, and subjecting elites in the Global South to the requirements of the West has undermined their legitimacy and increased tensions between governments and the people. However, the US world order is in decline and with it a decline in US and Western influence. US democracy cannot serve as a model when it is in crisis and that crisis is unlikely to be overcome short of a transformative change.

For the first time since the waning of the Non-Aligned Movement in the 1970s countries in the Global South are recognizing the limits of US power. This was evident in the rejection by two-thirds of the UN General Assembly of a resolution pressed by the West in support of Kiev in the Ukraine proxy war on 26 August 2022 (Sergey Latyshev, 26 August 2022). Many in the Global South have deeply felt anti-imperialist sentiments based on generations of Western power and arrogance and the Ukraine War has proven to be an opportunity to assert their independence, even if such actions are thus far largely symbolic. But the growing power of China, Russia, India, Brazil, Iran, Turkiye and other countries is not merely symbolic, and they and the peace agreements reached by China and Russia in the Middle East are upending the US international order.

A primary contention of this study has been the failure of Western, and particularly US, democracy to meet the needs of three countries in the Global South. Ultimately it is not procedure (elections) by which the viability of Western democracy is judged in the Global South, but outcomes and increasingly those outcomes do not impress. Western democracy is in crisis, increasingly dysfunctional and is rapidly losing support even in its US heartland. Such a democracy always had a weak claim to serve as a model for the Global South. In the present era it has none.

## Ethiopia and compromises with the West

According to Meles the EPRDF had no option but to accept capitalism and a parliamentary regime given the world configuration of power in 1991. This permitted, indeed in the view of Meles necessitated, reformism within capitalism and acceptance of the unipolar dominance of the United States rather than the transformative programme the TPLF and EPRDF had envisaged. But the basis for that shift was not due entirely to the reconfiguration of world power, but also to the limitations of the TPLF's commitment to the country's radical transformation. The TPLF began its existence as ideologically driven students, but during the armed struggle its leadership became accomplished political operatives, whose skills were used to ensure the unity of the broadest sections of Tigrayan society in the anti-Derg war. As a result, the TPLF did not distribute capital during the land reform, limited its commitment to women's liberation, did not focus exclusively on advancing poor and middle peasants, and maintained a respectful approach to the Ethiopian Orthodox Church, which even after the overthrow of the imperial regime represented the main exponent of feudal values. The EPRDF also did not upturn the state, and instead worked through institutions imbued with the authoritarianism, Amhara chauvinism, and militarism of the imperial and Derg regimes. This not only put a brake on policies and their implementation that threatened the bureaucracy, but also served to undermine any commitment to a transformative notion of democracy.

There were always good arguments for making these decisions, and it could be contended that they reflected the democratic sentiments of the community, but in every case, they involved compromising with the TPLF's revolutionary values. The objective of carrying out a social revolution while maintaining a broad alliance inevitably conflicted, and the TPLF invariably sided with keeping intact the alliance. This same pattern would be evident after the EPRDF assumed state power. TPLF leaders were well aware of the historical pattern of revolutionary parties compromising their ideals after taking state power but assumed that through self-criticism as part of their system of gim gima they could escape that trajectory. But they did not.

Although ideologically confused in the early years of its rule, the Meles-led EPRDF nonetheless refused Western demands that the Ethiopian economy be completely opened up. Instead, the EPRDF oversaw the construction of the developmental state which placed restraints on the market, land remained nationalized, national-based local governments were established, and a state plan directed development, all in opposition to the stipulations of neoliberal democracy. In response to Western demands that Ethiopia democratize, Meles claimed he was following the experience of the Asian Tigers and like them Ethiopia would in the future dispense with authoritarian governance and evolve into a fully developed capitalist economy with a liberal democracy. This was an illusion because there was little in common between the ethnically homogeneous Asian Tigers with their small populations, export-focused economies and ties to the United States in the context of the Cold War, and Ethiopia with its warring nations, large population, limited geo-strategic significance, few exports and still miniscule industrial sector at the time of Abiy's ascendency to power.

Instead of the Asian Tigers, the Ethiopian experience suggests comparisons to the People's Republic of China which has a thriving capitalist sector and welcomes foreign capital but retains ownership and direction of key areas of the economy, particularly the banking sector, and operates according to a national plan. It also ascribes a leading role in governance and the economy to the Chinese Communist Party, but unlike the EPRDF the CCP remained committed to socialism. China is nonetheless closer to the experience of the EPRDF whose leaders had their roots in the Ethiopian Student Movement and the Front's key tenants – revolutionary democracy, national federalism and the developmental state – were inspired and shaped by Marxism-Leninism. There was nothing in Ethiopia's economic or political development under the EPRDF that suggested it was moving towards a more market-oriented economy or Western democracy at the time of Abiy's counter-revolution as would be expected if Ethiopia was following the path of the Asian Tigers.

Unlike Ethiopia's relations with other countries, its relations with China were not only state-to-state, but also at the level of the EPRDF to the CCP. Moreover, after leaving his long-held position as foreign minister the late Seyoum Mesfin became Ethiopian ambassador to China, and Chinese developments were closely followed in Addis Ababa. Indeed, the EPRDF looked to China for advice on a wide variety of policies ranging from poverty alleviation to domestic economic development. It is thus likely that Meles had no intention of dissolving a highly successful model of state-led development and privatizing the economy or adopting liberal democracy.

But claiming to follow the Asian Tigers' model undermined suspicions in the West that the EPRDF was not fully committed to a market economy and democracy.

The failure of Meles, and by extension the EPRDF whose members permitted him dictatorial powers, is that he did not recognize that for economic development to be sustainable it needed to go hand in hand with political development and the involvement of the people in their governance. While the West restricts democracy to the political sphere and focuses on individual rights and the market, the EPRDF recognized that realizing the economic, social and national rights of its poverty-stricken constituents were critical elements in Ethiopia's democratization. But at the same time the EPRDF limited popular engagement in the political sphere. Meles' developmental state proved remarkably successful in growing Ethiopia's economy and raising the living standards of millions and it is highly unlikely that these achievements could have been made by following the stipulations of the IMF. But increasingly the developmental state usurped powers of the regions, undermined human rights and this produced tensions that eventually exploded.

Meles' narrow focus on economic development and the constraints imposed to maintain Western acceptance meant that socialist measures that could have dampened national tensions, addressed the problem of growing inequality and provided the basis to construct an alternative system of democratic governance were not considered. In 1990 Meles argued for giving primacy to politics, but instead he led a technocratic government of experts pre-occupied with the economic plan. Meles ascribed to a kind of techno-Marxism where reason, science and the economic plan for the country assumed a central place, and although improving the lives of the people was the principal goal, those same people were not permitted to have a major role in the process.

To be sure, the EPRDF devolved power to national-based governments and oversaw a cultural and linguistic renaissance among many long-marginalized communities. It also protected these communities from the economic dislocation of the market. But it did not take the next and crucial step of formulating a democracy based foremost on the peasantry, the large majority of the country's inhabitants and the group to which the EPRDF claimed leadership, together with an emerging working class. No less than Samuel Huntington, advocate of global democratization and staunch defender of US international hegemony, was prepared to accept the notion of a peasant-based democracy for Ethiopia providing there was respect for human rights in the urban areas. But the EPRDF and particularly Meles failed to make that leap.

Committing to capitalism foreclosed the formulation of a class-based democracy, even though that was the approach of leftist movements of all political stripes for more than one hundred years until they succumbed to neoliberalism. After adopting with few alterations the early Bolshevik system of national federalism, the EPRDF failed to unite under one umbrella all the nationally marginalized people on the basis of class. This failure served to generate a heightening of national consciousness which set nations against one another and led to the EPRDF being attacked as a TPLF front for the sole benefit of Tigrayans. This position could not be factually defended, but the EPRDF did little to challenge this perspective and never provided an alternative model. The TPLF and EPRDF had so compromised their revolutionary ethos that they rejected the Marxian insight that social classes transcend both nations and state borders and that mobilizing and constructing a society on that basis was far closer to the ideal of democracy, meaning the empowerment of the people, than the constricted elite version of democracy propagated by the West.

Despite Front opposition to neoliberalism, it developed deep roots in popular culture, the educational institutions and particularly the universities where Western social science faced almost no competition from alternative or Marxist analyses. As a result, the EPRDF failed to develop what Gramsci considered a 'counter-hegemony' of alternative values and ideology to the dominant bourgeois society (Antonio Gramsci, 1989). Under Meles the EPRDF and TPLF abandoned Marxism-Leninism which had served the Fronts well during the armed struggle, provided a guide for their key policies, and bound leaders and led. Once the fronts lost their ideology – indeed deliberately dispensed with it – they were reduced to a group of loosely connected individuals linked only by personal goals of enrichment and power and a belief in the unfailing wisdom of Meles.

Like many other leftist parties upon coming to power the EPRDF endeavoured to broaden its political base and brought in many new members who had no experience with the armed struggle or with the Front's Marxist-Leninist tenants that had long guided the organization. As a result, the Front was left ideologically adrift and even more vulnerable when the TPLF had to militarily confront the armies of Abiy and Isaias after November 2020. Indeed, the regression was so great that even many young Tigrayans had little understanding of their own long armed struggle against the Derg.

While the Chinese Communist Party emphasizes class politics, its leaders also highlight socialist morality (and hence Xi Jinping's anti-corruption campaign) and China's Confucian tradition to maintain national unity. The EPRDF came to power opposing Amhara chauvinism but failed to seriously challenge this pernicious doctrine ideologically and after Abiy took power Amhara chauvinism again came to the fore and the result has been disastrous. The EPRDF also failed to construct a pan-Ethiopian nationalism, and this is surprising because Tigray served as the historical foundation of modern Ethiopia and its people are very proud of that history. As a result, the EPRDF's narrow nationalist focus undermined the emergence of a non-Amhara-based supranational Ethiopian identity. Under the early Bolsheviks, upon which the EPRDF modelled its system of multinational federalism, national identities were superseded by a Soviet class-based identity, but the EPRDF failed to attempt a similar path.

Pan-Ethiopian nationalism was evident when the country's many national communities came together to successfully fight in the Ethio-Eritrean 1998–2000 War. However, the EPRDF only relied on national federalism and developmentalism to gain country-wide legitimacy, and that did not prove sufficient. Unlike Xi Jinping's popularization of the notion of socialism with Chinese characteristics, the EPRDF did nothing to bridge the gap. Moreover, since the 18th Congress in November 2012 the Chinese Communist Party has been devoted to overcoming inequality and achieving 'common prosperity', while Meles (and his successor, Hailemariam Desalegn) did little to overcome similar problems in Ethiopia.

Having officially committed Ethiopia to a capitalist future, the EPRDF virtually opened the door to the individual self-seeking of its cadres and followers as Meles effectively acknowledged when he spoke about some liberation fighters being corrupted after tasting the 'honey of the city'. Indeed, the EPRDF's first Prime Minister and former leader of the EPDM, Tamrat Layne, was dismissed from office by Meles and served twelve years in prison for corruption and abuse of power (Sudan Tribune, 21 December 2008). During its long years of armed struggle, the TPLF leadership was almost completely devoid of corruption, not only because there were few temptations while in the bush, but also because the Front ascribed to a strong socialist morality. But that morality was dispensed with after committing to capitalism and loyalty to the state, which Meles understood to mean himself as leader of the state, did not constitute an alternative system of ethics. Quite the contrary, it challenged fundamental TPLF values and provided the basis for a Meles personality cult that was beginning to emerge before he died.

While acknowledging its economic and development achievements, the EPRDF government was held internationally and by its domestic critics to be undemocratic. Indeed, the EPRDF explicitly rejected liberal democracy and held that it was not suitable for Ethiopia at its stage of development and that the government and ruling party needed to play a leading role in the economy which was not possible under a parliamentary regime. And that contention in opposition to the masters of the universe was correct. The Front was also mindful that opening the political and economic systems was the course chosen by the successors to the Soviet Union and the results were disastrous. Likewise, the enclosures and displacement of Europe's peasantry one hundred years earlier was equally calamitous and could only be carried out because Europe was dominated by oligarchies made up of landlords and capitalists.

Because of its weak position in the post-Cold War era the EPRDF felt compelled to respond to Western demands for 'democracy' which – following Huntington – were understood to involve multi-party elections, a functioning parliament, respect for a Western conception of human rights, the endorsement of capitalism and neoliberalism. The EPRDF assumed that accepting the forms of such a 'democracy' would be sufficient to gain it Western acceptance. Indeed, many US allies followed this pattern and some – notably the autocratic regimes of the Middle East and North Africa – did not even profess to being democratic and were not pressed by Washington which feared that any loosening of controls in these states would produce instability and the rise to power of regimes opposed to the United States. But Ethiopia was not of comparable strategic importance, had lost its access to the crucial Red Sea, and unlike the oil-rich Middle Eastern states the country was in desperate need of foreign aid and capital, which could be used as leverage to press the EPRDF to adopt Western democracy and an open market. Ethiopia did become of more interest with the rise of Western fears of Chinese penetration. The EPRDF was further mistaken in concluding that its opaque highly centralized decision-making would prove acceptable for people whose education levels rapidly developed due to Front policies providing it maintained high growth rates.

The EPRDF establishment of a parliamentary regime never gained it any bone fides, either in the West or among Ethiopians. Likewise, the provision of stability in war-torn Ethiopia, its considerable economic achievements and its peacekeeping role in the region did not win the EPRDF Western support, only a tentative tolerance and the rapid embrace of the anti-EPRDF Abiy Ahmed who espoused neoliberalism. At the core of the EPRDF mistake was using largely Leninist systems of governance and pursuit of the developmental state while at the same time committing to capitalism. It was an ideological mismatch, and the surprise is that it lasted as long as it did.

Added to that the EPRDF had become dangerously ideologically dependent by the late 1980s on one person – Meles Zenawi – and after 2001 he became the country's dictator. Meles' internal coup of 2001 degraded both the TPLF and EPRDF and led Medhane and me to raise the question of *TPLF Reform or Decline?* and it is clear that both fronts went into a decline because – so we argued – they did not undergo a democratic transformation. There is thus a direct thread between Meles' coup and Abiy's dissolution of the EPRDF in 2019 and the disastrous war that the TPLF conducted with Abiy, Isaias and the Amhara militias.

The TPLF's resort to violence to resolve its differences with the OLF in the 1990s meant that it lost an opportunity to demonstrate magnanimity, increase its national support and strengthen Ethiopia's weak democratic culture. Moreover, despite the TPLF's rejection of its secondary role in the historical Amhara dominated state, it nonetheless represented a continuation of the Abyssinian core which has long controlled Ethiopia and thus a TPLF-OLF strategic alliance would have constituted an important break from the country's past. Also hindering such an alliance was the TPLF's many military victories (first over the Tigray Liberation Front, and then the feudal Ethiopian Democratic Union, EPRP, Derg, OLF and EPLF) which fostered a false pride in a political environment where military success was assumed to represent the superiority of the victor's cause. This conclusion not only proved erroneous as the continuing popularity of the OLF demonstrated but made it more difficult for the Front to reconcile with opposing groups and share power.

Ethiopia was caught in an ideological bind that became increasingly tense after Meles died in 2012 and exploded in 2018 with the elevation to power of Abiy Ahmed who challenged the centre-pieces of the EPRDF – national federalism, the developmental state and revolutionary democracy. That Abiy's liberal democratic regime only lasted six months before it became more authoritarian than the EPRDF gives weight to the Front's contention that liberal democracy and centralized government are not a suitable model for Ethiopia. Abiy's rapid transformation from an international poster child for democracy to dictator proved just how difficult it is to transplant Western notions of democracy to the infertile environment of Ethiopia. Meles had also briefly been a darling of the international community, but his stardom was based on solid economic and social achievements, while Abiy's commitment to democratic change was quickly aborted and he, together with his comrade in arms, Isaias, unleashed a wholly unnecessary war.

## Sudan: Change without fundamental change

An overview of Sudan's post-colonial history suggests continuous dramatic change – military dictatorships to democratic governments, secular to Islamist regimes, a series of popular uprisings and the loss of one-third of the country with the secession of South Sudan. But a closer examination makes clear the continuity within this pattern of change, thus affirming the old Sudanese joke that the country's politics changes every week but if you come back after ten years it is exactly the same. State failure and systemic instability in Sudan are not due to rapid changes, but instead because of the absence of fundamental change and the devotion of its elites to a Western version of democracy that has consistently failed the country.

Note has been made of General Abboud's 1958 coup, but Prime Minister Abdalla Khalil asked the general to take power because of a political impasse among the country's ruling class. Abdalla was confident that under Abboud power would remain in Sudan's riverine core, the Arabist and Islamic orientation of the country would be protected and he would keep the rebellious southern Sudanese in line. Indeed, Abboud met all these expectations, but he developed a taste for power and did not want to relinquish it. The rule of Abboud was ended by what the Sudanese call the 'October Revolution' of October 1964. But was this event a revolution, was the 1969 'May Revolution' of Colonel Jaffir Nimeiri a revolution, and were the similar uprisings of 1985 and 2019 revolutions as the Sudanese typically call them?

The 1964 October Revolution produced a short-lived regime dedicated to implementing a Western version of democracy, but it withered on the vine and never posed a threat to Sudan's power structure. Indeed, it was the failure of the October Revolution to overthrow the traditional elites and end the exploitation of the peripheries by the centre that left it with declining support that virtually welcomed its displacement.

The resulting 'May Revolution' was not designed to carry out fundamental change, but to ensure that fundamental change did not take place. The weakness of the government, however, led Nimeiri into an alliance with the Communist Party which compelled him to introduce some of the most positive changes ever attempted in Sudan – the sidelining of Sudan's traditional elites, the peaceful resolution of the southern Sudanese conflict and granting the region autonomy, the establishment of a non-aligned foreign policy, nationalization of the banks, and efforts to construct a Sudanese identity not tied to Arabism and Islam. It is hard to imagine that any of these positive developments could have taken place under a Western-styled parliamentary democracy because that would have given power to political elites that Sudanese experience makes clear would block these initiatives.

In the event, Nimeiri's reformist zeal did not last long and the traditional political leaders who have always acted like they owned Sudan were again turning back the clock. Before Nimeiri left the political stage, however, he gave a special place in his government to al-Turabi's Islamists and declared himself an Imam. After Nimeiri was overthrown in a popular uprising in 1985, a Transitional Military Council held power from April 1985 to April 1986 under Lieutenant General Abdel Rahman Swar al-Dahab. The TMC did not represent a dramatic change, however, because Abdel Rahman was himself an Islamist who worked hard during his year holding power to improve the political prospects of al-Turabi's NIF (Haitham Nouri, 26 October 2018).

The Sadig al-Mahdi government was elected in 1986 after elections that were broadly free and fair, and Sudan met the conditions of a Western democracy. But the democratic regime did not represent the will of the people in any real sense because it was never devoted to improving their lives and the standard of living of most Sudanese declined during this period, power remained in the grip of a narrow elite and the government failed to end Sudan's second civil war. Instead, the preoccupation of the government was with enriching the politicians and their friends and replacing Nimeiri's 'September' Islamic laws with another set of Islamic laws, held to be superior (John Young, 2012, pp. 27–9). Although the West is forever singing the praises of democracy, Sudan's 1986–9 democracy had few defenders in the West, and indeed the US undermined Sadig's government.

Likewise, the military coup of Omar al-Bashir did not represent fundamental change because it inaugurated another Islamist regime, albeit one of a more violent character and like its predecessor it was corrupt, devoted to neoliberalism, continued the capitalist exploitation of the periphery and even intensified the southern war. However, the NIF briefly tried to carry out a transformative agenda that quickly fell by the wayside. First, despite their rhetoric, most Islamist leaders did not want to risk their well-being and wealth-enhancing attachment to the state by being removed from power because of al-Turabi's foreign adventures. Second, even the radical al-Turabi made no attempt to upturn capitalism – indeed, he was an ardent supporter of the market economy – and thus the same bankrupt system that had ill-served Sudanese from the colonial era continued without any significant changes, except that a different group of Islamists held a leading position at the trough.

When it appeared that the Islamist stranglehold would never end, the opposition elite lost confidence in its own capacity, gave up its Sudanese nationalism and anti-imperialism, and turned to the United States and the SPLM of Dr John Garang to dispatch the NCP. But the US-bequeathed CPA served as lifeline for the NCP, and even when northern Sudanese made up the majority of the SPLM, the movement's post-Garang leadership jettisoned its commitment to a united New Sudan and opted for the independence of South Sudan leaving the opposition elite high and dry. Another lifeline for the Islamists was oil-generated wealth which fostered a 'cappuccino-sipping new middle class in Khartoum' and further entrenched the regime and inequality already rampant in the country (James Copnall, 3 November 2014). This conservative class invested in property rather than in business which would create jobs and spread the national wealth, and as a result wealth was largely restricted to urban elites in the riverine core and little of it could be found in the periphery. This laid the basis for an effective agreement between the riverine urban elites who traded their enrichment for the devastation in the periphery and this precluded an urban-rural resistance alliance (Magdi El-Gizouli, 10 May 2022). In any case such a class and its political parties could never carry out the democratic transformation that Sudan needs.

Like the opposition elite, al-Bashir and the Islamists increasingly looked to the United States for security and worked to bring the regime's foreign and domestic policies in line with American requirements by winning the acceptance of United States and its client states in the Gulf. Although a simple soldier, al-Bashir was a Jalien, a community of the riverine elite, and after carrying out a coup he was supposed to step aside for al-Turabi who was to assume state power. But al-Turabi was not from the riverine core, and he attracted Darfuris to the Islamist movement. The Darfuris, however, learned that they would never be fully accepted by the riverine-dominated movement and began breaking away, the largest component forming the Justice and Equality Movement (Bob Zaremba, 2011). al-Turabi was himself of a darker hue than his colleagues and in his later years increasingly held that his marginalization in the NIF was due to his non-Arab origins.[1]

When al-Bashir was overthrown in 2019 by another generation of democracy espousing youth, continuity rather than fundamental change was again evident. First, the generals al-Bashir appointed held much of the power in the transitional government. Second, the transitional government had its origins in the country's riverine core, just like all of Sudan's post-colonial political leaders. Third, the domestic and foreign policies pursued by both the civilian and military components of the transitional government did not represent any significant change from those of al-Bashir. Indeed, like al-Bashir the transitional government worked to integrate Sudan into the US-dominated global economic and state system and win the favour and financial assistance of the rich Gulf states. And like all governments since the late 1980s, the transitional government looked to neoliberal restructuring which was impoverishing large numbers of Sudanese to resolve the country's economic decline.

Meanwhile, Prime Minister Abdalla Hamdok, a UN economist, appointed a cabinet with many links to the IMF and other international establishment bodies steeped in neoliberalism. He thus had no problem convincing Washington and the European capitals of his government's ideological bone fides and that his ministers could be trusted to carry out the West's bidding, beginning with the sacrifice of Sudan's national sovereignty. Having revoked Sudan's independence, the United States used Hamdok's weakness to demand further concessions, such as recognition of Israel and paying reparations for the alleged crimes of the former regime.

And when the transitional government found itself facing internal conflicts that could not be resolved, the military assumed a similar role to that in 1958. Thus, on 25 October 2021 General Abdel Fattah al-Burhan carried out a soft coup to keep the state afloat and ensure no disruptions by the unruly mobs on the streets of

---

1. During one meeting I had with al-Turabi in the company of two southern Sudanese, al-Turabi repeatedly referred to 'us niggers', presumably to distinguish himself and the southern Sudanese from the 'Arabs' who led the government.

Sudan's cities calling for democracy. While articulating the appropriate democratic rhetoric, the West was willing to deal with the coup government and the resulting agreement between al-Burhan and Hamdok, just as it did with Abboud's coup more than sixty years previously.

Many opposition groups have raised the democratic banner, only to ultimately seek refuge in compromises with the government or dictator of the day. The foremost challenge to successive Khartoum governments was by the SPLM which in its early years claimed an adherence to Marxism-Leninism, although its actions in the field suggested otherwise, and with the collapse of its Derg and Eastern Bloc backers it moved steadily to the right. This reached its height when the militarist General Salva Kiir formed the Government of South Sudan after the death of Garang. The rest of the SPLM's factions in Sudan have divided between individuals aligned with the Hamdok government, others with al-Burhan, and a handful of dissidents in Darfur and the Nuba Mountains and southern Blue Nile who continued armed struggles.

Apart from Abdelaziz's band, the only party that has had a consistent democratic vision not based in Islam or liberal democracy, supports secularism and rejects Western neo-colonialism is the Sudan Communist Party and some leftist factions. Although ascribing to Marxism-Leninism and committed to a National Democratic Alliance through the mobilization of the working class, peasantry and radical intelligentsia, the SCP largely operates as a social democratic party, except for its support for popular uprisings. The SCP has consistently opposed the colonial structures of the inherited state and struggled for the expansion of civil and political rights and a democratic resolution of the conflicts in the periphery, including southern Sudan (Yoshika Kurita, 23 May 2019). Although the SCP supported the struggle of the SPLA and endorsed Garang's vision of a united reformed New Sudan, it was deceived when the Salva-led SPLM opted for South Sudan's independence.

While playing a leading role in the 2019 uprising, the party holds that the failures of Sudan's three uprisings are due to the weakening of the working class by the NCP's destruction of the trade unions and this in turn weakened the SCP. Another weakness has been the failure of the SCP to bring youth into the party and it suffers from prejudices against a communist party in a traditional Islamic society and a leadership based in Sudan's riverine core. This in turn has led to the strengthening of the liberal professions – journalists, doctors and engineers – in the party and that has weakened the SCP's traditional class basis and emphasis on economic issues. Aware of this, the SCP has been working with the resistance committees and endeavouring to rebuild the trade union movement and popular associations to prepare for what it hopes will be a conclusive general political strike and mass civil disobedience.

The survival of the SCP in the face of opposition from military dictatorships, the Islamist regime and even democratic governments which were not above using the claim of atheism to dismiss its elected MPs from Parliament in 1967 (John Markakis, 1987, p. 83) is testimony to both the SCP's political skills, moderation and a constant struggle for survival. This has meant, however, tensions between holding to revolutionary democratic ideals and a practical politics which has often involved tactical cooperation with opposition groups of very different and even reactionary political persuasions.

Despite its important role in the 2018–2019 uprising, the SCP ended its participation in the opportunist FFC alliance after it agreed to a compromise with the generals and instead the party signed a political agreement with the two major armed groups, Abdel Aziz al-Hilu's Sudan People's Liberation Movement-North and Abdel Wahid al-Nur's Sudan Liberation Movement for regime change in Sudan (Radio Tamazuj, 23 May 2022). Two months later the SCP established the 'Forces for Radical Change' which included civil and trade union groups, but not the SPLM-N, the SLM or the resistance committees (Sudan Tribune, 24 July 2022).

The openness of politics in Sudan to the extent that ordinary citizens are often familiar with and talk about issues that in other countries are only considered by elites behind closed doors impresses but does not lead to substantive change. Also impressive is Sudan's elite's civility, charm, intellectual sophistication and capacity to find common ground across the political divide, and this sets it apart from Ethiopia's elite who can barely arouse themselves to speak to their political opponents.

While there have been periods of violence within the elite and the peripheries have frequently become killing fields, jailed members of the elite have usually reported that they were well cared for in prison and the experience served to bring people of different political persuasions together where they shared food and books, played football together and pursued the favourite Sudanese past time of endlessly talking. It is common for families to have political activists and cadres of different persuasions and there is a high degree of marriage within the elites that cross political boundaries. The family wants to preserve its unity, and this fosters tolerance, moderation, political realism and encourages the view that those who are politically marginalized today could be holding state power tomorrow.

However, the much-admired tolerance of the traditional Sudanese elite often leads to endless negotiations, compromises, backsliding, political opportunism and yet more meetings, in which the process is always in danger of becoming an end in itself, produces agreements which are heavy on rhetoric but light on substance or are simply ignored. This elite is also deeply paternalistic and considers that it alone can and has the right to determine Sudan's future. It uses democratic rhetoric but in practice abhors the masses and looks down on any potential leaders from outside the Sudanese core as it demonstrated with its mocking of former camel herder, Hemedti. The transitional government that came to power after the overthrow of the al-Bashir regime is a good example of that paternalism. Ironically it was an anonymous group in the NIF, almost certainly from the Darfur based Justice and Equality Movement led by the late Khalil Ibrahim, which authored the 'Black Book' which concluded that since independence Sudan governments and most of the leading figures in the Sudanese state had their origins in the country's riverine core (BBC, 24 February 2009). And there is little doubt that its analyses were substantially true. As a result, no matter what the political make-up of Sudan's post-colonial government, the interests of the riverine elite have predominated and have a vested interest in not sharing power.

Like the uprisings of 1964 and 1985, the 2018–2019 uprising was stimulated by declining economic conditions and the impact of an IMF austerity programme, but in the latter uprising the focus of the demonstrators' ire was solely on the demand that al-Bashir step down. Although centred in Khartoum, the 2018–2019 uprising began with demonstrations in Damazine in Blue Nile State and in the rail centre of Atbara, and when NCP ideologues attempted to discredit the uprising by claiming it to be Darfur based (that is, play to prejudices against Darfuris which were widespread among Sudan's elite), one of the chants of the demonstrators was 'we are all Darfuris'. Indeed, Darfuris figured significantly in the Khartoum demonstrators and had been challenging the government in Darfur for months before the outbreak of the uprising and had been largely ignored. But in the end their numbers and those from other Sudanese peripheries did not alter the fact that the FFC backers of the uprising were themselves dominated by conservative riverine leaders and it supported the transitional government.

An aroused people can break this cycle, ideally led by an organized working class in alliances with the peasants, but that has been forestalled by the successful efforts of the Islamist regime to break the trade unions and farmers' associations together with their links to the SCP. Without an organized working class focusing on the need to restructure the economy and oppose IMF interventions designed to protect the interests of global capital and their local representatives and not ordinary people, uprisings have been co-opted by different factions of the self-serving Sudanese elite and pursued – particularly in the 2019 and 2021–2022 movements – by politically immature youths. However, there are signs that this pattern may be breaking down.

In late 2018 and the first half of 2019 the youth went to the streets demanding that the al-Bashir regime be brought down. But this limited demand and the lack of appreciation of the interest of the Western-led international community in suppressing Sudanese democracy suggested that this movement would be co-opted even quicker than the uprisings in 1964 and 1985 which raised anti-IMF and anti-imperialist slogans. Moreover, while the SCP and other leftist parties played a major role in the uprising, they did so by largely responding to the demands of the youth for personal freedom, opposing dress codes and other restrictions on women, and not raising overtly socialist slogans, focusing on national sovereignty, highlighting issues of economic injustice and condemning the IMF which had pressed the austerity which was impoverishing the people of Sudan. When al-Bashir was imprisoned and a transitional government was established, the principal rationale for most of the uprising participants ended, and most of them left the streets.

The lack of political consciousness of the protestors is due to a number of factors: first, the post-Cold War collapse of the Eastern Bloc and the corresponding decline of leftist thought and movements; second, the effectiveness of the Islamist de-politicization campaign, particularly in the post-secondary institutions; third, the absence in the 2019 uprising of trade unions which would have given the movement a more economic and anti-imperialist focus; and lastly, the growing importance of professional associations that became the de facto leaders of the uprising and they have typically been infatuated with the West and Western democracy.

The resistance council members were also unduly influenced by the West, but they understood better than the politicians two things. First, there must be a united and unambiguous opposition to any involvement of the security forces in the Government of Sudan. Second, the resistance councils were correct in not making common cause with a fossilized political class that has failed Sudan since independence. What they failed to realize – despite ample evidence – is that a Western-led international community which places stability and protection of its autocratic allies in the Middle East above the concerns of Sudanese can never be allies in a struggle for a democratic transformation.

Without a democratic transformation Sudan will continue to suffer from tragedies such as the latest one which began on 15 April 2023 when the leaders of the Sudan Armed Forces and the Rapid Support Forces began a violent power struggle to the detriment of the civilian population. Prime Minister Hamdok did not prove to be an effective leader, but he may have been prophetic when he said, 'The big question today is will Sudan exist or not exist?'

## South Sudan and national self-determination

SPLM leader John Garang did not call for the national self-determination of southern Sudan until late in the day, only under pressure and almost certainly because he understood that with its polyglot of frequently antagonistic peoples and some of the lowest levels of economic and political development, southern Sudan was not a suitable candidate for independent statehood, much less Western democracy.

It is one thing to try and unite the disparate peoples of southern Sudan around the demand for regional autonomy within a transformed united Sudan and calls for a transfer of power from the riverine elite to the peripheries. It is also essential to demand respect for the repressed African cultures of southern Sudan, and to contend that the Arab identity of many northern Sudanese is destructive and should be replaced with a more holistic pan-Sudanese identity, even while also protecting local identities. These demands had the potential to overcome national tensions in southern Sudan, make common cause with similarly marginalized peoples in northern Sudan and construct a 'New Sudan'. But they were not realized because from its inception the SPLM did not have an ideology that had a popular basis, it lacked an institutional structure, was overwhelmingly dominated by Garang, and was a Dinka-led and -oriented movement that produced antagonism among many in southern Sudan.

Even after the SPLM committed to national self-determination for southern Sudan, by running for Sudan's presidency Garang could have undermined the demand of his own movement. Garang's victory in the 2010 presidential contest was a real possibility since he had considerable support in northern Sudan, and victory would have gone far to neutralize secessionist sentiments in southern Sudan. The separate British administration of southern Sudan (and adjacent territories in northern Sudan) and the war which led to the 1972 Addis Ababa Agreement and establishment of an autonomous southern Sudanese regional government made clear that the right of southern Sudanese to national self-determination was widely acknowledged. But South Sudan poses the difficult problem for democratic governance of which communities have a further right to secession and which do not, and how should national self-determination be handled when there is no competent party to realize the right, and the SPLM was clearly not such a party.

Under the CPA the Nuba Mountains and southern Blue Nile were granted the right of national self-determination (although never realized), but not the right to secession, while other areas which also rebelled against Khartoum governments such as eastern Sudan and Darfur were not granted any right to national self-determination. If the length of the armed struggle is the deciding criterion for granting the right to secession, then the Nuba have long since passed South Sudan because their struggle continues to the present. If marginalization and poverty are the critical criteria for granting the right to secession, then eastern Sudan should have that right.

Although the SPLM fought most of its long war against Khartoum under the banner of a united New Sudan, it was granted the right of secession because of the movement's change in political direction late in the day and because powerful international actors led by the United States endorsed that decision. There was no doubt as to the oppression that the southern Sudanese experienced in Sudan, but at no point during the long peace negotiations was the question ever raised as to whether the SPLM should have been the only designated southern Sudanese party to the negotiations, or in other words that it alone represented the diversity of southern Sudan. Also never entertained officially was whether the SPLM was capable of effectively ruling the country. My studies in southern Sudan, and I was not alone, led to the conclusion that the SPLM could not administer a national government because it could not administer its liberated territories and it did not have the support of the majority of South Sudanese (John Young, 2012 and 2019).

The Western-dominated IGAD and the Troika led by the United States only permitted the SPLM the right to participate in the peace negotiations and thus state power would be handed over to the SPLM, whether as head of an autonomous regional government or as the head of an independent state. While there were some in the international community and even in IGAD and the United States that questioned the capacity of the SPLM, that did not matter after the SPLM was officially accepted as the sole representative of the southern Sudanese because it alone would assume responsibility for realizing the right to national self-determination. Moreover, once the right of southern Sudan to secession and the holding of a referendum was granted by the CPA, no one could have seriously doubted that the vote would be overwhelmingly for secession.

To a considerable extent the hands of the US negotiators were tied because firmly entrenched narratives were in place in the United States which alternatively glorified the struggle for the rights of southern Sudanese led by the SPLM and its heroic leader Dr John Garang or held that Christian southern Sudanese needed to free themselves from rapacious northern Sudanese Arab Muslims. In either case the logical outcome was for southern Sudanese to break from northern Sudan. The fact that southern Sudan was of no strategic interest to the United States meant that it was of little concern for the 'blob', the establishment foreign policy experts, and thus lobby groups like the Friends of South Sudan had a disproportionate influence in shaping US government foreign policy. And that influence has been paternalistic, negative and informed by notions such as US exceptionalism.

These same outsiders with their devotion to American democracy determined that the new state would embrace liberal democracy as a mode of governance and neoliberal capitalism as an economic and development model. Although it is patently clear that both models have been failures in South Sudan, it is difficult to escape this legacy. And instead of starting the search for appropriate systems of governance and economy from within, South Sudanese have been led to believe that there is only one governance model which developed over many years in the West. There is growing disillusion if not despair among South Sudanese about conditions in their country, but change can only come when they turn their gaze from the West and begin to look to their own societies for inspiration and direction.

## Final words

Concern about national sovereignty and the rights of nations have long been at the centre of political and armed struggles in the HOA and the Global South generally, but they have little place in the Western understanding of democracy. Western governments and Western social science typically do not recognize the neo-colonial foundations of the Western dominated world state system and seem perennially surprised when this system breaks down in the periphery. In the past progressive elements within Western democracy championed parties that challenged the powerful on behalf of the downtrodden. But that is no longer the case. The version of democracy practised by the United States as formulated by Schumpeter and shaped by neoliberalism and the surveillance state is deeply conservative and closely linked to the intelligence services and a market economy which produces inequalities and social tensions. In the present era appeals for democracy are often taken up as a mantra by powerful interests in the West to pursue regime change, and as a result Western democracy has become an instrument to subjugate the Global South to the dictates of the United States.

The contradiction at the core of the Western understanding of democracy is exemplified by the example of the EPRDF. While Western commentators grudgingly acknowledge the Front's developmental successes, they largely discount its efforts in overcoming national oppression, and instead emphasize its authoritarianism.

But the EPRDF's successes in development, dramatically improving the living conditions of destitute Ethiopians, and its progress in overcoming national oppression are intrinsic to any genuine understanding of democracy, particularly as it is applied in the Global South. Moreover, the characterization of the EPRDF as authoritarian is implicitly based on a comparison with a supposedly democratic West which no longer exists in the wake of growing levels of inequality, restrictions on free speech, repression of the opposition, and collusion of the mass media, big tech and the intelligence services in manipulating the outcome of elections, long held to be the centre-piece of American democracy.

The failure of US democracy in the countries examined here does not, however, negate the need for a democratic transformation. In 1991 the EPRDF reluctantly endorsed Meles' argument that capitalism and a Western parliamentary regime had to be accepted because of the international configuration of power in which the United States and its Western allies assumed a global hegemonic position, while the rump Soviet state of Russia was a virtual vassal to the United States, and China had yet to flex its economic muscle. But three decades later liberal democracy and neoliberalism are in crisis, Russia stands militarily toe-to-toe with the United States and NATO, and China is expected to soon overtake the United States economically. Equally significant, the ethnocentric and once-confident West now suffers self-doubt, destabilizing societal divisions and a declining ability to impose its will on the Global South, all of which are evident in NATO's proxy war in Ukraine. To quote the remarkable insight of Samuel Huntington: 'the failure of the United States would inevitably be seen as the failure of democracy' and 'the central problem in the relations between the West and the rest [is] America's efforts to promote a universal Western culture and its declining ability to do so' (Huntington, 1996, p. 183).

This book is a case study of three states struggling over Western democracy during a period when US power globally is in decline. It is increasingly clear that critical elements of the US world order beginning with liberalism, elite-led elections, a market economy and an individualist focus on human rights – which collectively constitute the core of American democracy – have not developed roots in the Global South, not only because they do not address the most basic needs of the people and are alien imports, but also because they are in crisis. As Moeini emphasizes, Western liberal millenarianism is alien, quixotic and nonsensical to much of the world and the demise of *Pax Americana* presents a historic opportunity for cultural renewal and national rebirth (Arta Moeini, 8 July 2022). Moreover, Russia and China are using their growing power to undermine a US international order beset by increasing political and economic problems and this is already serving to restructure relations in the Middle East and the Horn of Africa. Indeed, we are currently in an era when, as Lenin reputedly said, 'there are decades where nothing happens, and there are weeks where decades happen'.

Until very recently Russia assumed a subservient position in a Western-dominated global system of trade and finance, but a harsh regime of Western sanctions in the wake of the West's proxy war in Ukraine has forced Moscow to end its attachment to neoliberalism and give the state a leading role in the economy.

While China does have a highly successful non-Western model of governance and economic development, it is a case of 'socialism with Chinese characteristics', and those characteristics are not easily transferable. Unlike the United States, the Chinese Communist Party does not claim to provide a universal model and instead the importance of China is in demonstrating that highly successful alternative modes of governance and development can be constructed. Neither Russia nor China can be considered democratic, but acquiring national autonomy is a crucial prerequisite for such a transformation. Moreover, the deepening conflict between the West and Russia and China means that the latter states can be expected to increasingly come to the assistance of countries attempting to break from US hegemony.

A multipolar world is emerging, and this provides opportunities for the Global South to break free from the neo-colonial shackles of the West and develop systems of governance and economic organization that best meet their needs and not those of the West. Margaret Thatcher contended that 'there is no alternative' and the West has endeavoured to ensure that there is no discussion about possible alternatives to the existing order it dominates. But despite their efforts, the question of alternatives has become the burning issue of the present era.

This study does not propose alternatives but does draw some conclusions. First, democracy is impossible without national sovereignty and that necessitates re-empowering states deliberately emasculated by neo-colonialism and neoliberalism and ensuring that the leading sectors of the economy, beginning with agriculture and banking, are under national control. Second, the rights of oppressed nations, other minorities and all the disadvantaged must assume a central place in a unifying class struggle. Third, the need to dramatically raise the standard of living of the people, overcome uneven development and address economic injustices must be considered primary tasks of governments carrying out their democratic responsibilities. Fourth, the UN was established in the wake of the Second World War and reflected Western power at that time, but for a genuine system of international law to emerge it needs to be reformed and reflect the current balance of power and the rise of the Global South. Finally, instead of imported Western governance models, the Global South must foster intellectual independence and political imagination that transcends present political reality and provides forward-looking and radical solutions rooted in local conditions. Or as Thomas Sankara summed up, 'We must dare to invent the future.'

# BIBLIOGRAPHY

Aaron Finch. (2021). 'What Did the 13th, 14th and 15th Amendments Do?' 16 November. https://sehiresnafi.com/what-did-the-13th-14th-and-15th-amendments-do/.

Aaron O'Neil. (2021). 'United States Share of Global Gross Domestic Product (GDP) 2026'.

Aaron Tesfaye. (2019). 'China-Ethiopia Relations and the HOA'. *Italian Institute for International Political Studies*. 20 September.

Abdi M. Abdullahi. (2007). 'The Ogaden National Liberation Front (ONLF): The Dilemma of Its Struggle in Ethiopia'. *Review of African Political Economy*. Vol. 34. No. 113. September.

Abdi Sheikh. (2021). 'Anger in Somalia as Sons Secretly Sent to Serve in Eritrea Military Force'. *Reuters*. 28 January.

Abdolgader Mohamed Ali. (2022). 'UAE, Turkiye, and Iran: Why Rival Powers Are Backing Ethiopia's Government'. *The New Arab*. 14 February.

Abdúllahi A. Gallab. (2001). 'The Insecure Rendezvous between Islam and Totalitarianism: The Failure of the Islamist State in the Sudan'. *Arab Studies Quarterly*. Vol. 23. No. 2. Spring.

Abdullaihi A. Gallab. (2018). *Hasan al-Turabi the Last of the Islamists*. Lexington: Arizona State University.

Abdullahi Osman El-Tom. (2011). *Darfur, JEM and the Khalil Ibrahim Story*. Red Sea Press.

Abdul Wahid al-Nur. Chairman Sudan Liberation Movement. (2018). 'Sudan's Removal from the Terrorist List Taints US Values'. *Sudan Tribune*. 14 November.

Abdur Rahman Alfa Shaban. (2018). 'Ethiopia Riot Police Deployed, Addis Deserted amid Flag Clashes'. *Africanews*. 14 September.

ACCORD. (2016). 'Conflict Resurgence and the Agreement on the Resolution of the Conflict in the Republic of South Sudan'. 19 October.

ACCORD. (2019). 'Reviving Peace in South Sudan through the Revitalised Peace Agreement'. 11 February.

AFP. (2015). 'Saudi Arabia Deposits $1bn in Sudan Central Bank'. 13 August. https://gulfnews.com/news/mena/sudan/saudi-arabia-deposits-1b-in-sudan-central-bank1.1566103.

AFP. (2017). 'In Russia, Sudan's Bashir Asks Putin for "protection" from US'. *yahoo!news*, 23 November.

Africa Center for Strategic Studies. (2021). '10 Years after Independence South Sudan Faces Persistent Crises'. 13 September.

African Union Commission of Inquiry on South Sudan. (2014). *Final Report*. Addis Ababa. 14 October.

Aggrey Mutambo. (2021). 'Africa Backs Addis Protest against UN Session on Ethiopia Human Rights'. *Zehabesha*. 14 December.

Ahmed Adel. (2023). 'About 20 Countries Now Interested in Joining BRICS despite Ukraine Crisis'. *The Intel Drop*. 28 February.

# Bibliography

Al Arabiya English. (2019). 'Sudan Military Council, Opposition Sign Political Agreement'. 17 July.

Alan Macleod. (2022). 'Most of the "Fact-Checking" Organizations Facebook Uses in Ukraine Are Directly Funded by Washington'. 2 August.

Alex de Waal. (1997). *Food and Power in Sudan: A Critique of Humanitarianism*. African Rights. London.

Alex de Waal. (2013). 'Review Article: The Theory and Practice of Meles Zenawi.' *African Affairs*. Vol. 112. No. 446. (January). Oxford University Press.

Alex de Waal. (2016). 'Writing Human Rights and Getting It Wrong'. *Boston Globe*. 6 June.

Alex Vershinin. (2022). 'The Return of Industrial Warfare'. *RUSI*. 17 June.

Alfred de Zayas. (2022). *The Human Rights Industry*. Clarity Press.

Alice Slater. (2018). 'The US Has Military Bases in 80 Countries. All of Them Must Close'. *The Nation*. 24 January.

Al-Jazeera. (2017). 'Turkey Sets up Largest Overseas Army Base in Somalia'. 1 October.

Al-Jazeera. (2019). 'Sudan Top Diplomat Says Removal from US Terror List Top Priority'. 9 September.

Al-Jazeera. (2021). 'Military Chief Says Sudan Reviewing Naval Base Deal with Russia'. 2 June.

Al-Jazeera. (2021). 'UN Calls on Sudan's Military to Restore Transitional Government'. 28 October.

Al-Jazeera. (2022). 'More than 7.7 Million Facing Food Crisis in South Sudan'. 9 April.

Allen Hertzke. (2004). *Freeing God's Children The Unlikely Alliance for Global Human Rights*. Boulder Co: Rowman & Littlefield Publishers, Inc.

Altaghyeer Archives. (2021). 'Sudan: «Hamdi Gone, but His Policies Sustained despite Revolution»'. 19 April.

Amac. (2020). 'Bozell to Levin: Survey Shows 4.6% of Democrats Would Not Have Voted for Joe Biden Had They Known Hunter Biden Story'. 12 November.

American Foreign Relations. www.americanforeignrelations.com/O-W/Post-cold-War-Policy-Isolating-and-punishing-rogue-states.html.

Andrew Edward Yaw Tchie and Jihad Mashamoun. (2022). 'After the Coup: Regional Strategies for Sudan'. *African Arguments*. 7 January.

Anis Chowdhury and Jomo Sundaram. (2017). 'Hunger in Africa, Land of Plenty'. *Inter Press Service*. 14 October.

Anis Chowdhury and Jomo Sundaram. (2021). 'Allow Least Developed Countries to Develop'. *JOMO*. 30 August.

Anis Chowdhury and Jomo Sundaram. (2022). 'Aid for Power in New Cold War'. *Challenging Development*. 12 July.

Antonio Gramsci. (1989). *Selections from the Prison Notebooks Reprint*. Hoare, Quintin and Smith, Geoffrey. (Editors and Translators). Chadwell Heath, UK: Lawrence & Wishart.

Antony Loewenstein. (2015). 'US Evangelicals in Africa Put Faith into Action but Some Accused of Intolerance'. *The Guardian*. 18 March.

Arab Press Updates. (2021). 'Countries Issue Joint Statement on the November 21 Political Agreement in Sudan'.

Arta Moeini. (2022). 'America: The Last Ideological Empire'. *Compact*. 8 July.

Assefa Fiseha. (2018). 'Federalism and Development: the Ethiopian Dilemma'. *International Journal of Minority and Group Rights*. Vol 25. No. 3. 333–68.

Assefa Fiseha. (2019a). 'Federalism, Development and the Changing Political Dynamics in Ethiopia'. *International Journal of Constitutional Law*. Vol. 17. No. 1.

Assefa Fiseha. (2019b). 'Local Level Decentralization in Ethiopia: Case Study of Tigray Regional State'. *Law and Development Review*. https://doi.org/10.1515/ldr-2019-0006.
Associated Press. (2019). 'US Bars Entry to International Criminal Court Investigators'. 15 March.
Asteris Huliaras. (2006). 'Evangelists, Oil Companies, and Terrorists: The Bush Administration's Policy towards Sudan'. *Foreign Policy Research Institute*. 1 September.
Ayah Aman. (2021). 'Sudan's Political Crisis Could Complicate Nile Dam Dispute'. *Al-Monitor*. 3 November.
Ayyaantuu News. (2021). 'Russia, Ethiopia Ink Military Cooperation Agreement'. 12 July.
Baker Institute. (2022). 'The OPEC+ Phenomenon of Saudi-Russian Cooperation and Implications for US-Saudi Relations'. 18 October.
Banafsheh Keynoush. (2022). 'Iran to Remain a Key Partner for Ethiopia in the Tigray Conflict'. *MEI*. 26 January.
BBC. (2009). 'Who Are Sudan's Darfur Rebels?' 24 February.
BBC. (2010). 'Yassir Arman Quits Sudan Presidential Poll'. 31 March.
BBC. (2016). 'US Shuts Down Drone Base in Ethiopia'. 4 January.
BBC. (2018). 'John Bolton Threatens ICC with US Sanctions'. 11 September.
BBC. (2019). 'Mueller Report: US Congress Given Key Findings from Attorney General Barr'. *BBC News*. 24 March.
Ben Aris. (2023). 'LONG READ: Russia the Mining and Minerals Titan of the Future'. *bne IntelliNews*. 16 April.
Ben Schott. (2020). *China Is More Democratic than America, Say the People*. Bloomberg. 26 June.
Benoit Faucon, Summer Said, and Joe Parkinson. (2021). 'Military Coups in Africa at Highest Level since End of Colonialism'. *Wall Street Journal*. 4 November.
Bereket Simon. (2012). 'A Tale of Two Elections: A National Journey That Averted Calamity'. Mega Enterprise. Addis Ababa. Parts of Which Were Translated from Amharigna in Daniel Berhane. 'A Look at Bereket Simon's Book: A Tale of Two Elections'. *HOA Affairs*. 4 February. Addis Ababa.
BGEA. (2018). 'U.S. Presidents Honor Their Pastor and Friend, Billy Graham'. *Billy Graham Evangelical Association*. 21 February.
Bill Allison and Sarah Harkins. (2014). 'Fixed Fortunes: Biggest Corporate Political Interests Spend Billions, Get Trillions'. *Sunlight Foundation*. 17 November.
Bill Vann. (2003). 'Bush Vows Decades of War for "Democracy" in the Middle East'. *World Socialist Web Site*. 8 November.
Bloomberg News. (2023). 'Putin Meets Assad as Russia Pushes for Syria-Turkey Accord. 15 March.
Bob Zaremba. (2011). 'Conflict in Darfur: Calculation and an Inadequate International Response'. *Journal of Theoretical and Philosophical Criminology*. Special Edition. Vol. 1: 43–6.
Brett Decker. (2019). 'Mueller Report: Findings Prove Donald Trump Never Colluded with Russia, Obstructed Justice'. *USA Today*. 18 April.
Brett Schaefer. (2000). 'The Keys to an African Economic Renaissance'. *The Heritage Foundation*. 10 May.
Briscoe Center for American History. (2015). 'Kagnew Station and Fluctuating Policy on Ethiopia'.
Bruce Dickson. (2003). *Red Capitalists in China: The Party, Private Entrepreneurs, and Prospects for Political Change*. Cambridge University Press.

Bruce Livesey. (2020). 'How Capitalism Is Destroying Democracy'. *CBC*. 8 December.
Bruce Mutsvairo, Mirjam De Bruijn, and Kristin Skare Orgeret. (2022). 'While the Focus Is on Ukraine, Russia's Presence in the Sahel Is Steadily Growing'. *The Guardian*. 3 February.
Cambridge Dictionary. https://dictionary.cambridge.org/dictionary/english/democracy.
A. Carl LeVan. (2010). 'The Political Economy of African Responses to the U.S. Africa Command'. *Africa Today*. Vol. 57. No. 1.
Carole Landry. (2019). 'China, Russia Block UN Action on Sudan'. *Yahoo News*. 4 June.
Cass Sunstein. (2004). 'Sunstein on FDR's Second Bill of Rights'. *The University of Chicago Law School*. 1 October.
Catalist. 'What Happened in 2020 National Crosstabs'. https://www.dropbox.com/s/ka9n5gzxwotfu1a/wh2020_public_release_crosstabs.xlsx?dl=0.
Celia Garrett. (2018). 'US Interventionist Policy in South Sudan Ineffective at Bringing Needed Improvement'. *The Kenan Institute for Ethics at Duke University*. 15 February.
Cesran International. (2016). 'Modernization and the Third Wave of Democracy'. http://cesran.org/modernization-theory-and-third-wave-democracy-internal-and-external-impediments-to-democracy-and-development.html.
CGTN Africa. (2021). 'Talk Africa: The Belt and Road Initiative in Africa'. *China in Africa*. 11 October.
Chair of the Commission on Human Rights in South Sudan, to the Human Rights Council'. (2022). 18 March.
Chalmers Johnson. (2004). *The Sorrows of Empire: Militarism, Secrecy, and the End of the Republic*. New York: Henry Holt and Company.
Charles Capito. (2017). 'Amid Wave of Final Executive Actions, President Obama Eases Sanctions against Sudan'. *Government Contracts Insights*. 24 January.
Charles Tilley. (1990). *Coercion, Capital, and European States, AD 990–1992*. Cambridge, MA: Blackwell.
Charlie Kimber. (2005). 'Aid, Governance and Exploitation'. *International Socialism*. Vol. 107. 27 June.
China.cn.org. (2019). 'Full Text of Xi Jinping's Report at 19th CPC National Congress' [in Chinese]. 6 November.
China Daily. (2021). 'China and Africa in the New Era: A Partnership of Equals'. 27 November.
Chris Bohner. (2022). 'Labor's Fortress of Finance'. *Radish Research*. Summer.
Chris Devonshire-Ellis. (2021). 'Russia Prepares for 2022 Africa Summit as Trade & Investment Increase'. *Russia Briefing*. 2 December.
Chris Maisano. (2020). 'The "Crisis of Democracy" around the World Is a Crisis of the Working Class'. *Jacobin*. 30 March.
Christian Lammert. (2020). 'The Crisis of Democracy'. In *The Emergence of Illiberalism. Understanding a Global Phenomenon* edited by Boris Vormann and Michael D. Weinman. London: Routledge.
Christopher Clapham. (2017). *The Horn of Africa: State Formation and Decay*. London: Hurst and Company.
Christopher Clapham. (2018). 'The Ethiopian Developmental State'. *Third World Quarterly*. Vol. 39. No. 6: 1151–65. DOI: 10.1080/01436597.2017.1328982.
Christopher Davidson. (2016). *Shadow Wars: The Secret Struggle for the Middle East*. London. One World Publication.

Christopher Rhodes. (2021). 'America and China Opened the Door for African Coups to Return'. *Al-Jazeera*. 3 December.
Chtatou Mohamed and Kester Kenn Klomegah. (2022). 'Russia-Maghreb Relations: Moscow's Geopolitical and Economic Objectives'. *Global Research*. 11 February.
Civil and Human Rights News. (2013). 'Where the United States Stands on 10 International Human Rights Treaties'. 10 December.
Claire Berlinski. (2011). *There Is No Alternative: Why Margaret Thatcher Matters*. New York: Basic Books.
CNN. (1999). 'Former US President Bush Urges Pinochet Release'. 12 April.
CNN. (2006). 'Judge: Ethiopian Forces Killed 193 Unarmed Protesters'. 18 October.
CNN. (2023). 'Donald Trump Pleads Not Guilty to 34 Felony Counts of Falsifying Business Records'. 4 April.
CNN. (2023). 'Biden Dismisses China's Proposed Peace Plan'. 24 February.
CNN Money. (2007). 'Bush Announces Sanctions against Sudan'. 29 May.
Collin Campbell and Deborah Scroggins. (1989). 'Officials: U.S. May Welcome Coup in Sudan; Military Rulers Might Improve Famine Relief'. *Atlanta Journal and Constitution*. 27 January.
Congressional Research Service. (2018). 'South Sudan's Civil War: Nearly 400,000 Estimated Dead'. 28 September.
Constitutionnet. (2018). http://www.constitutionnet.org/news/sudans-missed-opportunity-historic-peaceful-transfer-power-planned-removal-term-limits. 17 August.
Constitution of the Federal Republic of Ethiopia. (1994). Addis Ababa.
Contemporary Thinkers. (2022). https://contemporarythinkers.org/samuel-huntington/biography/.
Crawford Young. (1994). *The African Colonial State in Comparative Perspective*. New Haven and London: Yale University Press.
D. Reiter. (2001). 'Does Peace Nurture Democracy?' *The Journal of Politics*. Vol. 63, No. 3: 935–48.
Dabanga. (2014). 'Opposition Forces Sign "Sudan Appeal" in Addis Ababa'. Addis Ababa. 3 December.
Dabanga. (2017). 'Sudan Participates in US Africom Summit for First Time'. 18 April.
Dabanga. (2019). 'Burhan's Appointment Deplored in Central and West Darfur'. 15 April.
Dabanga. (2021). 'Sudan Public Order Law Still Being Implemented: SIHA Network'. 3 September.
Daily Nation. (2016). 'IGAD Accepts Riek Machar's Ouster as South Sudan's Vice President'. 26 August.
Dale Snauwaert. (2004). 'The Bush Doctrine and Just War Theory'. *The Online Journal of Peace and Conflict Resolution*. January.
Dan Merica. (2016). 'WikiLeaks Releases Transcripts of Clinton Goldman Sachs Speeches'. *CNN*. 17 October.
Daniel Benaim. (2019). 'Amid Revolutionary Change at Home, Ethiopia Is Remaking Its Middle East Ties'. *World Politics Review*. 9 April.
Daniel Stewart. (2023). 'Trump Claims He Could Resolve Ukraine War «in 24 hours» if He Were U.S. President'. *MSNBC*. 27 January.
Daniel Williams. (2023). 'US Failure in Iraq Opened the Door for China, Russia'. *Asia Times*. 20 March.
Daphne Psaledakis and Michelle Nichols. (2020). 'U.S. Blacklists ICC Prosecutor over Afghanistan War Crimes Probe'. *Reuters*. 20 September.

David Bauder. (2021). 'Outlets Hurt by Dwindling Public Interest in News in 2021'. *AP News*. 27 December.
David Blackmon. (2023). 'A Spate of Recent Deals Raises Chatter of a Fading Petrodollar'. *Forbes*. 2 April.
David Butter. (2020). 'Egypt and the Gulf Allies and Rivals'. *Chatham House*. London. 20 April.
David Deng, Sophia Dawkins, Christopher Oringa, and Jan Pospisil. (2022). 'National Survey on Perceptions of Peace in South Sudan'. PeaceRep: The Peace and Conflict Resolution Evidence Platform. The University of Edinburgh. 19 May.
David Efune. (2020). 'US Ramping Up Efforts to Combat BDS, 'Pursuing It Relentlessly'. *Americans United with Israel*. 10 September.
David Hendrickson. (2022). 'At the End of Its Tether: U.S. Grand Strategy of Advancing Democracy'. *Defense Priorities*. 30 June.
David Lake, Lisa Martin and Thomas Risse. (2021). 'Challenges to the Liberal Order: Reflections on International Organization'. *International Organization*. Vol. 75. No. 2: 225–57.
David Mageria. (2005). 'Ethiopia to Charge Leaders of Protest'. *Reuters*. 10 November.
David Shinn. (2011). 'US Policy towards the Horn of Africa'. The Center for African Development Policy. Kalamazoo. Michigan. 30 September.
David Shinn. (2014). 'Ethiopia and China'. *International Journal of Ethiopian Studies*. Vol. 8. No. 1 and 2.
David Shinn. (2021). 'China's Maritime Silk Road and Security in the Red Sea Region'. MEI@75. 18 May.
Declan Walsh. (2019). 'Amid U.S. Silence, Gulf Nations Back the Military in Sudan's Revolution'. *New York Times*. 26 April.
Diane Kunz. (1997). *Butter and Guns: America's Cold War Economic Diplomacy*. New York Press.
Dnvanesh Kamat. (2022). 'US Disengagement Reflects on Nile Dam Dispute'. *The Arab Weekly*. 25 April.
Donald Petterson. (1999). Former US Ambassador to Sudan. *Inside Sudan: Political Islam, Conflict, and Catastrophe*. Boulder: Westview Press,
Earl Conteh-Morgan. (2017). 'China's Arms Sales in Africa'. Oxford Research Group. 19 April.
Eastafro. (2021). 'China Eritrea, Ethiopia Foreign Ministers Meeting'. EastAFRO.com.
Economist. (2022). 'Chinese Loans and Investment in Infrastructure Have Been Huge'. 20 May.
Ed Broadbent. (2009). 'Barbarism Lite: The Political Attack on Social Rights'. *Toronto Star*. 21 February.
Edson Ziso. (2018). *A Post State-Centric Analysis of China-Africa Relations Internationalisation of Chinese Capital and State-Society Relations in Ethiopia*. London: Palgrave Macmillan.
Edward Newman, Roland Paris, and Oliver Richmond. (2009). *New Perspectives on Liberal Peacebuilding*. New York: UN University.
E.E. Evans-Pritchard. (1940). *The Nuer – A Description of the Modes of Livelihood and Political Institutions of a Nilotic People*. Oxford: Clarendon Press.
Ellen Nakashima and Shane Harris. (2018). 'How the Russians Hacked the DNC and Passed Its Emails to WikiLeaks'. *Washington Post*. 13 July.

Elliot Berg. (1981). 'Accelerated Development in Sub-saharan Africa: A Plan for Action'. *World Bank*.
Emma-Jo Morris and Gabrielle Fonrouge. (2020). 'Smoking-Gun Email Reveals How Hunter Biden Introduced Ukrainian Businessman to VP Dad'. *New York Post*. 14 October.
Enough Project. 'Founding Director John Prendergast'. https://enoughproject.org/about/john-prendergast
Eric Schewe. (2018). 'Why Is the U.S. Military Occupying Bases Across Africa?' *JSTOR Daily*. 11 April.
Ermias Tasfaye. (2022). 'Amhara Civilians Were Massacred in Tole, but Questions Remain'. *Ethiopia Insight*. 8 July.
Ermias Tasfaye. (2022). 'Oromo and Amhara Militants Battle on the Western Frontier'. *Ethiopia Insight*. 1 June.
Ethiopia Constitution. (1994). Ethiopia's Constitution of 1994. constituteproject.org. 19 September 2013.
Euractiv. (2011). 'EU Divisions Grow over Libya Operations'. 22 March.
European Tribune. (2022). 'Merkel's Explosive Interview Die Zeit'. 25 December.
Fabrizio Tassinari and Mehari Taddele Maru. (2021). 'Global Rivalry in the Red Sea'. *Danish Institute for International Studies*. 5 October.
Focus on Global South. (2000). *The Transfer of Wealth: Debt and the Making of a Global South*. Chapter 4. October.
Foundation for the Defense of Democracies. (2023). 'Saudi Arabi, Iran Agree to Reestablish Diplomatic Ties'. 10 March.
Fox News. (2022). 'FBI raids Trump's Mar-a-Lago'. 8 August.
Francis Fukuyama. (1989). 'The End of History'. *The National Interest*. No. 16. Summer.
Francis Fukuyama. (1992). *The End of History and the Last Man*. Glencoe, IL: The Free Press.
Frank Andrews. (2021). 'Sudan Coup 2021: What's at Stake for Neighbouring Powers'. *Middle East Eye*. 28 October.
Franklin Graham. (2010). 'Rev. Franklin Graham: Islam "evil"'. *Politico*. 3 October.
Gary Morson. (2022). 'The Cancellation of Russian Culture'. *First Things*. 14 March.
George Downes and Bruce Bueno de Mesquita. (2004). 'Gun-Barrel Diplomacy Has Failed Time and Again'. *Los Angeles Times*. 4 February.
George Eaton. (2021). 'Is the Neoliberal Era Finally Over?' *The New Statesman*. 16 June.
George Herring. (2008). *From Colony to Superpower; U.S. Foreign Relations since 1776*. Oxford University: Oxford University Press.
George Smith. (2016). 'Immanuel Kant on War and Peace'. Libertarianism. 20 June. https://www.libertarianism.org/columns/immanuel-kant-war-peace.
George H. W. Bush. (1990). 'Address before a Joint Session of the Congress on the Persian Gulf Crisis and the Federal Budget Deficit'. 11 September.
George W. Bush. (2005). 'Second Inaugural Address'. *Inaugural Addresses of the Presidents of the United States*. 20 January. https://www.bartleby.com/124/pres67.htmly.
Gerry Mackie. (2009). 'Schumpeter's Leadership Democracy'. *Political Theory*. 1 February.
Ghazi Salahuddin Atabani. (2018). 'Realising Sudan's Potential: Requisite Reforms and Challenges (2018-2060)'. A Round Table Meeting Chaired by Dame Rosalind Marsden. *Chatham House*. London. 17 June.
Gilles Kepel. (2002). *Jihad, on the Trail of Political Islam*. Cambridge, MA: Harvard University Press.
Giulia Paravicini and Maggie Fick. (2020). 'From Nobel Prize to Fighting Former Comrades: Ethiopia's PM Abiy'. *Reuters*. 11 November.

Glenn Greenwald. (2021). 'Democrats, Media Do Not Want To Weaken Facebook, Just Commandeer Its Power To Censor'. *Substack*. 10 May.

Glenn Greenwald. (2022). 'NBC News Uses Ex-FBI Official Frank Figliuzzi to Urge Assange's Extradition, Hiding His Key Role'. *Substack*. 2 January.

Glen Greenwald. (2023). *Twitter*. 12 April.

GlobalSecurity.org. (2000). 'National Security Report'. December.

Greg Sargent. (2007). 'There's Been Class Warfare for the Last 20 Years, and My Class Has Won'. *Washington Post*. 30 September.

Haitham Abdualaziz Almosharaf and Fung Deng Tian. (2014). 'The Causes of Sudan's Recent Economic Decline'. *Journal of Economics and Finance*. Vol. 2. No. 4. January.

Haitham Nouri. (2018). 'Sudan's Religious General'. *Ahramonline*. 26 October.

Hansen, Stig Jarle with Bradbury, Mark. (2007). 'Somaliland: A New Democracy in the HOA?' *Review of African Political Economy*. September.

Hany Besada. (2013). 'Assessing China's Relations with Africa'. *Africa Development/Afrique et Développement*. Vol. 38. Nos. 1–2. CODESRIA.

Harriet Alexander. (2023). 'Ex-acting CIA Director Reveals He Had 50 Spies Sign a Letter Saying Hunter Biden Laptop Scandal Was Russian Disinformation to HELP Joe "win the presidential election"'. *MailOnline*. 21 April.

Henry Kissinger. (2014). *World Order*. New York: Penguin Press.

Homeland Security. (2022). 'Summary of Terrorism Threat to the U.S. Homeland'. *National Terrorism Advisory System Bulletin*. 7 February.

Hone Mandefro. (2019). 'Old Habits Die Hard'. *Insight*. 4 July.

Hooper Hearst and Mustafa. (2019). 'EXCLUSIVE: Sudanese Spy Chief 'Met Head of Mossad to Discuss Bashir Succession Plan'. 1 March. https://www.middleeasteye.net/news/exclusive-sudanese-spy-chief-met-head-mossad-discuss-bashir-succession-plan.

Human Rights Watch. (2002). 'U.S.: "Hague Invasion Act" Becomes Law'. 3 August.

Human Rights Watch. (2010). '"One Hundred Ways of Putting Pressure" Violations of Freedom of Expression and Association in Ethiopia'. 24 March.

Human Rights Watch. (2015). 'Men with No Mercy'. 9 September.

Human Rights Watch. (2016). 'South Sudan: Killings, Rapes, Looting in Juba'. 15 August.

Hussein Aboubakr Mansour. (2023). 'The New Middle East Rules of the Rules-Based Order'. *Middle East Forum*. 23 March.

Ian Schwartz. (2023). 'Rubio: Adversaries Creating A Secondary Economy, Will Trade In Currencies Other Than The Dollar To Avoid Sanctions'. *RealClear Politics*. 29 March.

Intercept. (2016). 'New Nation, Long War: Hillary Clinton's State Department Gave South Sudan's Military a Pass for Its Child Soldiers'. 9 June.

International Commission on Intervention and State Sovereignty (ICISS) (2001). 'The Responsibility to Protect'. *International Development Research Centre*. Ottawa.

International Crisis Group. (2019). 'Managing Ethiopia's Unsettled Transition'. Report 269 Africa. 21 February. Brussels.

International Crisis Group. (2021). 'Oil or Nothing: Dealing with South Sudan's Bleeding Finances'. Report 305 Africa. 6 October. Brussels.

International Monetary Fund. (2015). 'The Federal Democratic Republic of Ethiopia Selected Issues'. November. Washington, DC.

International Monetary Fund. (2022). 'World Economic Data Base'. April. Washington, DC.

Iona Cable. (2021). 'The Complicity Of Human Rights In Neoliberalism: Beyond Redemption?' *Human Rights Pulse*. 27 April.

Ivar Iverson. (2007). 'Foreign Policy in God's Name: Evangelical Influence on U.S. policy towards Sudan'. *Norwegian Institute for Defence Studies*. 1 January.

J. Burr and Robert Collins. (2003). *Revolutionary Sudan: Hasan al-Turabi and the Islamist State, 1989–2000*. Leiden: Brill.

Jacob Sullum. (2020). 'The New York Times Belatedly Admits the Emails on Hunter Biden's Abandoned Laptop Are Real and Newsworthy'. *Reason*. 17 March.

Jale Richard. (2020). 'People Want Kiir, Machar to "step aside" – ND Report'. *Eye Radio*. 17 December.

James Copnall. (2014). 'The Decline of Sudan's Cappuccino-sipping Middle Class'. *How We Made Africa*. 3 November.

Jean-Nicholas Bach. (2012). 'Abyotawi Democracy: Neither Revolutionary nor Democratic. A Critical Review of EPRDF's Conception of Revolutionary Democracy in post-1991 Ethiopia'. *Journal of Eastern African Studies*. 1 November.

Jeff King. (2003). *An Activist's Manual on the International Covenant of Economic, Social and Cultural Rights*. Law and Society Trust.

Jeffery Herbst. (2018). 'Sudan Prospects of Economic Engagement'. *Atlantic Council*. Africa Center. March.

Jeffrey Migdal. (1974). *Peasants, Politics, and Revolution: Pressures towards Political and Social Change in the Third World*. Princeton, NJ: Princeton University Press.

Jennifer Hochschild. (2010). 'If Democracies Need Informed Voters, How Can They Thrive While Expanding Enfranchisement? *Election Law Journal: Rules, Politics, and Policy*. Vol. 9. No. 2: 111–23.

Jesse Marks. (2022). 'China's Evolving Conflict Mediation in the Middle East'. *MEI*. 25 March.

Jessica Campisi. (2019). 'Trump Called out for "My Favorite Dictator" While Awaiting Egyptian Leader at Summit: Report'. 13 September. *The Hill*.

Jessica Larsen and Finn Stepputat. (2019). 'Gulf State Rivalries in the Horn of Africa: Time for a Red Sea Policy?' *Danish Institute of International Studies*. 1 March.

Jessica Whyte. (2019). 'The Morals of the Market Human Rights and the Rise of Neoliberalism'. London: Verso.

Jevans Nyabiage. (2022). 'Somaliland Offers to Resist Growing Chinese Influence in Africa as It Seeks US Recognition'. *South China Morning Post*. 15 January.

Joan Leishman. (2016). 'International Criminal Court Facing Exodus of African Nations over Charges of Racism'. *CBC*. 16 November.

Joan Roelofs. (2016). 'NATO and the Bananazation of Western Europe'. *Counterpunch*. 19 February.

Joe Conason. (2007). 'Seven Countries in Five Years'. *Salon*. 12 October.

Johan Schaar. (2019). 'The World's 40 Million Invisible Refugees'. *IRIN*. 11 February.

John Bowden. (2019). 'Almost Half in New Poll Still Say Trump, Russia Colluded'. *The Hill*. 27 March.

John Fulton. (2019). 'China's Growing Presence in the Gulf'. *East Asia Forum*. 26 March.

John Markakis. (1987). *National and Class Conflict in the Horn of Africa*. Cambridge: Cambridge University Press.

John Markakis. (2021). 'The Afar'. In John Markakis, Guenther Schlee, and John Young. *The Nation State – A Wrong Model for the Horn of Africa*'. Max Planck Research Library for the History and Development of Knowledge Studies 14.

John Markakis, Guenther Schlee, and John Young. (2021). *The Nation State – A Wrong Model for the Horn of Africa*'. Max Planck Research Library for the History and Development of Knowledge Studies 14. https://www.mprl-series.mpg.de/studies/14/index.html.

John Mearsheimer. (2018). *The Great Delusion: Liberal Dreams and International Realities*. New Haven and London: Yale University Press.

John Mearsheimer. (2019). 'Bound to Fail: The Rise and Fall of the Liberal International Order'. *International Security*. 1 April. Vol. 43. No. 4: 7–50.

John Mearsheimer. (2021). 'The Inevitable Rivalry America, China, and the Tragedy of Great-Power Politics'. *Foreign Affairs*. November/December.

John Quincy Adams. (1821). *An Address Delivered At the request of a Committee of the Citizens of Washington; On the Occasion of Reading The Declaration of Independence on the Fourth of July*. Washington: Davis and Force.

John Young. (1998). *Peasant Revolution in Ethiopia: The Tigray People's Liberation Front. 1975–1991*. Cambridge: Cambridge University Press.

John Young. (2005a). 'John Garang's Legacy to the Peace Process, the SPLM/A & the South'. *Review of African Political Economy*. No. 106: 535–48.

John Young. (2005b). 'South Sudan Defence Force: A Challenge to the IGAD Peace Process'. *Occasional Paper*. Institute of Security Studies. Pretoria.

John Young. (2012). *The Fate of Sudan: Origins and Consequences of a Flawed Peace Process*. London: Zed Publications.

John Young. (2013). 'The Day After'. *Sudan Tribune*. 26 February.

John Young. (2016). 'Popular Struggles and Elite Cooptation: The Nuer White Army in South Sudan's Civil War'. In *Small Arms Survey*. Geneva: Graduate Institute of International Studies.

John Young. (2019). 'Sudan's Relations with Ethiopia'. *Small Arms Survey*. Geneva: Graduate Institute of International Studies.

John Young. (2020a). 'Conflict and Confrontation Transitions in Modern Ethiopian–Sudanese Relations'. Briefing Paper. *HSBA*. Geneva, Switzerland.

John Young. (2020b). Sudan Uprising: Popular Struggles, Elite Compromises, and Revolution Betrayed'. Report. *Small Arms Survey*. Graduate Institute of International and Development Studies, Geneva, Switzerland. June.

John Young. (2021a). 'Bolshevism and National Federalism'. In John Markakis, Guenther Schlee, and John Young. *The Nation State – A Wrong Model for the Horn of Africa*. Max Planck Research Library for the History and Development of Knowledge Studies 14.

John Young. (2021b). 'South Sudan: The Fractured State'. In Markakis, John, Schlee, Guenther, and Young, John. *The Nation State A Wrong Model for the Horn of Africa*. Max Planck Research Library for the History and Development of Knowledge Studies 14.

John Young. (2022a). 'Ethiopia's Abiy Ahmed: From Poster-Boy of the West to Poster-Boy of the Left'. *Global Research*. 4 January.

John Young. (2022b). 'Western Democracy Has Failed in South Sudan – Time to Consider Alternatives'. *Nyamilepedia*. 8 January.

John Whitbeck. (2022). 'The Territorial Integrity of States vs. the Self-Determination of Peoples'. *Counterpunch*. 24 February.

Johnathan Schanzer. (2012). 'Pariah State: Examining Sudan's Support for Terrorism'. *Foundation for Defense of Democracies*. 5 July.

Johnnie Carson and Zach Vertin. (2018). 'Sudan Politics, Engagement and Reform'. *Atlantic Council*. Africa Center. March.

Joseph Krauss. (2021). 'What Reinstating Sudan's Prime Minister Means for the Country'. *Associated Press*. 22 November.

Joseph Schumpeter. (1987). first published in 1947. *Capitalism, Socialism and Democracy*. Unwin Books.

Joseph Stalin. (1913). 'Marxism and the National Question'. In J. Stalin. *Collected Works*. Moscow: Progress Publishers.

Joseph Stiglitz. (2002). *Globalization and Its Discontents*. New York: Norton.
Joseph Stiglitz. (2011). 'Of the 1%, By the 1%, For the 1%'. *Vanity Fair*. May.
Josh Kron and Jeffrey Gettleman. (2011). 'South Sudanese Vote Overwhelmingly for Secession'. *New York Times*. 21 January.
Joshua Lee. (2023). 'Utah Rep. Chris Stewart Claims "Twitter Files" Show FBI Violated First Amendment'. *Desert News*. 10 March.
Jubilee Debt Campaign. https://jubileedebt.org.uk/countries/sudan.
Karl Marx. (1852). *The 18th Brumaire of Louis Bonaparte*. Moscow: Progress Publishers, 1937.
Karl Polanyi. (1944). *'The Great Transformation'*. New York: Farrar & Rinehart.
Karl Wycoff. (2004). 'Fighting Terrorism in Africa'. *U.S. State Department*. 1 April.
Keir Lieber and Robert Lieber. (2002). 'The Bush National Security Strategy'. *U.S. Foreign Policy Agenda*. U.S. Department of State. December.
Kelley Vlahos. (2022). 'US Bombs Somalia for the Third Time This Summer'. *Responsible Statecraft*. 18 August.
Ken Silverstein. (2005). 'Official Pariah Sudan Valuable to America's War on Terrorism'. *Los Angeles Times*. 29 April.
Kenneth Vogel, Katie Rogers and Glenn Thrush. (2022). 'Republicans Lay out Biden Investigations, but Democrat-Aligned Groups Promise Counteroffensive'. *New York Times*. 17 November.
Khalid Abdelaziz, Michael Georgy, and Maha El Dahan. (2019). 'Exclusive: Sudan Militia Leader Grew Rich by Selling Gold'. *Reuters*. 26 November.
Khalid Mukhtar Salim. (2022). 'How the Military Harnessed the African Union in the UNITAMS Process to Legitimize the Coup'. 30 July.
Khalil al-Anani. (2021). 'How Sisi Became a Role Model for Arab Coup Plotters'. *Middle East Eye*. 21 December.
Khalil al-Anani. (2021). 'Sudan Coup: The Regional Interference behind a Faltering Transition'. *Responsible Statecraft*. 22 December.
Kholood Khair. (2021). 'Sudan's Democratic Transition at a Crossroads'. *Al-Jazeera*. 3 September.
Kossaify Ephrem. (2021). 'UN Security Council Calls for "Utmost Restraint" from All Parties in Sudan'. *Arab News*. 28 October.
Lam Akol. (2021). 'Opinion What Makes an Uprising?' *Sudan Post*. 3 September.
Latana. (2022). 'Democracy Perception Index'. https://latana.com/democracy-perception-index/.
Laura Barber. (2020). 'China's Response to Sudan's Political Transition'. *United States Institute of Peace*. 8 May.
Lee Camp. (2022). 'Lee Camp: How US Government Was Bought for $14.4bn'. *RT*. 23 February.
Leopold Traugott. (2016). 'Outsourcing European Border Security – 'at the Whim of Foreign Dictators'. *Euractiv*. 21 September.
Library of Congress. 'Voting Rights for Native Americans'. https://www.loc.gov/classroom-materials/elections/right-to-vote/voting-rights-for-native-americans/.
Linda Heiden. (1979). 'The Eritrean Struggle for Independence'. *Monthly Review*. Vol. 30. No. 2: 15.
Lloyd Ambrosius. (2006). 'Woodrow Wilson and George W. Bush: Historical Comparisons of Ends and Means in Their Foreign Policies'. *Diplomatic History*. Vol. 30. No. 3. June.
Lorimer Wilson. (2023). 'Shift From U.S. Dollar as World Reserve Currency Underway'. *MunKnee*. 6 February.

Luca Ventura. (2022). 'Poorest Countries in the World 2022'. *Global Finance*. 5 August.

Macharia Munene. (2022). 'Geopolitical Dynamics in the Horn of Africa Region'. *The Horn of Africa Bulletin*. January-February.

Madeleine Albright. (1998). 'NBC-TV Interview'. Archived from the original on 8 March 2016.

Magdi El Gizouli. (2020). 'Mobilization and Resistance in Sudan's Uprising'. *Rift Valley Institute*. Briefing Paper. January.

Magdi El-Gizouli. (2022). 'Interview'. *Breakthrough News*. 10 May. https://www.youtube.com/watch?v=Ormq8xhEl08.

Magdi El Gizouli. (2023). 'Sudan's Unfinished Democracy'. *Elephant*. 20 April.

Mahmood Mamdani. (2010). *Saviors and Survivors: Darfur, Politics, and the War on Terror*. Crown.

Mansoor Ijaz. (2001). 'Clinton Let Bin Laden Slip Away and Metastasize'. *Los Angeles Times*. 5 December.

Margaret Sullivan. (2020). 'Ghosting the News: Local Journalism and the Crisis of American Democracy'. *Columbia Global Reports*. 14 July.

Marina Ottaway. (2020). 'As a Parting Gift to Israel, the Trump Administration Pushes Sudan and Morocco to Recognize Israel'. *Wilson Center*. 17 December.

Marshall Cohen. (2021). 'The Steele Dossier: A Reckoning'. *CNN*. 18 November.

Martin Cleaver and Mark Tran. (1986). 'US Dismisses World Court Ruling on Contras'. 28 June.

Martin Gilens and Benjamin Page. (2014). 'Testing Theories of American Politics: Elites, Interest Groups, and Average Citizens'. *Perspectives on Politics*. American Political Science Association. Cambridge University Press. 18 September.

Matt Ellentuck. (2017). 'Donald Trump Super Bowl Interview Transcript with Fox News' Bill O'Reilly. 5 February.

Matt Nashed. (2022). 'Sudan: Russian Influence and Ukraine War Stir Domestic Tensions'. *Al-Jazeera*. 18 March.

Matthew Spalding. (2010). 'Why Is America Exceptional?' *The Heritage Foundation*. 1 October.

Maximilian Forte. (2011). 'The Top Ten Myths in the War against Libya'. *Counterpunch*. 31 August.

Medhane Tadesse and John Young. (2003). 'TPLF: Reform or Decline?' *Review of African Political Economy*. Vol. 30. No. 97. September.

Mediterranean Defense. (2021). 'China's Naval Base in Djibouti'. 27 March.

Megan Leonhardt. (2022). 'The Top 1% of Americans Have about 16 Times More Wealth than the Bottom 50%'. *CNBC Make It.* 23 June.

Melani McAlister. (2008). 'The Politics of Persecution'. *Middle East Report*. 249. Winter.

Merisha Gadzo. (2023). 'Changing Global Order': China's Hand in the Iran-Saudi Deal'. *Al-Jazeera*. 11 March.

MERP. (2012). A US government official quoted. 'The Sudan Split How US Policy Became Predicated on Secession'. Mimi Kirk In: 262. Spring.

Michael Barnett. (1997). 'Bringing in the New World Order: Liberalism, Legitimacy, and the United Nations'. *World Politics*. Vol. 49. No 4.

Michael Barnett. (2021). 'International Progress, International Order, and the Liberal International Order'. *The Chinese Journal of International Politics*. Vol. 14. No. 1. Spring.

Michael Collins. (2018). 'How Financialization Is Starving Manufacturing'. *IndustryWeek*. 21 September.

Michael Crozier, Samuel Huntington, and Joji Watanuk. (1975). 'The Crisis of Democracy – Report on the Governability of Democracies'. *Trilateral Commission*.

Michael Mandelbaum. (2022). *The Four Ages of American Foreign Policy: Weak Power, Great Power, Superpower, Hyperpower*. Oxford University: Oxford University Press.

Michael Sainato. (2016). 'Wikileaks Proves Primary Was Rigged: DNC Undermined Democracy'. *Observer*. 22 July.

Michael Welton. (2022). 'Alternative Vision of a New Global Order'. *Counterpunch*. 2 May.

Michael Woldemariam. (2019). 'The Ethiopia-Eritrea Thaw and Its Regional Impact'. Current History, May.

Michele Flournoy. (2020). 'How to Prevent a War in Asia'. *Foreign Affairs*. 18 June.

Middle East Eye. (2019). 'EXCLUSIVE: Sudanese Spy Chief 'Met Head of Mossad to Discuss Bashir Succession Plan'. 1 March.

Middle East Eye. (2020). 'US Envoy Reiterates Support for Egypt in Its War on Terrorism'. 3 September.

Middle East Eye. (2021). 'US Receives $335m from Sudan as Compensation for Militant Attacks'. 31 March.

Miguel Brockmann. (2009). 'Thematic Dialogue'. Lecture delivered to UN General Assembly. 28 July.

Mike Pompeo. (2019). Video at an event at Texas A&M University. https://www.youtube.com/watch?v=DPt-zXn05ac. 25 April.

Mohamed Amin. (2022). 'Sudanese Protesters Accuse Cairo of Supporting Coup, Straining Relations'. *Middle East Eye'*. 31 January.

Mohamed Khair. (2013). 'Sudan's Implementation of Islamic Financing, A Story of Three Decades' Experience'. *Central Bank of Sudan*. 6–7 November.

Mordechai Chaziza. (2018). 'China's Approach to Mediation in the Middle East: Between Conflict Resolution and Conflict Management'. *Middle East Institute*. 8 May.

M.T. Geiger and L.C. Moller. (2015). 'Fourth Ethiopia Economic Update: Overcoming Constraints in the Manufacturing Sector'. *World Bank Group*.

Muhmmad Osman and Magdi El Gizouli. (2018). 'US-Sudanese Relations: Moths to the Fire'. *Sudan Tribune*. 25 November.

Murat Sofuoglu. (2022). 'Can Sudan's Hamdok Defend His Deal with the Military?' *TRT World*. 25 November.

Mustapha Dalaa and Halime Afra Aksoy. (2021). 'Russia's Wagner Group Reportedly Deployed in Africa'. *AA World*. 5 March.

Muzan Alneel. (2021). 'The People of Sudan Don't Want to Share Power with Their Military Oppressors'. *Jacobin*. 24 November.

Nancy Fraser. (2017). 'From Progressive Neoliberalism to Trump—and beyond'. *American Affairs Journal*. Winter 2017/Vol. I. No. 4.

National Security Council. (2018). 'Remarks by National Security Advisor Ambassador John R. Bolton on the The Trump Administration's New Africa Strategy'. *Heritage Foundation*. Washington. 13 December.

nazret.com. (2016). 'Ethiopia: State of Emergency Risks New Abuses – HRW'. 31 October.

NBC-TV. (1998) 'The Today Show'. *NBC News*. 19 February.

Nehanda Radio. (2019). 'US Refuses to Remove Sudan from Terror List While Military Rules'. 17 April.

Neta C. Crawford (2021). 'The U.S. Budgetary Costs of the Post-9/11 Wars'. Watson Institute. Brown University. 1 September.

New Partnership for Africa's Development. (2001). 37th Session of the Assembly of Heads of State and Government. Lusaka, Zambia.New World of Wealth. nw-wealth.com. Republic of South Africa.

New York Times. (1957). 'SUDAN SHUNS DOCTRINE; Plans No Reply to U.S. on Eisenhower Proposals'. 29 May.
New York Times. (1986). 'Fragile Democracy in the Sudan'. 10 May.
New York Times. (2014). 'In Iraq Crisis, a Tangle of Alliances and Enmities'. 13 June.
New York Times. (2018). 'Why NATO Matters'. 8 July.
New York Times. (2020). 'Trump Announces Sudan Will Move to Normalize Relations With Israel'. 23 October.
New York Times. (2022). 'As Faith Flags in U.S. Government, Many Voters Want to Upend the System. 13 July.
Nicholas Lemann. (2008). 'Worlds Apart Obama, McCain, and the Future of Foreign Policy'. *The New Yorker*. 13 October.
Nick Turse. (2015). 'The United States Is Supporting an Army That Is Recruiting Child Soldiers'. *The Nation*. 18 May.
Nick Visser. (2020). 'More than 50 Former Intel Officials Say Hunter Biden Smear Smells Like Russia'. *Huffington Post*. 20 October.
Noam Chomsky. (2006). *Failed State: The Abuse of Power and Assault on Democracy*. Metropolitan Books.
Northern California Citizenship Project. (2004). 'U.S. Voting Rights Timetable'. https://a.s.kqed.net/pdf/education/digitalmedia/us-voting-rights-timeline.pdf.
Oleg Shchedrov. (2008). 'Russia Comes in from Cold, Medvedev Says in Berlin'. *Reuters*. 5 June.
Oliver Richmond. (2008). 'Understanding the "Liberal Peace"', *Conflict in Focus*. Regional Centre on Conflict Prevention. Issue #22. July.
One World. (2019). '20 Years Of Proxy Wars Divided Sudan & Turned It Into A Top Exporter of Mercenaries'. 27 December.
Open Secrets. 'Did Money Win?' https://www.opensecrets.org/elections-overview/winning-vs-spending?cycle=2020.
Osman Suliman. (2007). 'Current Privatization Policy in Sudan,' Policy Brief #52. *The William Davidson Institute*. University of Michigan. 1 January.
Ousman Murzik Kobo. (2013). 'A New World Order? Africa and China'. *Origins*. March.
Paulos Milkias. (2001). 'Ethiopia, TPLF and Roots of the 2001 Political Tremor'. *Northeast African Studies*. Vol. 10. No. 2.
Peter Jackson. (2021). 'The Indispensable Madeleine Albright Defends Democracy'. *Fair Observer*. 29 October.
Peter Van Buren. (2020). 'Hunter Biden's Guilty Laptop'. *The American Conservative*. 31 December.
Peter Walker and James Sturcke. (2008). 'Darfur Genocide Charges for Sudanese President Omar al-Bashir'. *The Guardian*. 14 July.
Pew Research Center. (2021). 'What People around the World Like – and Dislike – about American Society and Politics'. 1 November.
Philipp Jahn and Gerrit Kurtz. (2021). 'What Comes after the Revolution?' *IPS Journal*. 9 April.
Phyllis Bennis. (1996). *Calling the Shots: How Washington Dominates Today's U.N*. New York: Olive Branch Press.
President of Russia. (2017). 'Russia-Sudan Talks'. Sochi. 23 November.
Public Citizen. (2010). 'Citizens United: The Supreme Court Ruling'. 3 February.
Queerroo. (2020). 'The Oromo Struggle Headed by the OLF Will Not be by a Croaking Frogs and Tick Bites'. 16 September.

Rachael Bunyan. (2022). 'Denmark, New Zealand and Finland Top List of Least Corrupt Nations While South Sudan Is the Worst and US Drops Out of Top 25 Amid 'Continuous Attacks on Free and Fair Elections'. *Daily Mail On Line*. 25 January.
Radio Free Europe. (2012). 'Sudan Says Israeli Planes Hit Khartoum Arms Factory'. 24 October.
Radio Tamazuj. (2022). 'SCP Signs Agreement with SPLM-N Al-Hilu and SLM Al-Nur'. 23 May.
Radio Tamazuj. (2022). 'Extension of Coalition Government Set at 24 Months'. 28 July.
Rakesh Krishman Simha. (2015). 'How Lee Kuan Yew and Putin Exposed the Democracy Bogey'. *Russia Beyond*. 24 March.
Ramzy Baroud. (2021). 'Denying the Inevitable: Why the West Refuses to Accept China's Superpower Status'. *Middle East Monitor*. 30 December.
Raven Rakia. (2015). 'IMF's Involvement Fuels Sudan's Continued Unrest'. *Truthout*. 25 March.
Rebecca Hamilton. (2011). 'U.S. Played Key Role in Southern Sudan's Long Journey to Independence'. *The Atlantic*. 9 July.
Rebecca Hamilton. (2011). 'Inside Colin Powell's Decision to Declare Genocide in Darfur'. *The Atlantic*. 17 August.
Rebecca Strong. (2022). 'The Monopoly on Your Mind (Part 1): Six Media Companies Control 90% of What You Read, Watch and Hear'. *Transcend Media Service*. 18 April.
Refworld. (2015). 'South Sudanese President Salva Kiir Threatens to Kill Journalists'. 17 August.
Relief Web. (2012). 'First Paved Highway in South Sudan Constructed by USAID, Officially Opened'. 13 September.
Rene Lefort. (2018). 'Leba! Leba! Abiy Inspires Farmers' Revolt in North Shoa Village'. *Ethiopian Insight*. 21 November.
Renewal. (2001). Addis Ababa. November.
Report to Congress on United States Policy Toward South Sudan. (2022). Section 6508 (b) of the National Defense Authorization Act for Fiscal Year 2022 (P.L. 117–81).
Reuben Brigety. (2018). 'A Post-American Africa The U.S. Is Falling Behind'. *Foreign Affairs*. 28 August.
Reuters. (2007). 'Ethiopian PM Praises Blair as 'Friend of Africa'. 16 May.
Reuters. (2018). 'Bolton Wants to Sanction ICC Judges Who Probe Alleged U.S. War Crimes'. Washington. 10 September.
Reuters. (2019). 'Russian Contractors Are Training the Army in Sudan'. 23 January.
Reuters. (2019a). 'Attempted Coup Leaves Ethiopia's Army Chief and 3 Senior Officials Dead'. 23 June.
Reuters. (2019b). 'Sudan's Military Rulers Say Protest Site Threatens Stability – TV'. 30 May.
Reuters. (2021). 'Biden: Democratic Nations in a Race to Compete with Autocratic Governments'. 13 June.
Reuters. (2023). 'Syria's Assad Arrives in United Arab Emirates in Official Visit'. 19 March.
Richard Posner. (2011). *The Crisis of Capitalist Democracy*. Cambridge, MA: Harvard University Press.
Rita Abrahamsen. (2000). *Disciplining Democracy: Development Discourse and Good Governance in Africa*. London: Zed Books.
River Page. (2021). 'The CIA and the New Dialect of Power'. *American Affairs*. Winter. Vol. 5. No. 4.
Robert Bates. (2010). 'Democracy in Africa: A Very Short History'. *Social Research*. Vol. 77. No. 4: 1133–48.
Robert Lynch. (2023). 'Pay Attention, Class'. *The American Conservative*. 18 March.

Rogers Winters. (2009). 'Testimony before the Subcommittee on Africa and Global Heath'. Committee on Foreign Affairs, House of Representatives. 111th Congress. Sudan: U.S. Policy and Implementation of the Comprehensive Peace Agreement. 29 July.

Rosa Luxemburg. (Reprinted 1961). *The Russian Revolution and Leninism or Marxism?* Westport. Greenwood Press.

RT. (2021). 'Pentagon Says World Will Have Three 'Great Powers' – and US Will Be 'Challenged'. 3 November.

RT. (2023). 'The Battle for African Hearts and Minds: Here's Why the West Is Upset about Russia's Growing Influence on the Continent'. 18 March.

Ryan Grim and Alex Emmons. (2017). 'How Sudan Got Off Trump's Latest Travel Ban List'. *The Intercept*. 25 September.

Ryan Saavedra. (2019). 'New York Times Reporter on Burisma Scandal: Joe Biden's VP Position, Ukraine Activities Gave Burisma Its "Rationale" to Put Hunter Biden on Its Board'. 28 November.

Sam Hamad. (2021). 'All be endorsing Sudan's coup, Biden puts US back in bed with region's autocrats'. *The New Arab*. 15 December.

Sami Moubayed. (2017). 'Turkish Base in Sudan a Problem for Arab Powers'. *Gulf News*. 28 December.

Samuel P. Huntington. (1991). 'Democracy's Third Wave'. *The Journal of Democracy*. Vol. 2. No. 2.

Samuel Huntington. (1993). Submission to the Ethiopian Constitutional Commission. 'Political Development in Ethiopia: A Peasant-Based Dominated Party Democracy?' Addis Ababa.

Samuel Huntington (1996). *The Clash of Civilizations and the Remaking of World Order*. New York: Simon & Schuster.

Santiago Zabala and Claudio Gallo. (2022). 'NATO's Philosophers'. *Al-Jazeera*. 10 May.

Sarah Vaughan. (2003). 'Ethnicity and Power in Ethiopia'. PhD Dissertation. University of Edinburgh.

Sergey Latyshev. (2022). 'A Sensation That Went Unnoticed: The UN "Cancelled" Ukraine'. 26 August.

Shaio Zerba. (2014). 'China's Libya Evacuation Operation: A New Diplomatic Imperative—Overseas Citizen Protection'. *Journal of Contemporary China*. November.

Simon Marks. (2020). 'How an African State Learned to Play the West Off China for Billions'. *Politico*. 7 February.

Simon Marks, Michael Kavanagh, and Verity Radcliffe. (2021). Dubai Is Growing on the Back of Smuggled African Gold'. *Business Day*. 28 December.

Simon Springer, Kean Birch, and Julie MacLeavy. (2016). *The Handbook of Neoliberalism*. New York and London: Routledge.

Simon Watkins. (2022). 'China And Saudi Arabia Intensify Energy Cooperation with Critical Deal'. *OILPRICE*. 9 August.

Skye Wheeler. (2008). 'South Sudan Anti-corruption Body "Struggles" against Graft'. *Reuters*. 13 March.

Small Wars Journal. (2011). 'The Terrorist Climate of Sudan'. 9 April.

Sohu. (2018). Sohu.com/a/246480323_726570. 10 August.

Somtribune Africa. (2021). 'Ethiopia: Major Oromo Group Strikes Alliance with TPLF'. 12 August.

Sophie Mann. (2023). 'Has the Penny Finally Dropped for CNN? Anchor Erin Burnett Admits Bank Transactions Revealing Biden's Family Members Received More than $1m in Chinese Cash 'Don't Look Good'. *MailOnline*. 19 March.

Statista. https://www.statista.com/statistics/248004/percentage-added-to-the-us-gdp-by-industry/. *Statista*. 23 November.
Stephen Chan. (2012). 'Meles Zenawi Obituary'. *The Guardian*. 21 August.
Stephen Mbogo. (2008). 'Clinton Spurned Bin Laden Offer Because He Didn't Want to Work With Sudan, Analyst Says'. *cnsews*. 7 July.
Stephen McBride. (2022). *Escaping Dystopia Rebuilding a Public Domain*. Bristol: Bristol University Press.
Stephen McGlinchey. (2010). 'Review – A Second Look at Huntington's Third Wave Thesis'. *E-International Relations*. 23 September.
Stephen Weisman and David Sanger. (2005). 'THE INAUGURATION: DEMOCRATIZATION; Bush Speech Not a Signal Of New Policy, Aides Say'. *New York Times*. 22 January.
Steven Levitsky and Daniel Ziblatt. (2018). *How Democracies Die*. Broadway Books. New York.
Stockholm International Peace Research Institute. (2021). 'International Arms Transfers Level off after Years of Sharp Growth; Middle Eastern Arms Imports Grow Most, says SIPRI. 15'. March.
Stratfor. (2010). 'US Offers to Remove Sudan from State Sponsors of Terrorism List'. 9 November.
Sudan Democracy First Group. (2018). 'Banking System in Sudan: Political Influence and Personal Interests Breed Corruption and Lack of Transparency'. December.
Sudan Democracy First Group. (2019). 'Sudan Banking System'. 29 May. https://democracyfirstgroup.org/2019/05/29/sudan-banking-system/.
Sudan Tribune. (2008). 'Ethiopia Release Ex-Prime Minister after 12 Years in Jail'. 21 December.
Sudan Tribune. (2010). 'SPLM Nominates Yasir Arman to Contest against Bashir'. 14 January.
Sudan Tribune. (2012). 'Foreign Advisor to South Sudan's President Flees Juba after Disclosure of Corruption Letter'. 12 August.
Sudan Tribune. (2013). 'Amnesty International Says More than 200 Killed in Sudan Protests'. 4 October.
Sudan Tribune. (2017). 'CIA Office in Khartoum Is the Largest One in the Middle East: Official'. 1 February.
Sudan Tribune. (2019). 'Sudanese Communists Denounce U.S. Efforts to Secure Soft Landing for al-Bashir Regime'. 5 January.
Sudan Tribune. (2019). 'Sudan's Revolution Is the Result of Civilian-Military Alliance: Hamdok Says'. 25 December.
Sudan Tribune. (2021). 'Sudan, Egypt Sign Joint Military Cooperation Agreement'. 26 June.
Sudan Tribune. (2021). 'Sudan Releases Islamists Leaders from Prison'. 31 October.
Sudan Tribune. (2022). 'Communist Party Establishes New Coalition for Radical Change in Sudan'. 24 July.
Sudan Tribune. (2022). 'Sudan, Russia Agree to Expedite Implementation of Signed Agreements'. *Sudan Tribune*. 25 February.
Sudan Tribune. (2022). 'U.S. Ends Support to South Sudan Peace Implementation Mechanisms'. 31 July.
Suliman Baldo. (2018). 'Sudan's Self-Inflicted Economic Meltdown'. *Enough Project*. November.
Susan Woodward. (2017). *The Ideology of Failed States*. Cambridge University: Cambridge University Press.

Suzanne Mettler and Robert C. Lieberman. (2020). *Four Threats: The Recurring Crises of American Democracy*. New York: St. Martin's Press.

Sydney Morning Herald. (2021). 'Congo in, China out Biden's Democracy Summit Raises Eyebrows'. 11 December.

Taylor C. Boas & Jordan Gans-Morse. (2009). 'Neoliberalism: From New Liberal Philosophy to Anti-Liberal Slogan.' *St Comp Int Dev*. 21 February.

Ted Dagne. (2002). 'Sudan: Humanitarian Crisis, Peace Talks, Terrorism, and US Policy'. Washington. *Congressional Research Service*. US Library of Congress. 11 December.

Teller Report. (2019). 'Al-Tayeb Saleh Asks: Where did they come from?' 22 April.

Teller Report. (2023). 'Putin Cancels $20 billion Debt Owed by Africa, Pledges to Supply Grain for Free'. 21 March.

Tesfa-Alem Tekle. (2021). 'Ethiopia Downplays TPLF, OLF Military Alliance'. *The East African*. 13 August.

The Carter Center. (2009). 'Observing the 2005 Ethiopia Elections: Final Report'. Atlanta. Georgia.

The Carter Center. (2010). 'Observing Sudan's 2010 National Elections.' *Final Report*. 11 – 18 April.

The Comprehensive Peace Agreement Between The Republic of the Sudan and The Sudan People's Liberation Movement/Sudan People's Liberation Army. (2005). 9 January.

The Diplomat. (2022). 'China's Xi Proposes Global Security Initiative'. 7 May.

The Economist. (2020). 'Somaliland and Taiwan Establish Diplomatic Ties'. 3 October.

The Financial Times. (2018). 'Growing Partisan Differences in Views of the FBI'. 26 July.

The Guardian. (2020). 'Facebook and Twitter Restrict Controversial New York Post Story on Joe Biden'. 15 October.

The Guardian. (2021). 'Clinton Lawyer Charged with Lying to FBI during Trump-Russia Inquiry'. 16 September.

The Guardian. (2021). 'US Democracy Faces a Momentous Threat, says Joe Biden – but Is He up for the Fight?' 17 July.

The Guardian. (2021). 'Sudan's Ongoing Struggle: "a Revolution in the Making."' 13 September.

The Intercept. (2023). 'U.S. Counterterrorism Efforts Destabilizing African Nations'. 12 April.

The Irish Times. (2002). 'The Great Slave Scam'. 23 February.

The New Humanitarian. (2010). 'Countdown to the Southern Referendum'. 23 November.

The White House. (2009). 'President Bush Meets with First Vice President of the Government of National Unity of the Republic of Sudan and President of the Government of Southern Sudan Salva Kiir Mayardit'. 5 January.

The White House. (2022). 'US. Strategy toward Sub-Saharan Africa'. National Security Council. Washington, DC. 8 August.

Thomas Piketty. (2018). 'Brahmin Left vs Merchant Right: Rising Inequality & the Changing Structure of Political Conflict (Evidence from France, Britain and the US, 1948-2017)'. *WID.world WORKING PAPER SERIES N° 2018/7*. March.

Tim Weiner and James Risen. (1998). 'Decision to Strike Factory in Sudan Based Partly on Surmise'. *New York Times*. 21 September.

Times of Israel. (2020). 'Palestinians Say Sudan-Israel Normalization Meeting Is a "Stab in the Back"'. 4 February.

Timothy Carney. (2002). 'Intelligence Failure? Let's Go Back to Sudan'. *Washington Post*. 30 June.

TIPP. (2022). 'Info On Hunter Biden Laptop Could Have Swung The Election'. 13 December.

# Bibliography

Tirfe Mammo. (1999). *The Paradox of African Poverty*. Asmara: Red Sea Press.
Trita Parsi. (2023). 'The U.S. Is Not an Indispensable Peacemaker'. *New York Times Guest Editorial*. 22 March.
Tom Casier. (2018). 'Gorbachev's "Common European Home" and Its Relevance for Russian Foreign Policy Today'. *Debater a Europa*. January.
Tom Fowdy. (2022). 'America's Hypocrisy on China's Overseas Military Bases Is Breathtaking'. *RT*. 14 February.
Tom Parker. (2021). 'YouTube CEO: It's Easy to 'Make up Content and Post It from Your Basement' So We Boost 'Authoritative Sources'. *Reclaim The Net*. 8 April.
Toward Freedom. (2022). 'Conversations with Sudanese Activists on the Sudan Coup'. 17 January.
Tuvia Gering and Heath Sloane. (2021). 'Beijing's Overseas Military Base In Djibouti'. *MEMRI*, 16 July.
Ty McCormick. (2015). 'Unmade in the USA: The Inside Story of U.S. Foreign-Policy Failure in South Sudan'. *Pulitzer Center*. 26 February.
UN Development Program. (2019). 'Ethiopia Human Development Report'. 19 December.
UN Security Council. (2011). 'Security Council Approves "No-Fly Zone" over Libya, Authorizing "All Necessary Measures" to Protect Civilians, by Vote of 10 in Favour with 5 Abstentions'. *Department of Public Information*. New York. Security Council. 17 March.
United Nations. 'Responsibility to Protect'. Office on Genocide Prevention and the Responsibility to Protect.
United Nations. (1992). *An Agenda for Peace: Preventive Diplomacy, Peace-Making and Peace-Keeping*. New York.
United Nations. (1995). *Supplement to an Agenda for Peace*. New York.
United Nations Development Program. (2017). 'Legal Provisions Related to Gender Equality and Sexual Gender Based Violence in South Sudan. August.
United Nations Human Rights Office of the High Commissioner. (2022). 'Statement by Yasmin United Nations Security Council Report. (2011). Security Council Approves "No-Fly Zone" over Libya, Authorizing "All Necessary Measures" to Protect Civilians, by Vote of 10 in Favour with 5 Abstentions'. 17 March.
United Nations Peacekeeping. https://military-history.fandom.com/wiki/United_Nations_peacekeeping
United Nations Security Council. (2022). 'Letter Dated 28 April 2022 from the Panel of Experts on South Sudan Addressed to the President of the Security Council'. 28 April.
UPI Archives. (1991). 'End of Ethiopian Civil War Paves Way for Opposition Groups'. 8 June. https://www.upi.com/Archives/1991/06/08/End-of-Ethiopian-civil-war-paves-way-for-opposition-groups/8390676353600/#ixzz5bCoGqkyF.
USAID. (2021). 'South Sudan History'. 1 December.
US Department of Defense. (2017). 'Africom Uses Whole-of-Government to Engage Nations'. 7 February.
US Department of State. (1973). 'Foreign Relations of the United States, 1969–1976, Volume E–6, Documents on Africa, 1973–1976'. June.
US Department of State. (1986). 'Sudan." Country Report on Human Rights for 1986'. Washington, DC: United States Government Printing Office.
US Department of State. (2003). http://www.UStreas.gov/ofac/legal/sudan.html
US Department of State. (2011). 'Country Reports on Human Rights Practices for 2011'. www.state.odocuments/organizations/18790.pdf.
US Department of State. (2014). ForeignAssistance.gov. South Sudan.

US Department of State. (2017). 'United States Lifting Select Sanctions on Sudan'. January 13. https://2009-2017.state.gov/r/pa/prs/ps/2017/01/266946.htm.

US Department of State. (2021). 'Joint Statement by the Kingdom of Saudi Arabia, the United Arab Emirates, the United States of America and the United Kingdom, on the November 21 Political Agreement in Sudan'. Office of the Spokesperson, 16 December.

United States Institute of Peace. (2020). 'China's Impact on Conflict Dynamics in the Red Sea Arena'. Washington, DC. April.

Unterberger, Betty. (2002). 'Self-Determination'. *Encyclopedia of American Foreign Policy*.

Veronica Nmoma. (2006). 'The Shift in Sudan United States Relations. *The Journal of Conflict Studies*. Vol. 26. No. 2.

Vladimir Danilov. (2021). 'Erdogan Is Actively Trying to Score Points in Africa'. *New Eastern Outlook*. 24 December.

Vladimir Lenin. (1905). Republished in 1962. 'Two Tactics of Social-Democracy in the Democratic Revolution', *Collected Works*. Moscow. Volume. pp. 15–140.

Vladimir Lenin. (1916). 'Imperialism, the Highest Stage of Capitalism'. *Selected Works*. Progress Publishers. 1963. Moscow.

Wael Gamal. (2019). 'Lost Capital: The Egyptian Moslem Brotherhood's Neoliberal Transformation'. *Carnegie Middle East Center*. 31 January.

Walter Rostow. (1960). *The Stages of Economic Growth: A Non-Communist Manifesto*. Cambridge University: Cambridge University Press.

Washington Post. (2017). 'Obama Administration to Lift Some Sanctions against Sudan'. 13 January.

Washington Post. (2021). 'Renewed Scrutiny of Wuhan Lab Scrambles the Politics of the Pandemic'. 27 May.

Wikileaks. https://wikileaks.org/plusd/cables/08ADDISABABA82_a.html.

Wikipedia. (2023). '2009 Sudan Air Strikes'. https://en.wikipedia.org/wiki/2009_Sudan_airstrikes.

William Howell and Terry Moe. (2020). *Presidents, Populism, and the Crisis of Democracy*. University of Chicago: University of Chicago Press.

William Worley. (2022). 'Exclusive: Russia, China Foiled UN Meetings on Tigray famine, says Lowcock'. *Devex*. 21 June.

Wolfgang Merkel. (2014). 'Is Capitalism Compatible with Democracy?' Springer Fachmedien Wiesbaden. 26 July.

World Bank Group. (2015). *Ethiopia Poverty Assessment 2014*. Washington, DC. https://openknowledge.worldbank.org/handle/10986/21323.

WorldData.info. (2018). 'Corruption in Ethiopia'. www.worlddata.info/africa/ethiopia/corruption.php.

World Inequality Report. (2022). 7 December 2021.

World Leaders Forum. (2010). 'Meles Zenawi'. Columbia University. September.

Worldometer. (2021). 'Covid-19 Coronavirus Pandemic Weekly Trends'. 4 October. https://www.worldometers.info/coronavirus/#countries.

World Population Review. (2022). https://worldpopulationreview.com/countries/ethiopia-population.

World Trade Organization. 'The 128 Countries That Had Signed GATT by 1994'. https://www.wto.org/english/thewto_e/gattmem_e.htm.

Xi Jinping. (2019). 'Full Text of Chinese President Xi Jinping's Speech'. 3 September.

Yahoo! News. (2021). 'India at UNSC: Ethiopia Needs All Support from International Community'. 26 August.

Yascha Mounk. (2019). *The People vs. Democracy*. Cambridge, MA: Harvard University Press.
Yasir Zaidan. (2021). 'Sudan's Democratic Transition Needs a Jumpstart'. *World Politics Review*. 13 July.
Yoshiko Kurita. (2019). 'The Sudanese Communist Movement'. *African History*. 23 May. https://doi.org/10.1093/acrefore/9780190277734.013.14.
Youtube. (1961). https://www.youtube.com/watch?v=94N2wK4zUaM. 4 October.
Zach Vertin. (2019). 'Red Sea Rivalries: The Gulf, the Horn, & the New Geopolitics of the Red Sea'. *Brookings Doha Center*. August.
Zachary Cohen. (2021). 'CNN Exclusive: US Intel and Satellite Images Show Saudi Arabia Is Now Building Its Own Ballistic Missiles with Help of China'. *CNN*. 23 December.
Zachary Karabell. (1996). 'Fundamental Misconceptions: Islamic Foreign Policy'. *Foreign Policy*. 105. Winter.
Zeenat Hansrod. (2016). 'The UAE Expands Military Presence In The HOA'. *Saxafimedia*. 25 December.

## Interviews

Author email from Leenco Lata. (2018). 13 March.
Author email from Negasso Gidada, late and former President of Ethiopia. (2017). 1 March.
Author interview with al-Maboob Abdelsalem. (2018). Khartoum, 28 November. al-Maboob is a leading Sudanese Islamist intellectual, author, and former confidant of Hassan al-Turabi.
Author interview with Bereket Simon. (2018). Addis Ababa. 10 November. Bereket was jailed shortly after this interview and has not been seen since.
Author interview with Gebru Asrat. (2018). 9 November, Addis Ababa. Gebru was a senior member of the TPLF and governor of Tigray from 1991 until 2001, when he was the victim of Meles' purge.
Author interview with Leencho Lata. (2018). Addis Ababa. 2 November. Leencho was a member of the ESM and subsequently a leader of the OLF.
Author interview with Lt-General and Chief of Staff Gebretsadkan Gebretensae. (2002). Addis Ababa. 18 February.
Author interview with Lt-General Gebretsadkan Gebretensae. (2018). Former Ethiopian Chief of Defense Staff. Addis Ababa. 1 November.
Author interview with Sebhat Nega. (2020). Former leader of the TPLF. Mekelle. 2 March.

# INDEX

Abboud, Ibrahim 98, 100, 131, 160, 163
Abdallah, Asmaa 126
Abdallah, El Shafee 122
Abraha, Siye 60, 78
Adams, John 29
Adawi, Emadeldin 113
Addis Ababa Agreement (1972) 134, 167
Afar National Democratic Front (ANDF) 59
Afghanistan 1, 4, 6, 15 n.2, 18, 27, 102, 107, 133, 151
Africa 7, 19, 45, 58, 63, 80, 86, 105–6, 108, 116, 120, 135. *See also* Horn of Africa (HOA)
   China in 41–2, 52–3
   food imports 19
   Strategy 108
   US direct investment 38
Africa Command (AFRICOM) 41, 53, 113
African Development Bank 118
African Renaissance 80
Afwerki, Isaias 48–9, 55, 77, 80, 89, 92, 157, 159
Agreement for the Resolution of Conflict in South Sudan (ARCSS) 146
Ahmari, Sohrab 32
Ahmed, Abiy 7–8, 42, 44, 46–9, 55–6, 71, 73, 79, 93–4, 96, 123, 157, 159
   counter-revolution 82–92, 155
Akol, Lam 135, 149
Albright, Madeleine 16, 29, 39, 102–3
All-Ethiopia Socialist Movement (MEISON) 58
Amac 26
American hegemony 1, 3, 5, 12, 34, 52–3, 170
American Revolution 11, 20
American Servicemembers Protection Act (2002) 15
Amhara 57 n.1, 59, 70, 73, 77, 87–8, 90, 92, 94, 159

chauvinism 77, 154, 157
domination and national self-determination 8, 70, 94, 159
pan-Ethiopian nationalism 69
Amhara National Democratic Movement (ANDM) 59, 78
al-Amoudi, Mohammed Hussein 86, 86 n.4
anachronism 57
anti-imperialism 81, 109, 111
anti-Semitism 112
Anya-Nya. *See* South Sudan Liberation Army (SSLA)
Arabization 98
Arab Spring 28, 51
Arman, Yasir 142
Asian Tigers 62, 74, 82, 94, 155–6
Asrat, Gebru 78
al-Assad, Bashar 27, 37–8, 45, 53
Assange, Julian 23, 31
Australia, UK and the United States (AUKUS) 13
*Awlad al bahr* 134

Bab al-Mandab Strait 40
banking system 115–17
al-Bashir, Omar 7, 9, 42–3, 46–51, 97–8, 100, 102–3, 104, 106, 110–12, 114, 119, 122, 124, 132, 139, 161–2, 165
Beijing Olympics (2008) 43
Belt and Road Initiative 38
Benishangul-Gumuz People's Democratic Unity Front (BGPDUF) 59–60
Bennis, Phyllis 17
Bensouda, Fatou 15 n.2
Bereket, Simon 76, 82–3
Berger, Sandy 102
Biden, Hunter 24–6, 36
Biden, Joe 1, 22, 24–5, 47, 52, 54, 108, 148
bin Laden, Osama 101–2

bin Zayed Al Nahyan, Mohammad 49, 123
Black Lives Matter (BLM) 137
Blair, Tony 80
Blinken, Antony 25, 30 n.4, 127
Bolshevik revolution (1917) 5
Bolsheviks 8, 68–72, 83, 94, 157
Bolsonaro, Jair 22
Bolton, John 15 n.2, 108
Bonapartism 77
Booth, Donald 113
Boycott, Disinvestment, and Sanctions (BDS) campaign 112
Brazil, Russia, India, China and South Africa (BRICS) 39
Brennan, John 25
Buffet, Warren 33
al-Burhan, Abdel-Fatah 46, 50, 122–3, 126, 128–30, 162–3
Burisma Holdings 25
Bush Doctrine 29
Bush, George H. W. 16
Bush, George W. 16, 27, 29, 80–1, 105–7, 113, 131, 136, 138–9, 141

capitalism 2–4, 5, 11, 17, 26, 32, 34, 61, 69, 87, 92–3, 95, 97, 154, 156, 158–9, 161, 168–9
   embraced 61–3
   and foreign interventionism 30
   golden age of 5, 26
   surveillance 12
   United States and Islamists 114–21
   and Western liberal democracy 20, 32, 34
The Carter Center 23, 23 n.3, 81, 142, 142 n.4
Carter, Jimmy 23, 105
censorship 12, 31–2, 88
Child Soldiers Prevention Act 145
China 2, 4, 6–7, 29, 34–5, 53, 75, 79, 92, 108, 154–5, 169–70
   ascendent 38–46
   authoritarianism 7, 34, 40
   development and investment 42
   economic influence 37
   economic power 43
   Global Security Initiative 39
   'Go Out Strategy' 75
   military strategy 40

   peace initiative 54
   rising status 38
China National Petroleum Corporation (CNPC) 42–3
Chinese Communist Party (CCP) 59, 79, 155, 157, 170
Christian Solidarity International (CSI) 102, 138
Civil Rights Act 21
Clapper, James 24
Clark, Wesley 103
Clinton, Bill 9, 16, 29, 80, 101–4, 101 n.1, 107, 133, 136, 138, 145
   National Security Strategy document 35
Clinton, Hillary 23, 145
Clooney, George 137
CNN 24, 81
Cohen, Herman 63
Cohen, Yossi 112
Cold War 4, 6, 10–11, 13, 16, 20, 23, 29, 34, 46, 57, 61–2, 74, 91–3, 99, 103, 109, 138, 151, 153, 155
   'Eisenhower doctrine' 98
Comprehensive Peace Agreement (CPA, 2005) 107, 110–11, 118, 140–1, 143–4, 161, 167
Congressional Budget Justification (2013) 145
Constitutional Document 130
*Convention on the Prevention and Punishment of Genocide* (1948) 15
Corruption Perceptions Index (2021) 147
Covid-19 pandemic 34, 40, 53

Daglo, Mohamed Hamdan. *See* Hemedti
Dagne, Ted 137
Darfur 43, 48–9, 100, 104–6, 111, 113, 119, 122, 141–2, 163–5, 167
Darfuris 162, 165
Demeksa, Kuma 78
democracy (US) 1–3, 5–6, 9–10, 16, 20–3, 26–8, 30, 36, 53, 97–8, 100, 118, 126, 150–1, 153–4, 168–9
   and authoritarianism 7
   decline of 30–4
   pursuit of 105–8
Democracy Perception Index (2022) 12

democracy promotion 1, 11, 17, 30, 36, 50, 80, 98, 131, 148
   nation-building and 133
   Western failures at 27
Democratic Party 9, 12, 23–4, 26, 31–3, 36, 136, 138
Deng, Francis 17
Deng, Taban 146
Derg 55–6, 58–61, 64, 70–1, 73–4, 91, 97, 99, 134, 136, 138, 154, 157, 163
Desalegn, Hailemariam 76, 83–4, 88
d'Escoto Brockmann, Miguel 18
developmental authoritarianism 75
de Waal, Alex 100–1
de Zayas, Alfred 16
*Die Zeit* newspaper 36
Dinka 10, 133–5, 140 n.3, 144, 149, 166
Djibouti, foreign military base 40–1
D'Silva, Brian 137
Dubowitz, Mark 39
Dulles, John Foster 56
Duterte, Rodrigo 22

Eastern Bloc 11–12, 14, 20, 46, 99, 134, 136
   collapse 61, 136, 163, 165
   and socialism 153
Egypt 47, 50–1, 112, 118, 122, 124, 127, 129, 136
Eibner, John 138
Elbadawi, Ibrahim 123
elections (US) 2, 10, 12, 30, 62, 133, 169
   and economic liberalism 36
   rise and decline 20–6
Enough Project 137
Eritrea 3, 46–8, 56–8, 71 n.3, 73, 77, 84, 87–9, 110, 135, 144
   Eritrean peace process 89
   front line states 101
Eritrean Liberation Front (ELF) 44
Eritrean People's Liberation Front (EPLF) 8, 58–9
Ethio-Eritrean War (1998–2000) 43, 64, 73, 77, 87, 102, 157
Ethiopia 2, 44, 47, 50, 55, 57 n.1, 101, 114 n.5, 119, 127, 135–6, 139, 144, 159, 164. *See also* Tigray People's Liberation Front (TPLF)
   Abiy counter-revolution 82–92

Addis Ababa 7, 38, 40, 44–5, 47
   capitalism (reluctantly) embraced 61–3
   and compromises with West 154–9
   democratization 156
   EPRDF (*see* Ethiopian Peoples Revolutionary Democratic Front (EPRDF))
   Human Development Index 85
   national federalism 69–73, 76, 89, 92, 94, 157
   poverty 8, 55, 76, 83, 85
   radical transformation 57
   revolutionary *vs.* liberal democracy 63–9, 83, 95
   self-determination 3, 7, 43, 55–9, 63, 70, 73
   state-led development 55, 73–6
   Tigrayans and Oromos 7, 70, 86–8
   Zenawi, Meles (*see* Zenawi, Meles)
Ethiopian Peoples' Democratic Movement (EPDM). *See* Amhara Democratic Movement (ANDM)
Ethiopian Peoples Revolutionary Democratic Front (EPRDF) 4, 8, 42, 44, 46, 55–6, 59–71, 73–5, 77–81, 83–6, 89–96, 110, 154–9, 168–9
   Great Ethiopian Renaissance Dam (GERD) 75
   industrialization 68, 74, 82, 85, 94
   key tenants 155
   national aspirations 72
   sub-state nationalism 95
Ethiopian People's Revolutionary Party (EPRP) 58
Ethiopian Somali People's Democratic Party (ESPDP) 59
Ethiopian Student Movement (ESM) 55–8, 69, 155
Ethiopia-Somali War (1977–8) 70
ethno-nationalism 8, 68, 72, 75, 83, 85

Farmajo, Mohamed Abdullahi 48
Fawcett, Louise 1
First Amendment 31
First World War 5
Five-Track Engagement Plan (2016) 113
Flournoy, Michele 40

Forces for Freedom and Change (FFC) 122–4, 127, 129, 131, 164
foreign policy 16, 23, 27–31, 37, 45, 47, 97, 99, 104–5, 111, 114, 129, 168
    analysis 17
    weakness 53
    Western 18
*Foreign Policy* journal 121
Fraser, Nancy 32
Friedman, Milton 34
Friends of South Sudan 136–7, 143, 145, 168
Fukuyama, Francis 16, 66
    *The End of History and the Last Man* 20

Gaddafi, Muammar 27, 35, 37, 49, 99–100, 111
Gadet, Peter 146
Gambela People's Democratic Movement (GPDM) 59
Garang, John 9–10, 97, 100–1, 109, 134–7, 141, 161, 166–8
garrison socialism 56
Gatluak, Tut 126
Gebremichael, Debretsion 88
Gezira Scheme 116
Gidado, Negasso 78
gim gima 67, 79, 84, 93, 155
Ginbot-7 89
El Gizouli, Magdi 118, 121
Global South 5–6, 10, 36, 53, 62, 74, 100, 103, 153–4, 168–70
    modernization theory 18–19
    neo-colonialism 153
    political processes 2
    Western interventions 17–18
Global War on Terror (GWOT) 6, 12, 28, 46, 52, 80, 86, 104–7, 112–13, 120
Gorbachev, Mikhail 13, 16
Gosh, Salah 50, 106, 112, 124
Graham, Billy 138
Graham, Franklin 138–9
Gramsci, Antonio 5
    counter-hegemony 157
Gration, Scott 107, 107 n.3
Great Depression 5
Greenspan, Alan 22
Gulf Cooperation Council (GCC) 38
Gulf War (1990–1) 6, 101, 109

Habash, George 109
Habre, Hissen 99–100
Haftar, Khalifa 49–51
Haile-Selassie, Emperor 44, 56–7
Hamas 23, 27–8, 102, 111–12, 131
Hamdi, Abderrahim, Hamdi Triangle 115, 115 n.6
Hamdok, Abdalla 50, 123–5, 127–31, 162–3, 166
Harari National League (HNL) 59
hate speech/disinformation 32
Hayden, Mike 25
Heavily Indebted Poor Country (HIPC) Initiative 118, 124
Hemedti 48, 50, 111, 122–3, 128–9, 164
Heritage Foundation 29
al-Hilu, Abdel Aziz 126, 164
Hochschild, Jennifer 22
Hollande, Francois 35–6
Horner, Jonas 50
Horn of Africa (HOA) 1–3, 5, 37–40, 50–1, 54–5, 99, 113, 120, 168–9
    Confucius Institutes 43
    Middle Eastern states in 46–52
    regional and international dimensions 6
    self-determination and secession 3, 7
Houthis 48, 111
human rights 3, 6, 11, 14, 16, 35, 45, 66–7, 75, 87, 90, 92, 97, 105, 114, 153, 156, 158, 169
    abuses 9, 22, 48, 52, 67, 99, 101, 107, 111, 118, 131, 136, 138, 144, 149
    commission 144
    democracy and concerns 98, 131, 153
    language of 14, 19
    neoliberalism 11–12, 15
Human Rights Watch (2016/2021) 27, 84, 146
Hundessa, Hachalu 90
Huntington, Samuel 21–3, 27, 30, 36, 64, 66, 138, 142, 156, 158, 169
    clash of civilization thesis 109, 138, 139 n.2
Hussein, Saddam 1, 27, 103, 109
hyper-capitalism 3

Ibrahim, Khalil 164
*Imam* 99

imperialism 2, 5, 13, 42, 57, 136
  militarism 13
  slavery and 18
individual rights 8–9, 64, 156
Information Network Security Agency 88
Inter-Governmental Authority on Development (IGAD) 42, 105, 108, 139–40, 146–7, 167
Inter-Governmental Authority on Drought and Development (IGADD) 105
Internal Displacement Monitoring Center 90
International Commission on Intervention and State Sovereignty (ICISS) 17
*International Covenant on Economic, Social and Cultural Rights* 14
International Criminal Court (ICC) 14, 15 n.2, 105, 110, 112
International Crisis Group, slush-fund governance 147
International Financial Institutions (IFIs) 28, 74–5, 92, 118, 123, 127, 130
internationalism/humanitarianism 17
International Monetary Fund (IMF) 3, 8, 19, 38, 42, 44, 64, 73–4, 85, 99–100, 116–19, 121, 124–5, 156, 162
  austerity programme 165
  Heavily Indebted Poor Country Initiative 124
International Religious Freedom Act (1998) 138
Iranian Revolution 4
Iraq 1, 6, 27–8, 53, 133
Iraq War 1, 6, 36, 80
Islamization 98
Israeli Boycott Act (1958) 126
Israeli war (1967) 98

Al-Jazeera 47
Jefferson, Thomas, empire of liberty 28–9
jihadi groups 28, 35, 103–4
Jinping, Xi 39, 42 n.2, 79, 157
Johnson, Hilde 145 n.5
Jolie, Angelina 137
Juba 148
Justice and Equality Movement 162, 164

Kagame, Paul 80
Kant, Immanuel 16
Keane, John 22
Kennedy, John F. 98
Kerry, John 107, 146
Keynesian economics
  decline of 3
  policies 5
  rejection of 26, 74
Khair, Kholood 50
Khalil, Abdalla 160
Khartoum 44, 48, 100, 102, 103 n.2, 105–8, 111, 113, 115, 118–24, 126–7, 131, 135, 137, 139, 139 n.2, 143, 149, 161, 163, 165
Khashoggi, Jamal 47
Kisho, Abate 78
Kiir, Salva 10, 42, 107, 126, 137, 139, 141, 144–9, 150 n.6, 163
Kissinger, Henry 20
Kong, Gordon 135
Kurita, Yoshiko 131

Layne, Tamrat 158
Lata, Leenco 66, 70
Lavrov, Sergey 35, 46, 128
Lenin, Vladimir 58, 60, 169
  democratic centralism 96
  *Two Tactics of Social-Democracy in the Democratic Revolution* 65
Lewinski, Monica 103
liberal peacekeeping 3, 10–11, 16–17, 104, 120, 139, 143, 148
Lincoln, Abraham 33
Lukyanov, Grigory 45
Luxemburg, Rosa 96

al-Maboob, Abdelsalem 109
Machakos Protocol 140–1
Machar, Riek 10, 107, 135, 139, 144–5, 149, 150 n.6
al-Mahdi, Sadig 97, 99–100, 109, 115, 119, 121, 128, 131, 161
Mandelbaum, Michael, *The Four Ages of American Foreign Policy* 29
Manning, Chelsea 31
al-Marouf, Kamal Abd 113
Marxism-Leninism 57, 60–2, 93, 96, 155, 157, 163

Marxist-Leninist League of Tigray (MLLT) 60, 77
Marx, Karl 15, 68–9, 77, 84
Matieb, Paulino 135
McCain, John 22
Mearsheimer, John 12, 16
Medvedev, Dmitri 13
Mekonnen, Walelign, 'On the Question of Nationalities in Ethiopia' 57
Menelik II 56, 89
Merkel, Angela 35–6
Mesfin, Seyoum 155
Milley, Mark 36
Minsk II agreement (2015) 35–6
Modi, Narendra 22
Moi, Daniel arap 139
Morell, Mike 25
Morsi, Mohamed 28, 128
Mubarak, Hosni 110
Mueller, Robert 24
Mugabe, Robert 128
multilateralism 29
multipolarity 4
Museveni, Yowri 80, 146
Muslim Brotherhood/Brothers 27–8, 47–8, 51, 97, 115, 131

Nafi, Nafi Ali 110, 110 n.4
National Congress Party (NCP) 101, 105–6, 109, 111–12, 115–16, 118–20, 129, 131, 140–2, 161, 163, 165
National Democratic Alliance (NDA) 102, 137, 140, 163
National Dialogue 149
national federalism (Ethiopia) 55, 69–73, 76, 89, 91–2, 94, 96, 155–7, 159
National Islamic Front (NIF) 4, 97, 100–4, 108–12, 115 n.6, 116–19, 121, 161–2, 164
*National Security Strategy* 29, 35
Nega, Sebhat 77
neo-colonialism 3, 41, 45, 53, 63, 151, 153, 163, 170
neoliberalism 3, 6, 6 n.2, 14, 19, 20, 26, 28, 30, 33, 44, 55, 62, 66, 74, 85, 95, 97, 115, 119, 124, 126, 141, 153, 156–9, 161–2, 168–70
financialization 33–4

human rights 11–12, 15, 67
pace 67
progressive 32
Netanyahu, Benjamin 50, 126
New Partnership for African Development (NEPAD) 19, 80
*New York Post* tabloid 24–5
*The New York Times* newspaper 13, 24–5, 39, 102
Nimeiri, Jaffir 98–100, 115–16, 118, 131, 160–1
9/11 6, 27, 41, 52, 104–6
Nixon administration 39
Non-Alignment Movement 10, 154
North Atlantic Treaty Organization (NATO) 1–2, 5–6, 12–14, 17, 35–6, 53, 169
al-Nur, Abdel Wahid 126, 164

Obama, Barack 22, 24, 28, 31, 105, 107–8, 107 n.3, 120, 141, 145
October Revolution (1964) 98, 160
Ogaden National Liberation Front (ONLF) 58, 70
Operation Enduring Freedom 113
Orange Revolution 81
O'Reilly, Bill 36
Organization of African Unity 110
Oromo Federalist Congress 90
Oromo Liberation Army (OLA) 71, 71 n.3, 73
Oromo Liberation Front (OLF) 8, 58, 66–7, 69–71, 71 n.3, 87–91, 93, 159
Oromo People's Democratic Organization (OPDO) 59, 70–1, 78, 87, 91, 93
Oslo Agreement 112

pan-Ethiopian nationalism 58, 69, 84, 157
Panetta, Leon 25
Parsi, Titra 39
*Pax Americana* 23, 169
Petterson, Donald 103
Piketty, Thomas 33
Pinochet, Augusto 15
Podesta, John 23
Polanyi, Karl, *The Great Transformation* 16
Pompeo, Mike 15 n.2, 32
Popular Congress Party (PCP) 110

post-Cold War 4, 9, 13, 17, 27–9, 39, 46, 62, 69, 74, 106, 153, 158, 165
Prendergast, John 137
progressive neoliberalism 32
Prosperity Party 8, 44, 55, 89–90
*Public Citizen* 31
Puritans 28
Putin, Vladimir 23, 36, 46, 48

*al-Qaeda* network 102, 114
Qatar 41, 47
Queerroo 88

Rand Corporation 62
Rapid Support Forces (RSF) 46, 48–50, 98, 122, 166
Reeves, Eric 137
Responsibility to Protect (R2P) doctrine 3, 9, 11, 17–18, 138
Revitalized Agreement on the Resolution of the Conflict in South Sudan (R-ARCSS) 146–8
Rice, Susan 102, 107, 136–7
Rockefeller, David 30
Roosevelt, Franklin D. 14, 29
  'Four Freedoms' 27
Rostow, Walter, *The Stages of Economic Growth: A Non-Communist Manifesto* 18
Rubio, Marco 35
Russia-Africa Summit 45
Russian disinformation 25–6
Russia/Russian Federation 4, 6, 11, 13, 23–5, 35, 38–9, 45–8, 52–3, 108, 121, 128, 154, 169–70. *See also* Ukraine War

Sadat, Anwar 99
Sahrawi Arab Democratic Republic 126
Salahdien, Ghazi 109
Salih, Tayeb 121
Salman, Mohammed bin 47, 122
Sanders, Bernie 23
Sankara, Thomas 19, 170
Satellite Sentinel Project 137
Saudi Arabia 37–9, 43, 45, 47–9, 51, 53, 86 n.4, 108, 111–12, 114, 120, 122, 130
Saudi-UAE war 47, 111
Saudi Wahabism 109

Schumpeter, Joseph 21–3, 30, 36, 64, 142, 168
  *Capitalism, Socialism and Democracy* 21
Second World War 2, 5, 11, 13, 26–7, 40, 56, 170
al-Shabaab 49, 80
Shanghai Cooperation Organisation 39
Sharia law 99
Shellenberger, Michael 31
Shinn, David 102
el-Sisi, Abdel Fatah 28, 122, 128, 130
slave trade 102
Snowden, Edward 31–2
Snyder Act (1924) 21
social media 31, 39, 83, 86, 149
soft power 43, 53, 76
Somaliland 3, 41–2
Southern Ethiopia Peoples' Democratic Front (SEPDF) 59, 78
South Sudan 2–3, 7, 9–10, 47, 50, 107, 113, 117–18, 133, 140 n.3, 150, 160–1, 163
  civil society 149
  civil war and 107, 113, 145–8
  conflicts, mythologizing 137–9
  democracy promotion 30, 133, 148
  diversity of 167
  future 148–50
  historical context 134–5
  Kiir dictatorship in 42
  national self-determination 135–6, 143, 166–8
  peace process 47, 53, 107–8, 114, 139–45
  with Tel Aviv 50
  UN peacekeeping mission 43, 52, 80
  US engagement 135–7
South Sudan Defense Forces (SSDF) 135–6, 135 n.1, 140
South Sudan Liberation Army (SSLA) 134
Sovereign Council 123, 126
SPLM-In Opposition (SPLM-IO) 107, 146
Stalin, Joseph 58, 84
  *Marxism and the National Question* 69, 94
Steele, Christopher 24–5
Stiglitz, Joseph 33, 74

Stockholm International Peace Research Institute (SIPRI) 43
Strategic Initiative for Women in the HOA (SIHA) 125
Structural Adjustment Programs (SAPs) 19, 74, 117, 124
Sudan 2, 7–9, 17, 44, 50–1, 134, 138, 142–3, 148, 160, 166–7
  change without fundamental change 160–6
  civil war 134, 136, 161
  democratic transformation 140, 166
  dictatorships 9
  elections 10, 23
  National Islamic Front 4
  national sovereignty 162
  peace process 18, 47, 53, 143
  US relations with (see Sudan, US relations with)
Sudan Appeal 121
Sudan Communist Party (SCP) 98–9, 116, 123–4, 163–5
  Forces for Radical Change 164
Sudan Liberation Movement 126, 164
Sudan Peoples Liberation Army (SPLA). See Sudan People's Liberation Movement (SPLM)
Sudan People's Liberation Movement (SPLM) 9–10, 44, 97, 100–4, 108–10, 126, 133–8, 140–9, 145 n.5, 151, 161, 163–4, 166–8
Sudan Public Order Law 125
Sudan, US relations with 97
  capitalism 114–21
  civil society 132
  democracy and peace 105–8
  economic crisis 108
  historical context 98–100
  Islamist radicalism, decline of 106, 108–14
  Islamists 100–4
  post-al-Bashir era 121–31
  youth movements 132
Sumbeiywo, Lazarus 139
Summits for Democracy (2021) 22
Supreme Allied Commander Europe (SACEUR) 13
surveillance capitalism 12
Swar al-Dahab, Abdel Rahman 161

Tadesse, Medhane 93
Taha, Ali Osman 110
Taibbi, Matt 31
Taliban 1, 4
Talisman 42
Thatcher, Margaret 20, 66, 170
Tigray 3, 57 n.1, 58–61, 60 n.2, 67–8, 70, 72, 87–9, 92–4, 157
  Abiy's humanitarian blockade of 44, 47
  Ethiopian National Defense Force in 44, 51, 91
  Marxist-Leninist League of 77
Tigray Defense Force (TDF) 67, 91
Tigray People's Liberation Front (TPLF) 44, 46, 48–9, 51, 55, 70, 76, 83, 87–9, 91–4, 154–7, 159
  Central Committee 78
  gim gima 67, 79
  leadership and dogmatism 93
  origins and development of 56–61
  *The TPLF Manifesto* 59
Tigray War (2020) 43, 47, 73, 89
TIPP Insights survey 25
Transitional Military Council (TMC) 99, 110 n.4, 122–3, 160–1
Trans-Saharan Counterterrorism Initiative 113
Trilateral Commission 30, 30 n.4
Truman, Harry 29
Trump, Donald 1, 23–5, 28, 32, 36, 108, 113, 120, 126, 131, 133, 145–6
  and Abrahams Accords 50
Tsadkan, Gebretensae 60, 78
Tsehai, Abay 60, 60 n.2
Tsige, Asaminew 90
al-Turabi, Hassan 98, 101, 104, 106, 108–10, 116, 119, 161, 162 n.1
Turkish Exporters Assembly 51
Turkiye 7, 28, 45, 47–9, 51–3, 121
Turksom 48
Twitter Files 31

Uganda 98, 101, 110, 135, 139, 144, 147
  Lord's Resistance Army 113–14
Ukraine War 4, 35–6, 38–9, 45, 52–3, 154, 169
*UN Covenants on Civil and Political Rights, and on Economic, Social and Cultural Rights* 14

UN Human Rights Council 43, 45
United Arab Emirates (UAE) 7, 37, 41, 43, 47–9, 53, 55, 111–13, 120, 122, 128, 130
United Nations
    *An Agenda for Peace: Preventive Diplomacy, Peace-Making and Peace Keeping* 16
    *Supplement to an Agenda for Peace* 17
*United Nations Charter* 13–14
United Nations Development Programme (UNDP) 144
United Nations Mission in South Sudan (UNMISS) 148
*Universal Declaration of Human Rights* (*UDHR*) 14
UN Panel of Experts on South Sudan 148
UN peacekeeping mission 15, 43, 52–3, 86, 130
US Agency for International Development (USAID) 126, 137, 147, 150
US exceptionalism 29, 36, 138, 168
US Federal Reserve 22, 26, 34
US Indo-Pacific strategy 40
US invasion of Iraq 6, 18, 103
US liberal international order 3, 5–6, 10–20, 34, 125, 148, 151, 154, 169
    establishment and development 20
    failed state 18
    Great Powers 12
    human rights 14–16
    peacemaking 17
    political and moral bankruptcy 54
    protectionism 19

Vietnam War 6, 57
Voting Rights Act 21

Wagner Group 45–6, 48
*Wall Street Journal* 130
War on Terror 108
Washington Consensus 117

Washington, George 12–13, 20, 41, 46, 98–9, 107
*Washington Post* newspaper 24, 47
Weapons of Mass Destruction (WMD) 1
Weber, Max 21–2
welfare state, decline 6
Western democracy 1–2, 5, 7, 9–11, 16, 32, 34–5, 55, 61, 63, 92, 96, 117, 150, 153–5, 158–61, 166, 168–9
    failure of 1, 9
    propagation of 3, 5, 12, 26–30
Western parliamentary system 95
Whitbeck, John 126
whole-of-government approach 41
Wilson, Woodrow 29, 105
    'Fourteen Points' 27
Winters, Rogers 137
Wojcicki, Susan 31
Wolde Mariam, Tewolde 60, 77–8
Wolfowitz, Paul 103
World Bank 3, 12, 19, 42, 44, 74, 85, 114, 118, 124
World Food Program projects 150
World Inequality Report (2022) 33
World Trade Organization (WTO) 12, 19

Xiaoping, Deng 79

Yew, Lee Kuan 82
Yi, Wang 44
Yohannes IV, Emperor 59
Yunis, Samora 78

Zedong, Mao 59
Zenawi, Meles 46, 55, 60–2, 65–6, 68, 74–83, 87, 89–92, 94–6, 154–6, 158–9, 169
    autocrat, making 77–82
    *The Question of Building an Independent National Economy in Ethiopia* 62